# Suttons Seeds

## *A History*
## *1806–2006*

### EARLEY LOCAL HISTORY GROUP

# Suttons Seeds

## A History
### 1806–2006

EARLEY LOCAL HISTORY GROUP

EARLEY LOCAL HISTORY GROUP
2006

Published by
Earley Local History Group
48 Harcourt Drive
Earley
Reading RG6 5TJ

ISBN 0 9540041–2–4


Designed and Typeset by the
Department of Typography & Graphic Communication
The University of Reading
Printed and bound by
Cromwell Press, Trowbridge
2006

.

*Front and back cover*

A collection of Suttons Seeds catalogue covers

# Contents

Banana

Castor Oil

Cotton x2 magnification

Chinese Water Chestnut

Strychnine

Devil's Claw

Kapok

A selection of unusual seeds (actual size). See page 53.

# Acknowledgements

The idea to produce this book resulted from a casual conversation between Gerry Westall and Grahame Hawker. It has been researched and written by former employees of Suttons, Gerry Westall and Ron Butler and by members of the Earley Local History Group; Grahame Hawker, Liz Vincent, Elaine Watts and Gerry Westall.

In addition to the main authors, valuable contributions and assistance have been given by John Cox, former Suttons Company Secretary; Jane Sutton, daughter of Martin Audley Sutton, (foreword and personal memories), the staff at The Museum of English Rural Life especially Roy Bridgen, Caroline Benson, Caroline Gould, Jonathon Brown, Will Phillips and Zoe Watson, the staff of Suttons at Paignton, especially Alex Grenfell (Managing Director), Ann Boswell and members of the design and publicity department; a number of retired Suttons staff; staff of Earley Town Council, especially Mary Sutherland and Diana Collins; David Cliffe from Reading Local Studies Library; the Berkshire Records Office; David Chelley former Company Secretary at Torquay for help with the 'On to Devon' chapter; Tom Ratcliffe, former Chief Analyst and Personal Manager (for his contribution to the 'Seeds and Plants' chapter); Mike Smallwood (India and Kashmir); John Trigg (Arthur Warwick and the Bucklebury 'Fireside Club'); Keith Jerome (Edith Sutton); Professor Eric Paulson, University of Canterbury, Christchurch, New Zealand (Export of agricultural grasses to New Zealand in the 1840's); Julian Vincent and Bill Watts.

We would especially like to thank Jean and Brian Hackett for their tireless work in checking the text so thoroughly for us, and the staff of the Department of Typography & Graphic Communication at Reading University, especially Mick Stocks, Paul Odell, Geoff Wyeth and Michael Johnston.

Victoria Chalard and Niki Dadou, students in Typography & Graphic Communication, contributed to the design of the book.

Whilst we have gathered material for the book from many sources, most of the photographs and documents have come from the personal collection of Gerry Westall, with additional material from the Museum of English Rural Life.

*This very act of planting a seed in the earth has in it to me
something beautiful, I always do it with a joy
that is largely mixed with awe.*

Celia Thaxter 1835–1894

# Foreword

I count it a privilege to be asked to write the foreword to this book. So many other companies have been taken over and their names have disappeared, like Suttons' neighbour, Huntley and Palmers; but Suttons has survived under its own name for 200 years, and is still known worldwide for the quality of its products. Many packets of Sutton's seeds are literally 'worth their weight in gold'!

Leaving Cemetery Junction in Reading and going along the A4 eastwards, a traveller by car comes to the bridge under the old Southern Railway line to Waterloo. In my childhood, that bridge had an advertisement for Sutton's Seeds painted on it that filled me with pride when I saw it. Beyond it, to the left, was the vista of assorted colours of the trial grounds that later had the offices built in the centre. Today the office block remains, surrounded by numerous other buildings. It is good, however, that Reading remembers its connections with the company by calling the area 'Suttons Business Park'. There are also other reminders of the family in the town. There is a bust of Martin Hope Sutton in Greyfriars Church, and Alfred Sutton still has a primary school on Wokingham Road named after him.

I am privileged to belong to this family, a family that always sought to honour God first. Board meetings always started with prayers, and time was set aside each week for any staff members who wished to attend morning worship led by ministers from the town. My father, Audley Sutton, took prayers regularly, and I remember attending with him on more than one occasion. As this book shows, these businessmen did not seek only to further their commercial interests, but contributed to the Borough of Reading in their many civic responsibilities. They were also active in Christian witness through the life of Reading churches and societies, such as the Bible Society.

We now live in an age where people are often valued only for what they can contribute financially. If a company is not doing well, it is the staff first who are made redundant in a cost-cutting exercise. It is increasingly rare for someone to remain in one company for all of his or her working life. It has, however, been a privilege for me recently to meet retired employees who spent many years working at Suttons. Some of them had the vision to rescue material that would have been thrown out when the firm moved from Reading to Torquay. Now, as members of the

Earley Local History Group, they have felt inspired to compile and write this book, *Suttons Seeds*. I am personally grateful that this team should have cared enough about the company both for the sake of agriculture and horticulture, as well as the Borough of Reading.

I hope many people will enjoy reading this history.

*Jane Sutton.*

The Maiwand Lion Memorial as referred to in Jane Sutton's memories.

# 1. Introduction

The famous seed company, Suttons, celebrated its bicentenary in 2006 after 200 years of continuous service to agriculture and horticulture. Its name reflects the family who founded it and the tradition of high standards instigated from the start: hard work, attention to detail and great care given to seed and plant production and to its staff. The company has changed from one supplying local farmers and vegetable growers to an international firm supplying the world. For well over 150 years, the company was run by five generations of the same family but, for the last quarter of a century, none of the Sutton family has been involved in the firm.

The firm, which was founded in Reading in 1806 by John Sutton, now sells more than 40 million packets of seed a year. It was the flair,

John Sutton – the Founder of Suttons Seeds.

energy and love of botany of John's second son, Martin Hope Sutton, which drove the company forward. Over the years the name of the company has changed from John Sutton, to John Sutton and Son, then to John Sutton and Sons, then Sutton and Sons Ltd; then when the last member of the Sutton family left the board of the company, it became Suttons Seeds, and most recently, Suttons.

This book has been written by members of the Earley Local History Group and employees who worked for the firm in Reading, Earley, Torquay and Paignton. Many of the papers that would otherwise have been lost were saved by the quick thinking of a few employees when the company was leaving Reading. These archives are now safely stored in the Museum of English Rural Life at Reading University.

---

### The Museum of English Rural Life (MERL)

The Museum of English Rural Life (MERL) was founded by the University of Reading in 1951. The aim of the museum was to reflect and record the changing face of farming and the countryside.

Over the past 50 years the museum has been collecting a wide range of objects including tools, farm wagons, carts, carriages, horse-drawn ploughs, books, photographs and archives, which now comprises the single largest collection of rural history materials in the country. The museum houses designated collections of national importance and is a major resource and research centre for the history of food, farming and the countryside. It is the repository for the archives of some major companies with interests in agriculture and food; not least it houses the Suttons Seeds Archive.

The museum recently (2005) moved to a new location in Redlands Road, the main part of which is East Thorpe House, the residence of Alfred Palmer, (of the Reading firm of Huntley and Palmers, famous for their biscuits and cakes) which was built for him in 1880 by the famous architect Alfred Waterhouse. This building, with various additions, formed St Andrew's Hall, one of the university's halls of residence, until 2001. Since then the building has been refurbished with a grant from the Heritage Lottery Fund, funding from the university and from public appeal. Today it forms part of the university's museums and collections service.

Researchers are welcome to visit and consult the archive, library and gallery free of charge. Further information can be found on the web site www.merl. org.uk ; e-mail merl@reading.ac.uk ; The Museum of English Rural Life, The University of Reading, Redlands Road, RG1 5EX; telephone 0118 378 8660.

# 2. Setting the Scene

It is helpful to put the start of the firm by John Sutton, in 1806 at 13 King Street, Reading, in its historical perspective. The turn of the eighteenth to the nineteenth century was an important time in the history of agriculture and horticulture in England. In the previous 100 years, most of the open fields of England had been enclosed, and many of the commons were enclosed over the next 50 years or so. The open-field strip system was replaced by modern scientific agriculture. In the early eighteenth century, Jethro Tull invented the seed drill and the 4-coulter plough which could rip up turf and produce a friable seedbed. Less seed produced greater grain yields. The seed drill was used to sow grassland with clover and grass, and fields with turnips. Farmers could now produce enough food to feed their stock during the winter, and beef became available all the year round. Viscount Raynham (known as 'Turnip Townshend') developed the four-course system of cultivation: wheat – oats (or barley) – greenstuffs – turnips. Thomas Coke of Holkham Hall in Norfolk continued this work when he inherited his family's estate in 1776. Coke improved cattle (Devon Red) and sheep (Southdown) breeds by selective breeding, Robert Bakewell produced a dual-purpose beef and dairy Longhorn and bred the Leicester sheep. The Board of Agriculture was formed in 1793. Without these changes in food production, Britain would not have been able to feed her people during the Napoleonic Wars (Kay, 1952).

> The Swedish Turnip seed *(Ruta baga)*
> *Transplanted seed of the real original growth to be sold from one bushel to five sacks at Demezy's, the White Lion, Hertford-bridge, from 1s 6d per lb to 1s 3d according to quantity purchased. Turnips from seed of the same quality may be seen from 10lb to 12lb weight, the seed to be paid for on delivery.*
> Reading Mercury, *10th February 1806*

> Swedish Turnip seed
> *Of the true Yellow sort, from transplanted turnips of last year's growth may be had at the low price of 3 shillings per gallon by applying either to George Holloway, Porter, Reading; Mrs Winter, Newbury; or to the grower Mr Law, Bucklebury.*
> Reading Mercury, *21st April 1806*

> *R Swallow, seedsman, etc, Maidenhead, Berkshire [begs] to inform his friends and the public, they may be supplied with yellow, Swedish, Long White, Tankard, and Norfolk white turnip war-*

*ranted transplanted of the truest and best quality.*
*He returns thanks to his numerous friends, and hopes to insure*
*their future favours, by supplying them with the best Articles, on*
*the lowest terms.*
Reading Mercury, *9th June 1806*

Bread prices were high during the Napoleonic wars; after war broke out, wheat prices rose from 50 shillings a quarter to 160 shillings, and a loaf from 6 pence to 1 shilling and 5 pence in 1801. The prices dropped after the wars and, this combined with bad harvests, led to the 'Hungry Forties'.

Tastes in garden design were changing from the landscapes of Capability Brown and Humphrey Repton and controlled wildernesses of the landed gentry to the more domestic gardens designed by Loudon for the nouveau riche who had made their money during the war and, later on in the century, for the rising middle classes. Loudon started publishing *The Gardeners' Magazine* in 1826 and, in the first editorial, stated 'Landscape gardening about a century ago was as much the fashion as horticulture is at present' (Gorer, 1979). These people wanted plants and seeds of vegetables and flowers for their new gardens. A catalogue of 1804 lists 994 species of herbaceous plants and the 1869 list 582 species, with many of the non-ornamental species listed in the earlier catalogue no longer being offered. This was the start of the period of the plant hunters who brought back many new genera and species from around the world, particularly Asia. The forerunner of the Royal Horticultural Society, the Horticultural Society of London, was formed in 1805 by John Wedgewood and Sir Joseph Banks among others, reflecting the increase in interest in plants and gardens (Hodder, 1956). John Wedgewood mooted the idea of a society to award prizes for excellence in gardens, as well as presenting papers on all aspects of horticulture.

At this period, Reading was in an excellent geographical position to make full use of the trading routes around the country. Transport was improving, with the newly-opened canals being used to move goods between north and south via Oxford and the Thames to London. Improvements in the navigation of the river Kennet opened up a route from Newbury to Reading, and later the building of the Kennet and Avon canal, which was finished in 1810, allowed for the movement of goods between Bristol and London. The Bath Road and the newly-built Forest Road were both fast routes to the capital and the former also to the west. Numerous coach services and carters were available along these routes.

Plant breeding was in its infancy at this period, since little attention had been paid to it. Wholesalers in London controlled the market, and the seed industry as the eighteenth turned into the nineteenth century was riddled with the practice of seed adulteration.

*'From beginning to end of the entire business general laxity reigned. Poor stocks were sown for seed crops, and these for the most part were carelessly grown and they were sent to the stores imperfectly cleaned. Eventually they were sold to the farmers and horticulturists by shopkeepers who knew nothing whatever of the history or value of the seeds.*

*'As each harvest was received it was mixed with older seed of the same kind, unless by way of change it happened to be mixed with some other variety. It was the practice never to sell seed of the latest harvest, but always to incorporate the new with the old stock, the alleged object being to ensure a certain average growth which would meet the moderate expectations of the gardeners and farmers of that day. Even under these circumstances, the growth in some years was so far beneath the average that the remaining stock was practically worthless!'* (Cheales).

Thus Suttons came into being at a time of tremendous change, both in the country itself and in agricultural and horticultural practices, and also when the seed industry desperately needed someone to champion the cause of honesty, integrity and quality.

# 3. The Reading Years

Around the turn of the eighteenth century, two young men came to Reading. James (1776–1826) and John Sutton (1777–1863) were the second and third surviving sons of the late James Sutton (1744–89). Their forebears were millers in Newbury, Berkshire, and they had been apprenticed as millers to their late father's partner in London before coming to Reading around 1800 to manage a family mill or mills by the river Kennet. Their grandfather, Charles Sutton (mayor of Newbury in 1749), had died in 1750, and his son had moved to London where he became a partner in the flour company Winckworth and Sutton of Queenhithe in Southwark. James (the father) died in Bath in 1789, when he went to take the waters, and was buried in Bristol Cathedral (Corley, 1991–3).

John Sutton set up a shop called the 'House of Sutton' at 13 King Street in 1806 dealing in flour, agricultural seeds, corn (wheat) and pasture seed.

John Sutton is recorded in 1820, 1826, 1832 and 1835 on the voters' list for Reading as living in King Street trading as a corn dealer, and in 1837–39 and 1840–42 in Market Place, at the latter date with Martin Hope Sutton (RLSL). John Sutton rented the King Street and Market Place properties, but must have been a land or property owner elsewhere to have been on the voters' list. In 1859 he was living at Southampton Villa, Southampton Street, and Martin Hope was at Cintra Lodge, (Christchurch Road) (RLSL).

Unfortunately for James and John, two disasters hit them in 1814–15. Firstly, the Napoleonic Wars ended, and agricultural prices dropped dramatically. In addition, at the start of that year, the bad weather halted road and water transport, and the summer weather was so hot and dry that the harvests were badly hit, and the water in the canals was so low that boats could not move. Secondly, in January 1815, the Marsh, Deane & Co. Bank, Reading, collapsed. James had an overdraft of £1500 and was declared bankrupt. He continued to work as a baker, and died of alcoholism, a poor man, 11 years later. John was more fortunate in only having an overdraft of £960, and was able to make a deal with the receivers. It was in this disastrous year of 1815 that John's second son, Martin Hope, was born on the 14th March (Corley, 1991–3).

> 'As an expression of faith that a bright future was in store for the son, his parents named him Hope, and certainly the birth of this child proved to be the greatest blessing the family could have received at this severe crisis in its fortunes.' (Cheales)

Martin Hope Sutton took a great interest in botany from an early age, reading about the subject as well as growing plants in the garden. He left Miss Paget's Infant School in 1820, and became a scholar at a school on Church Street run by Joseph Huntley. In 1825 he attended Castle Street Academy, run by Thomas Greathead, for two years. At this time, John Sutton's company was running down and both his parents were in poor health, so his schooling was brought to an end and he was brought into his father's company. He started work in the granaries, and moved to the counting-house in 1829.

John's third son, Alfred Sutton, joined the firm in 1832, and in 1836 Martin Hope, aged 21, became a partner with his father, and the company was renamed John Sutton and Son. Later, in 1843 when Alfred was made a partner, the company became John Sutton and Sons.

All references mention Martin Hope's love of botany and his father's reluctance to let him study the subject.

> 'He found recreation in reading botanical works and in the practical study of botany, especially in relation to flowers, grasses, and forage plants. In these pursuits no encouragement was given him by the father. On the contrary, parental anxiety became acute when it was discovered that books on botany were smuggled to the bedroom, and that in early morning, before the household rose, the garden had been employed as an experimental ground for comparative trials of seeds.' (Cheales)

From an early age, Martin Hope carried out trials comparing various seeds. Funds were limited, and holidays were utilized as walking tours of trial grounds. He began making trips to visit local nurseries, mainly on foot, reading as he walked along. In the 1830s on one occasion, he visited over three days the grounds of Brown at Slough, Ronald at Brentford, on through Staines and Sunninghill to the Knaphill and Woking nurseries, and Waterers at Bagshot, examining the work of other growers. Of this trip he wrote:

> 'I walked back during the night in order to be at my desk at the proper time in the morning'.

This driven behaviour inspired Hodder (1956) to write 'this expedition was made on foot, making a round journey of well over seventy miles and obviously to that earnest young man it was nothing remarkable that he should walk twenty-five miles during the night, to start his normal day's work at 7 a.m.' In 1831, he opened an account in his father's name with the London wholesale seed firm of Beck, Allen and Shearman in the Strand. A year later, he produced his first printed broadsheet to advertise his growing list of seeds, and on the 3rd December of the same year he placed his first advertisement in the *Reading Mercury* under his father's name.

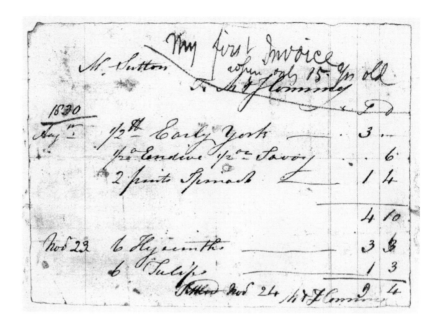

Copy of Martin Hope Sutton's first invoice for seeds and bulbs purchased 1830.

During the first half of 1833, Martin became very ill and, for the sake of his health, his father accepted that he would have to change career. Martin was a good artist, and friends of his father suggested that he should be employed somewhere using this talent. So in September 1833, his father decided that he should become a surveyor, and he went to work for F. Hawkes and Sons, estate agents, auctioneers and surveyors of West Street. But Mr Hawkes used him as a clerk and, after three months, brought his own son into the firm, so Martin Hope returned to his father's business (Corley, 1991–3).

His father, John Sutton, sold turnip seed to farmers from whom he bought corn. Recalling one such transaction, Martin Hope wrote:

> 'I well remember one Saturday evening [1833], his great concern at discovering that he had by mistake, served a farmer out of the wrong sack of turnip seed. It was decided that he and I would rise extra early next morning, which we did and carried with us a bag of the proper sort to the farmer, about 7 miles off, walking all the way and arriving in time to go to church with him, after having received hearty thanks for our painstaking – this was one of the most enjoyable Sundays I ever remember. After church we dined at the farmhouse, and walked home in the evening; so that part of the business which my father carried on was evidently established long before the year 1833.' (MERL)

Cheales, Hodder and Corley mention a seed chest that was the most treasured possession of Martin Hope. On top of the chest was a brass plate.

Martin Hope Sutton's original seed chest.

Below: Descriptive brass plate on the chest.

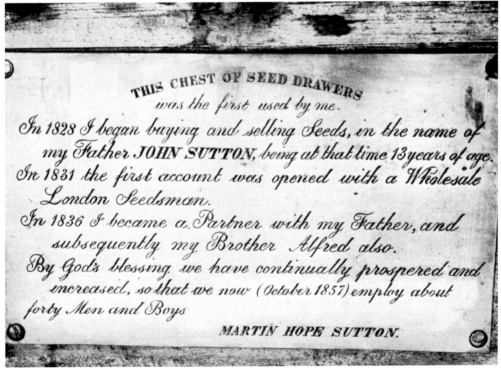

THIS CHEST OF SEED DRAWERS
*was the first used by me.*

*In 1828 I began buying and selling Seeds, in the name of my Father* JOHN SUTTON, *being at that time 13 years of age.*

*In 1831 the first account was opened with a Wholesale London Seedsman.*

*In 1836 I became a Partner with my Father, and subsequently my Brother Alfred also.*

*By God's blessing, we have continually prospered and increased, so that we now (October 1857) employ about forty Men and Boys*

MARTIN HOPE SUTTON.

Directories from the time show that Reading had many corn dealers, making Martin Hope's desire to diversify the company a sound business move.

| In 1830, there were | 13 Corn Dealers |
| | 14 Gardeners and Seedsmen |
| In 1840, there were | 17 Corn Dealers |
| | 10 Gardeners |
| | 2 Seedsmen |
| In 1850, there were | 21 Corn Dealers |
| | 17 Gardeners and Seedsmen |
| In 1860, there were | 15 Corn Dealers |
| | 4 Nurserymen |
| | 25 Gardeners |

Martin Hope Sutton began to expand his father's company by selling vegetable and flower seed. Records show that he was buying seeds and bulbous flower roots in 1833. He expanded the garden seed side of the business rapidly. In 1832, they represented only 2% of the stock, but they had risen to 42% by 1833. In 1834, he became a member of the Reading Horticultural Society.

Coincidentally, the Royal Horticultural Society had been founded only a year before Suttons, and the society's collectors had sent back a large number of new plants from all over the world. Together with the fashion change from Capabilitiy Brown's landscape style of gardening which required few seed-raised plants compared to the more formal Victorian styles which required much denser plantings, this created a rapidly-expanding horticultural market for the ambitious Suttons to exploit. Plant breeding was in its infancy at the start of the nineteenth century, and Martin Hope Sutton was one of a number of growers who started selecting lines of agricultural and horticultural plants for improvements in germination, vigour, yield and quality. The breeding of animals, begun in the previous century, was now matched by the breeding and development of root crops, grasses, garden vegetable and flower seeds in the nineteenth century.

In 1836, the company had purchased the goodwill of the nursery and seed trade of Mrs Conning at 7 and 8 Market Place, at the rear of which Martin Hope had a small trial ground, and a nursery on land in Queens Road. At these grounds, trained and standard fruit trees and roses, American tree species and other species were grown.

This picture is reproduced from an old woodcut of Suttons shop in the Market Place, Reading in 1837.

**J. Sutton & Son**
## NURSERYMAN, SEEDSMEN & ETC

Having in November 1836, purchased the goodwill of the Nursery & Seed trade of the establishment, numbers 7 & 8 Market Place, Reading, formerly in the occupation of Mrs Conning, and having recently taken more nursery ground, erected a new greenhouse, pits & etc and greatly enlarged the above premises, they beg respectfully to inform the nobility, clergy and gentry, that they have now removed from King Street, and earnestly solicit a continuance of their esteemed orders, which will always receive their personal attention, and be executed with the very best articles, at the lowest possible prices.
*Reading Directory, E Yorke, 1839*

1836–7 proved to be a pivotal period for the firm. In mid-summer of 1836, when he turned 21, Martin was made a partner and the firm became John Sutton and Son; the firm produced a three-figure credit balance for the first time; and it moved into new premises in Market Place. Martin gambled that the better position of the Market Place shop would more than offset the £50 a year rent for the new property (the King Street shop had been £23). Once again, Martin's health failed him and, during the move in January 1837, he had to be carried over to the new premises in a hospital ambulance wrapped in blankets.

In 1837, he persuaded his father to allow him to incorporate his seed and plant trade into the business under the title of John Sutton & Son (MERL). Also in this year Martin Hope advertised a large display of tulips at the rear of their premises in Market Place.

Mary Russell Mitford, a local author, wrote:

> 'We visited the nurseries, from Brown's, at Slough, a princely establishment, worthy of its regal neighbourhood, to the pretty rural gardens at South Warnborough, not forgetting our own most intelligent and so obliging nurseryman (Mr Sutton of Reading), whose collection of flowers of all sorts is amongst the most choice and select that I have ever known.' (Cheales)

The Market Place shop with its double-fronted windows and prominent position overlooking the vegetable and general market held each Saturday was well placed to gain the patronage of visiting farmers and market growers.

Suttons' Market Place premises eventually occupied some six acres of land. Originally this area belonged to the monks of Reading Abbey, which had been built in 1121. One of the two gardens of the Abbey was in the centre of what was to become Suttons' business complex. The early plant trials carried out by Martin Hope Sutton were almost certain to have been on part of this ancient garden, which was eventually covered by the Sutton establishment.

After the dissolution of the country's abbeys by King Henry VIII, this and other areas of Reading and district came into the hands of the Blagrave family. It is known they were leasing property and land as early as 1714; leasehold areas were found within the company up to the 1950s. As the leases became available, they were purchased by the company. The Blagrave Estate sold the last two of its leases in the Reading area in July 1988.

The Abbey stables were on land adjacent to the south gate of the Abbey bordered by the Holy Brook (a small diverted tributary of the river Kennet). It appears these were rebuilt between 1380 and 1420, and were known as the Queen's Stables in 1620. The land on which the stables were situated was redeveloped about 1869 when a school and other buildings, which included a restaurant and commercial hotel, and a grist mill, were built. Suttons purchased these buildings and spent £4,435 converting them into their Seed Potato Department. Later on, a bridge was built connecting this department with the main building on the opposite side of Abbey Square. The land around this area was known as Hookers Green from before Victorian times. When Suttons built a hall for the staff and for renting out, it was aptly named Abbey Hall.

*'I remember Harry Jermey, the deputy head of the Potato Department, telling me their department was built over part of the Abbey stables and that Suttons was responsible for the preservation of any of the ruins. These were in fact strengthened by inserting steel girders and additional brickwork.'*

(Gerry Westall, personal reminiscences)

From 1911 this was Suttons Potato Department. Some time later a bridge was constructed to connect with the main building. The boarded gate to the right gave access to the Holy Brook. On the extreme right is the rear of the York House Pub, much frequented by some staff, after work on Saturday mornings. The site is now occupied by the Reading Central library.

In the winter of 1962–3, the majority of the Suttons' buildings were demolished to make way for road developments which would have gone through the centre of their premises; although the road was built, it was never completed and the area became a car park for many years. The site of Suttons' Potato Department eventually became the main library for Berkshire and subsequently Reading.

As time went on, John Sutton's advancing years and failing health meant that, in reality if not on paper, Martin Hope began to assume effective control of the company, with his brother Alfred as his right-hand man; between 1840 and 1875, he built up the company from a small and none-too-profitable concern into the largest retail enterprise in Britain's seed trade (Corley 1994–7). By the late 1870s, Martin Hope 'went further, and claimed to have the most considerable retail seed business in Europe, measured both by turnover and by the number of customers.' (MERL)

The company distributed its seed, plants and tubers by carters, and became well-known in the south-east part of the country. *Kelly's Directory of Berkshire* of the 1840s and '50s shows that places as far away as Andover, Guildford, Newbury, Oxford, Thame, Windsor and Wycombe were served by a network of horse-drawn carriers' carts and wagons. It might have remained a small regional company if it had not been for two innovations. On 10th January 1840, with the implementation of the penny post, money orders for sending small sums of money through the mail became available through the Post Office: the almost-simultaneous arrival of the railway, in the form of the London to Bristol Great Western line to Reading, meant the company was able to receive consignments of seeds from its growers and send out seeds and plants to buyers reliably and speedily. Martin Hope Sutton was at Reading Station on 30th March 1840, to see the first train depart for London, and took advantage of the crowds to sell flower seed to spectators and passers-by (Cheales).

The money order system was taken over by the General Post Office from the banks in 1838. Fees for transferring money were reduced further, making the money order system profitable. '... by which the Public are enabled to remit small Sums of Money through the Post Office by means of Money Orders ...' *Regulation concerning Money Orders,* 10th August 1840, Section 38.

Advice had to be sent to pay the Post Office before payment could be tendered to the recipient of the order. This drawback was probably the primary incentive for the establishment of the Postal Order system on 1st January 1881.

1840 was a pivotal year in the history of the company; as well as being the year the penny post started and the railway arrived in Reading,

THIS INDENTURE *Witnesseth that James Messenger poor boy born in the Parish of Saint Laurence in the Borough of Reading in the County of Berks with the consent of his Father William Messenger of the Parish and Borough aforesaid Labourer, doth put himself apprentice to Martin Hope Sutton of the Borough of Reading Nurseryman and Seedsman to learn his arts and with him as an apprentice to serve from the day of the date thereof for the term of seven years during which time the said apprentice his Master shall faithfully serve his secrets keep his lawful command everywhere gladly do, he shall do no damage to his said Master nor see it to be done of others but to his power shall prevent or give notice to his said Master of the same he shall not waste the goods of his said Master nor lend them unlawfully to any he shall not contract Matrimony within the said term nor play at cards or any other unlawful games whereby his said Master may have any loss with his own goods or offers during the said term he shall not haunt Taverns or playhouses or absent himself from his said Masters service day or night unlawfully but in all things as a faithful Apprentice he shall behave himself towards his said Master and all his Family during the said term. And the said Martin Hope Sutton in consideration of such services and of the sum of Twenty pounds of lawful money of Great Britain to him paid by the Trustees of certain public charities in the Borough of Reading aforesaid denominated Church Charities which sum is public charity money and the gift of the Late William Laud formerly the Archbishop of Canterbury deceased the receipt whereof it hereby acknowledged his said apprentice in the arts of Nurseryman and Seedsman shall teach and instruct finding unto his said apprentice sufficient and proper meat drink and lodging and apparel of all sorts (and the washing and mending thereof) and all other necessaries whatsoever in sickness and in health during the said term and the said Martin Hope Sutton for himself his executors and administrators doth covenant to and with the present Trustees of the said Church Charities and the Trustees of the same Charities for the time being not to assign or part with his said apprentice to any other Master during the said term without the consent of the said present Trustees or the Trustees of the said charities for the time being thereto first had and obtained in writing In witness whereof the said parties to these presents have hereunto set their hands and seals this first day of August in the year of our Lord One thousand eight hundred and forty two.*

Signed sealed and delivered
By all the said parties

In the presence of The Mark of
William Messenger
William Walker
Junior Clerk to Mr Blandy
Solicitor Reading

Indenture of James Messenger.

MEMORANDUM DATED 1ST AUGUST 1842
CONCERNING INDENTURE FOR JAMES MESSENGER

*It is understood and agreed between us that James Messenger (the boy named in the annexed Indenture) is not to be provided with any food, drink lodging wearing apparel or washing by his Master, but these and all other necessaries are to be provided by himself or his friends.*

*It is also agreed the wages James Messenger shall receive from Martin Hope Sutton or the Master to whom he is assigned shall be as follows:–*

*From the first year from the date here of three shillings per week, for the next year four shillings, for the next year five shillings, for the next year six shillings, for the next year seven shillings, for the next year nine shillings and for the seventh year the wages to be mutually agreed upon at the expiration of the sixth year if he remains in the service of the same Master.*

*The hours of working are to be from six o'clock a.m. to nine o'clock p.m. in the months of April, May, June, July, August and September; and from seven o'clock a.m. to nine o'clock p.m. in the months of October, November, December, January, February and March; and the aforesaid James Messenger will have to perform such work as is absolutely necessary for the preservation of the plants in the Greenhouse Pits from the weather also on Sundays.*

*(signed) Martin Hope Sutton*
*James Messenger*
*The Mark of William Messenger X [sic]*

it was also the year that Suttons established its first seed-testing laboratory to test seed for germination and purity. The business was doing so well by this time that extra help was required. In accordance with his Christian principles, Martin Hope decided to take apprentices recommended by local church charities, and here is the indenture (agreement) for James Messenger. James Messenger was indentured as an apprentice to Martin Hope in 1842 under the Church Charities, a gift of William Laud, Archbishop of Canterbury (a native of Reading and a scholar at Reading School).

William Deane was indentured as an apprentice to Alfred Sutton in February 1851 under the Rich bequest, Sonning. He was paid similar weekly payments as James Messenger (see previous page). But by September 1851 in a Memorandum it was recorded that: '… having been guilty of diverse misdemeanours and miscarriages and ill behaviour in his service …', William Deane was threatened with being discharged from his apprenticeship. He expressed 'deep contrition' and Alfred Sutton forgave him but 'upon the express conditions that he shall be at liberty at any time to discharge the said William Deane and to cancel the Indenture.'. (MERL)

The seed trade that Martin Hope was trying to enter was effectively managed as a closed cartel by long-established seed merchants mostly based in London. They ensured that production (the majority from East Anglia) and prices were tightly controlled through their London Seed Association. In order to break into this club, Martin Hope was forced to develop his own network of growers and suppliers. These were mainly on land west of London, which made it easy for him to maintain the personal contact necessary to ensure the high standards he demanded.

During the terrible Irish potato famine in 1846–7, the British Government asked Suttons to supply seed of fast-maturing vegetable crops. The famine encouraged Martin Hope to put to use his knowledge of cultivating and selecting vegetables for food. Suttons continued to send seed to Ireland and to the highlands of Scotland, where the crofters had also suffered from potato blight. The company sent out the seed that was left over at the end of the year, as it had a rule that seed would be on sale for one year only. Public men of the day had discovered the value of Martin Hope's labours, resulting in the firm receiving substantial orders for seed of turnip, beetroot, cabbage and other quick-growing items to alleviate the severity of the famine. The company started to become internationally known with its exhibit at the 1851 Exhibition in London, and seed was supplied to gardeners across Europe.

At the time that Martin Hope was entering the seed trade, seed adulteration was commonplace. There was a lot of money to be made by mixing expensive seed such as broccoli (worth 10 shillings per pound weight) with rape seed rendered sterile to prevent germination (worth 3 pence per pound), and by mixing old seed with new seed. Indeed special seed-killing machines were widely advertised and available for purchase, and there were even accepted proportions for the mixing of live and dead seeds. From the start, Martin Hope worked to rid the trade of adulterated seed. He was so disaffected with the mixing of old and new seed, which was the normal situation with the wholesale seed market at that time, that in 1839 he organised a peaceful campaign to overcome the modest scruples of the seed growers in Essex, offering them higher prices for crops to be grown solely for him. To start with, he was a lone voice, but gradually he gathered enough other powerful people around him to ensure that his honest methods won the day. In 1840, he established a procedure for testing the purity and germination of seed. The fact that a number of the London seed-houses were making huge profits out of seed adulteration meant that Martin Hope's campaign turned out to be more protracted than he had first hoped. However, in 1868, the London Seed Association at last held a meeting on this issue, but even then many of its members cited lack of legislation as a reason for doing nothing. Fortunately in the same year, a sub-committee set up by the Royal Horticultural Society visited Martin to look at his extensive file of offers of killed seed and also threats that had been made against him! The covert evidence collected by this sub-committee forced the government to act. Martin Hope had the satisfaction of being in the gallery of the House of Commons as the new Bill was debated. In 1869 when the Seed Adulteration Act was passed, Suttons was one of only five firms lobbying for this reform, but nevertheless it became law. The company had to wait another 50 years, however, for the 1920 Seeds Act to be passed which covered the sale of agricultural and vegetable seeds, and for the first Government-funded seed-testing station to be set up. In spite of opposition from the London seed-houses, Martin Hope had won the day and established a good name for quality (*The British Trade Journal*, 1st Feb 1877). '[His] determination was that he would sell no seed unless of 'the highest purity and of full germination.' (Hodder, 1956)

The 1850s and 1860s were a boom period for Suttons. After a decade and a half of laying the foundations, Martin Hope began to see the fruits of his labour. 1849–50 had seen sales to the value of £4,700 and profits of £1,240, but only a decade later, with an annual growth rate of 22%, these had grown to sales of almost £35,000 and profits of nearly £10,000. Another ten years saw the 1869–70 sales reach £73,000, with profits of £21,000 (Corley, 1994–7).

Suttons' trade increased with the improved reliability of the seed it was offering for sale. The company paid great attention to the growing, selection and production of seed at all stages of the process. The partners in the business were involved at all these stages, and they prided themselves on close personal contact with their customers.

By 1852, Sutton and Sons was considered to be an important seed establishment. Seed was sold in labelled packets, which were an innovation at the time. There were extensive warehouses behind the shop where garden and agricultural seeds (particularly turnip and grass) were grown. Seed vigour was tested in the glasshouses and pits, and pot plants such as pelargonium and cineraria were grown with pots of bulbs plunged in old tan. Potted and bare-root conifers were available, and ivies: 'Ivies are much wanted, and therefore cultivated in pots here; both walls of a passage connecting the two gardens just mentioned being covered with them.' (*Gardeners' Chronicle*, 1852)

Roses, fruit trees, evergreens and conifers were cultivated at Portland Place (between Kendrick Road and Crown Place); valuable crops such as turnip, grass and many horticultural crops (lettuce, broccoli, cabbage, beetroot, carrots and 30 pea cultivars) were grown for seed, and potato cultivars such as the early cultivars Sodens Early Oxford and Walnut-leaf Kidney and the second early cultivars Red Ash-leaf, Doctor Nelson's Favourite and British Queen were grown for seed potatoes.

The company could reach every county of the UK by post by 1862, and discontinued the practice of calling on all its customers as it had become physically impossible to do so. It received further advertising and endorsements when its cultivars won top prizes in agricultural shows e.g. in 1857 the swede Suttons Champion won many prizes for local Berkshire farmers, and the Benyon (Englefield) estate won a silver cup, value 10 guineas, for a collection of long and globe mangels, swedes and carrots grown from Suttons' seeds at the Birmingham Show (30th November to 3rd December). The Royal Horticultural Society presented the company with the prestigious Lawrence Medal for its remarkable series of exhibits in 1918.

Royal patronage began in the 1850s when Queen Victoria requested that Martin Hope supply seeds to the Royal Household. The honour of the Royal Warrant was bestowed by the Prince of Wales (later King Edward VII) in 1871 and by Queen Victoria in 1884, and has continued ever since.

Expansion meant that the character of the firm changed over time. In the early 1840s, it was mainly staffed by members of the Sutton family. As well as John, Martin and Alfred, John's eldest daughter worked in the shop and, with the help of her two sisters, also made the seed packets and labels and wrote up bills. By the 1860s, Sutton and Sons was still family-controlled but was becoming less family-run, with production and sales run by managers as departmental heads. In 1863, John Sutton died and his daughter's assistance was no longer required. In 1866, Martin Hope's son Martin John left school and began an apprenticeship with the firm. Alfred's son, somewhat confusingly also called Alfred, also joined the firm at about the same time, but died of typhoid soon after becoming manager of the nurseries. In 1870, Martin Hope's son Arthur joined the firm and was made a partner in 1876. In 1871, Martin John Sutton became a partner, and his father Martin Hope took over the post of head of the executive from Alfred. Both Martin Hope and Alfred retired in 1888.

Compared with their father Martin Hope, Martin John's, Arthur's and Leonard's education was more orthodox in that they went to

Print of 1873 showing the new Market Place frontage.

fee-paying schools followed by college or university. Arthur Warwick Sutton took over responsibility for the vegetable side of the business producing many new varieties over the years, while his brother Leonard Goodhart Sutton, the youngest son, ran the flower seed department. He too, introduced many new selections, specialising in South African native plants.

## Suttons Seeds New Buildings, January 1873

'During the last few years, nearly the whole of the extensive premises has been remodelled or re-built. The frontage to the Market Place remained, however, until quite recently, as heretofore but, having obtained possession of two houses immediately adjoining, the present handsome structure has been raised.

'The various blocks of buildings extend from the Market Place. In an easterly direction, then branching southward through Abbey Square, they join the new diversion of Kings Road, opened in 1869 by the Prince and Princess of Wales, and known as the '"Prince of Wales buildings"'.

'The building in the illustration is made of white Mansfield stone and the basement is constructed of pressed bricks from Wheelers & Sons, Reading.

'The fascias are of Forest of Dean stone, with sunk letters gilded; the columns [are] of Bristol blue stone and red Bishop's Lydeard alternated. Royal green slates are used for roof coverings, with ornamental cast-iron curb and hip plates, by Walter MacFarlane & Co., of London, and wrought iron created by Margaretts, of Reading. The stall plates are of grey polished granite, sunk-lettered in gilt.

'Of the three lower arches of the front, two are windows lighting the retail departments, while the third (somewhat more elaborate in design) forms, in connexion with a corridor, the main entrance to the establishment.

'The first floor reached by a flight of Portland stone steps, is devoted entirely to a library and recreation room and toilets. On the second floor are two large rooms, which may be used as private offices, or for other business purposes. There is a lofty well-lighted upper floor, partly in the roof, which by means of a lift can be connected with the ground floor and basement.

'The whole of the joiner's work, including fittings, is of oak and pitch pine, slightly relieved with walnut; all French polished, and prepared from the architects' special designs.

'The whole complex is terminated by a handsome and capacious lecture hall, completely fitted, with open-timbered roof, stained and varnished and plastered between the rafters.

'In nearby Abbey Square the company has built and fitted up a coffee and refreshment house, which is used, not only by their own men, but by many others who prefer getting their meals there rather than resorting to an ordinary public house.

'On an adjacent portion of Kings Road, the company have erected another large store for agricultural seeds, three floors in height. The superficial area of the floor space is 5,474 square feet.

'The total cost exclusive of land and fittings was £17,000.'
(Builder Magazine, 1873)

Top left: Market Place frontage 1950's.
Top right: Market Place shop 1973.
Bottom left: Interior of Suttons Garden shop 1890's.
Bottom right: Interior of Market Place shop 1962.

The company was rapidly outgrowing its premises in Market Place, so in 1873 new offices and warehouses replaced the original premises which covered a large area behind Market Place. As well as a shop, offices and warehouses, it had its own manual fire engine, stables, a residence for the head groom and a nursery for sowing stocks of high-class plants.

With the exception of the Garden Shop, these premises were demolished in the winter of 1962–3. The company moved to a purpose-built building in the autumn of 1962, on land which had been their trial grounds since the 1880s. The shop was vacated in 1973. A garden centre adjacent to the new buildings was opened in the mid-1960s.

Imports of grain from the New World had resulted in low wheat prices, which forced many British farmers to put their land under pasture. In 1861 Martin Hope was asked to write an article entitled 'Laying Down Land to Permanent Pasture' for the *Journal of the Royal Agricultural Society of England*. This rekindled his interest in grasses, and he began looking at the composition of grass species and cultivars for different soil types. He made up special mixtures for farmers according to their requirements so that, in the period 1875–1890, Suttons sold sufficient to sow 30,000 acres per annum with '... in many cases 50% increases in hay crop yields.' (*The Times*, 1906)

His son Martin John continued this work by looking at the nutritional value of grasses and clovers. Martin John's book *Permanent and Temporary Pastures* (published 1886) became a standard work, and he received the gold medal at the Paris Exhibition of 1900. He received further honours from the French Government for his work on the nutrition of grasses.

The introduction of the potato Magnum Bonum in 1876 revolutionised the cultivation of potatoes (*The Times*, 1906). In 1894 this cultivar proved to be the most disease-resistant one in a year when the potato crop was a disaster.

Suttons ceased to have stands at the big agricultural and horticultural shows after 1887 (Millard diaries, MERL) because of the huge costs involved: '... for instance just as 10 years ago, after holding an annual root show for over 30 years, we decided that such a display was no longer necessary as a means of pushing the business, so now we have come to the conclusion that our trade is no longer dependent on agricultural shows and international exhibits and therefore we shall in future almost entirely dispense with such methods of advertising. Consequently the Exhibition Department has been reduced to a minimum...' (MERL)

Instead the company concentrated on selling via catalogues and travelling salesmen who visited the big estates in the UK, on the Continent and even the eastern USA. Suttons always dealt directly with the large estates; its connection with allotment holders and commercial growers came much later. The decision to abandon agricultural and horticultural shows was rescinded later, and the company became renowned for its exhibits at the Royal Show, Chelsea Flower Show and many others over a very long period.

Typewriters were introduced in 1898; until then, all letters were hand-written. A telephone system was installed between departments in the private offices in 1899. It took another 9 years (25th October 1908) before Sutton's decided to have the telephone number published in the directory. On the 8th February 1905, it was decided that the Packing Floor and Flower Seed Room were to be lit by electricity. Later that year in October, incandescent lights were installed in Mr Kinchin's department in place of flares. The Electric Light Company on hearing about this sent a deputation to discuss any improvement, to test the wiring and write a report as to how the electric light in various departments could be improved, and at less cost. It was also suggested that the 100-volt system should be replaced by 200 volts.

In 1913 the company purchased the seed business and trials grounds (at Slough) of J Veitch and Sons. Basic seed was propagated from the best plant specimens in the company's nurseries around the Reading area and Essex in particular, and then sent to specialist growers for bulking up. Graphic details are given of the difficulties in journeying across Europe to Italy to check on the growing of broccoli seed. At different periods, the company owned or rented trial grounds at Portland Place and Southcote Manor, Reading, Dysons Wood, south Oxfordshire, land between the GWR line and London Road, Earley (1880s), Slough and Gulval, Cornwall.

Suttons expanded from a plant nursery and seed company to include a design department and a construction department. It held a register of experienced gardeners and provided the labour and materials, including seeds, to provide a complete service for garden design and construction from concept to completion.

From 1806, the company had been completely owned by the family, but the untimely death of Martin John in 1913 and the tragic deaths of four of Leonard's five sons during World War One depleted the family and business tremendously, since only Leonard Noel Sutton was left to join the company. In 1921, Mr Salmon came from GEC to be Company Secretary, the first non-family person to hold this post. He brought the company up to date following the two Company Acts in the late 1920s and early 1930s. The partnership consisted of four partners who formed the Board, and each of the partners held the ordinary (voting) shares. If a partner wanted to sell any shares, he had to offer them to another partner. Other members of the family held preference shares, or 'loans'. They did not share in the profits, but had a fixed income of 5% from them. The company was run by the partners and, by the early 1930s, it was formed into a limited company.

Martin Hope Sutton was a practising Christian: morning work started with prayers (which were optional), and his Christian philanthropy was continued by his heirs. Suttons was a good employer and looked after its staff well. In 1918, it paid a minimum wage of 40 shillings a week, compared with the 44 shillings that Huntley and Palmer paid for a much longer day (MERL). The board discussed giving pensions to the staff as early as 1898, and a full contributory pension scheme was instigated in 1922. Prior to this, the partners awarded non-contributory pensions to their employees. Young men who went to war (Boer War, World War One and World War Two) were given extra monies (MERL). They were given separation allowances if married men, and unmarried men with dependants were given special consideration (Millard's diaries, MERL). From early on, they organised days out for the staff by train to seaside towns, as well as giving half-day holidays for royal events and for family marriages although, if there were lots of orders to process, work had to come first. In April 1911, Phil Sutton married Miss Douglas Jones '… during this busy time [of year] it is impossible to grant a general half day holiday but one will be arranged later on' (MERL). They encouraged their men to join their local unions (General Workers, Clerks and Firemen's Unions) (MERL). Profit-sharing was discussed in 1920. After due consultation with the partners and staff, a committee was set up with representatives of the partners and the unions (15th June 1920). It was decided that heads of departments were to receive 2.5% of the profits, and all staff with one year of service an 8.5% bonus; the bonus was distributed in 1921.

In 1864, the firm had 44 employees, and this number rose to over 100 in the late 1860s and 243 by the late 1870s; of these, 69 were office staff. Between 1880 and 1884, the work force totalled 256, of which 94 were office staff. The business saw rapid expansion: it had an annual turnover of £216,000 in 1900, and employed considerably more people.

The numbers of staff in the various departments from 1880 to 1884 were:

| | |
|---|---|
| *Ledger Office and Invoicing* | 46 |
| *Despatch Office* | 19 |
| *Growers' Office* | 22 |
| *Private and Pay Offices* | 7 |
| *Vegetable Seed Room* | 51 |
| *Flower Seed Room* | 22 |
| *Packing Floor* | 31 |
| *Granaries* | 22 |
| *Nursery and Farm* | 15 |
| *Potato Dept and Stables* | 13 |
| *Show Department* | 5 |
| *Shop* | 3 |

The highest-paid was a Mr Andrews of the Show Department (52/- per week). Junior office staff earned 6/- per week, and more senior staff 36/- per week. Junior warehouse staff earned 5/5d per week, and senior staff up to 32/6d.

The family belonged to the evangelical branch of the Church of England. Mr and Mrs Martin Hope Sutton contributed much time and money in supporting the repair of Greyfriars Church in Reading as, after the Reformation, the flint-walled church had been used as a town hall and a prison and had no roof on it. The Suttons played their part in the life of Reading: both Martin John and Leonard G Sutton were mayors in Reading, and other members of the family were councillors. Noel Sutton was a member of the Yeomanry in World War I and was, at one time, Lord Lieutenant of Berkshire.

In 1914 the partners sent Mr Stevens to India with a view to opening a branch there. He confirmed the usefulness of his journey by letter and, on his return, had further discussions so that full preparations were in place for the opening in May 1916 (Baskett's diaries, MERL). 'With the coming of the Suttons brand in India, the Indian farmers and other amateur gardening enthusiasts were exposed to the modern and professional ways of farming and horticulture. Suttons was the pioneer company which introduced the concept of high-yielding flower and vegetable seeds in India' (www.suttonseedsindia.com). The company came under Indian management as Sutton and Sons (I) Pvt, Ltd in 1969. It has consolidated its position, and Suttons has become a household name in India.

In January 1918, Arthur Warwick Sutton suggested that the time had come when the trade would have to protect itself by forming a Retail Seed Trade Association; as a first step, he drafted a letter to all the retail firms which had attended a large meeting at the Windsor Hotel in the autumn of 1915.

Between the wars the Flower Seed Room was altered to improve the efficiency of the execution of orders, with pigeon-holes replacing the old system of drawers. Also at this time a new automatic telephone system costing £525 was installed (MERL).

In the years after the Second World War, Suttons provided expertise and seed for the British Army on the Rhine which was involved with the horticultural industry in Germany.

After World War Two, high-quality seed was more readily available from many sources, and sales to large private houses were much reduced. Suttons had to consider other outlets for its various products. The company continued with main agents in towns and cities around the country; the first one had been Barrow's Stores in Corporation Street, Birmingham, in 1934. This was followed by the first stockists in shops and garden centres. During the 1960s, the number of stockists increased rapidly up to a maximum of 6,000, although demand by mail order still made up a considerable part of the total sales.

Shortage of workers was very acute after the war and, in March 1947, the Company Secretary attended a meeting of the Reading & District Employment Committee. The meeting was held in connection with the shortage of labour in Reading. It was reported that there were 400 unemployed people in the area, but that there were 2,800 job vacancies. The following suggestions were made to help alleviate the problem:

1. Women should be asked to return to industry, and employers should consider the employment of part-time female workers.
2. Employees due to retire should be encouraged to remain, if fit and able to work.
3. Foreign labour should be employed.

This problem was highlighted again in March 1961: there were 1926 vacancies in Reading and 645 applicants, compared with 995 and 1271, respectively, in 1958.

Prior to June 1952, vegetable and flower seed orders were executed in separate departmental rooms; this also applied to orders for garden sundries, which were executed in the Sundries Department. The Seed Rooms were amalgamated into a much larger Vegetable Seed Room, which included a section for small garden sundries, with a double row of pigeon-holes, one for each cultivar, running the length of the room. The catalogue contained a comprehensive printed order form, which although expensive, was easier to read when making up the customer's order. One person (he or she was known as the thrower-out) was responsible for a section, passing the order on in a tin tray. The order would be placed on a large bench ready for checking which, in those days, was a task done only by men. He would check every packet, and woe betide anyone if a mistake was found: he or she would be called to collect the correct packet or packets immediately. The order then continued its journey on the metal rollers to the packing department. This department also contained pre-packed seed potatoes which, if required, would be added to the order. At the height of the busy season, the noise from tin trays on metal rollers was quite deafening. If an order was required urgently, a large red label with 'immediate today' printed with black lettering was attached to the order, which ensured it would be despatched that day. Adjoining this department was the Grass Seed Department, from where larger quantities of agricultural and amenity grass seed were supplied.

# 4. The Earley Years

In the early 1960s, Reading Borough Council had planned road improvements which would have driven a road through the centre of the six-acre Suttons site behind the shop at Market Place. The directors decided that this was a good opportunity to move from the centre of the town to the site of the main trial grounds at London Road, Earley, on the east side of the town, a site the company had occupied since the 1870s. This was not the first time that such a move had been contemplated. The possibility of building new offices and warehouses at the trial grounds in Earley had been discussed on 11th September 1928, as Reading Corporation was looking for a site in the centre of the town. The idea proved somewhat premature, although to Suttons it was an attractive proposition.

An aerial view of Suttons Trial Grounds, 1965, showing the new headquarters building, glasshouse complex and bowling green. The 'Ideal Casement' factory can be seen between the river and the Great Western Railway. North of the river Thames a large area of gravel extraction can be seen (top left), this is now the site of a modern marina.

As early as October 1961, it had been decided that the company would move from Market Place in the centre of Reading to a brand-new building on land at the trial grounds in Earley. The Personnel Officer took many measurements of the distances from various bus stops which the staff used while working in Market Place, and compared them with the bus stops nearest to the new premises. He also calculated that staff who lived to the north, west and south would be 3/4d per week out of pocket. A census at the time indicated 206 out of 400 staff would be affected.

Sutton's new building, in the foreground their new garden centre. Mid 1960's.

With the exception of the garden shop, the firm moved into purpose-built premises in August 1962. The building was officially opened by Lord Aberconway VMH, the then-President of the Royal Horticultural Society. At the time they were the most up-to-date buildings of their kind in the country, and measured 350 feet by 330 feet, giving a total floor space of over 150,000 square feet.

A promotional pamphlet produced at the time stated:

> 'Over the years the number of varieties [cultivars] of both vegetable and flower seeds had increased to the extent that there were now some 12,000 separate pigeon-holed divisions for seed packets. The roller system was still operating, but they had less distance to travel to the packing areas. It was a very good working environment being surrounded by many acres of open land filled with such an array of beautiful flowers and we must not forget the vegetable trials which may not be as pretty, but were equally as important to the Company. The range of greenhouses was also an attraction, with their many thousands of flowers, particularly colourful in the days just prior to the Chelsea Flower Show in May'
>
> (Gerry Westall, personal collection).

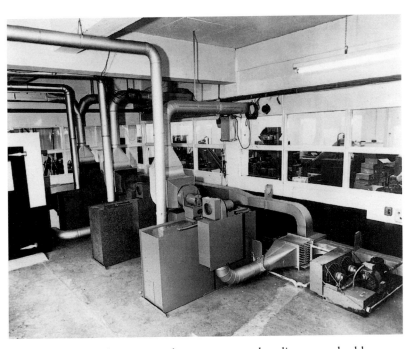

'Harvest Fresh' 'Dryomatic' machines which operate continuously day and night maintaining temperature and humidity levels.

Some 12 months prior to the move, a new bowling green had been constructed at the trial grounds for the firm's active bowling club (established 1906); this was followed by tennis courts. The sports facilities at Cintra Avenue, the firm's sports grounds, were vacated in the late 1950s, and were presented to the town as a recreation ground for the benefit of the inhabitants of the area (MERL).

This was the period when the company began to resume its efforts to increase the number of main agents and also to appoint stockists. During the summer Suttons catered for many hundreds of visitors from around the UK and abroad to its trial grounds.

In the early 1960s Phil, Noel, Audley and Owen Sutton were the four directors: Phil and Noel Sutton were the major shareholders. Within the previous 2 or 3 years, the board had appointed three senior members of staff as directors. In 1964 Douglas Collins, who had recently sold his Goya perfume company for more than £1 million, was invited in as a consultant to advise on publicity and to help with sales. He had previously been Chairman of British Lion Films, at the time when it was the largest film studio in Europe, and was looking for a new business venture. With all his business knowledge, it was felt he could introduce new ideas which might benefit the company. He transformed Suttons from a company with an ageing agricultural base to a thriving horticultural business aimed at the amateur gardener. Douglas Collins realised that the company had a lot of assets in buildings, land and goodwill, but sales

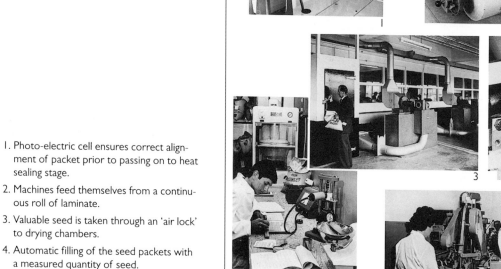

1. Photo-electric cell ensures correct alignment of packet prior to passing on to heat sealing stage.

2. Machines feed themselves from a continuous roll of laminate.

3. Valuable seed is taken through an 'air lock' to drying chambers.

4. Automatic filling of the seed packets with a measured quantity of seed.

5. Recording moisture content of freshly harvested seed with rapid moisture meter.

6. Left facing Mr Owen Sutton, Director and right facing Mr Douglas Collins, Managing Director.

were low and expenses were increasing, while profits were very small. He was initially allowed to buy a few ordinary shares, and then went on to acquire more from each of the directors. He suggested that Mr Phil, who was then in his eighties, should retire; and he bought the shares of the late Martin Audley who died in 1963, Leonard Noel, who died in 1965, and Owen Sutton, who owned a much smaller number of shares. In this way he came to own 51% of the shares, and within a year or so of his arrival, only one Sutton, Owen, was left on the board

Not only was he a very astute business man, but Douglas Collins was a very good boss who spoke to everyone in the company. By this period, the company had diversified into many areas, but Douglas Collins decided that the core part of the business was the sale of packets of seeds. The unit price of packets of seeds was very low. Before World War II, a packet of seed cost 6d, 1s or 2/6d, so a large number of packets had to

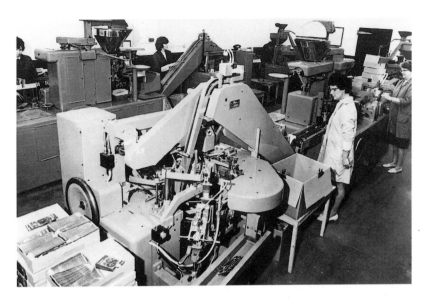

A general view of the packeting machines.

be sold to cover costs, particularly the wages. As a great deal of accurate hand-labour was needed for this work, Douglas Collins brought in mechanisation for counting seeds and filling packets. He withdrew from the annual Chelsea Flower Show held in May, to the dismay of the Royal Horticultural Society (many other seed companies then followed Suttons' lead). A lot of time and effort was spent producing plants out of season for Chelsea: specialist foremen were needed to grow each plant correctly; everything had to be perfect, so it was therefore very labour-intensive. Other departments such as the Garden Construction Department, the Sports Ground Department, the Nursery Trade Department and the Farm Seed Department were also closed. Many of these staff were re-employed within the company. Those who were made redundant were paid well above the statutory entitlement, and on the whole were satisfied with the arrangements.

On 30th September 1965, the 'Harvest Fresh' range was launched. The added publicity increased considerably both the number of stockists and orders from the general public. The harvested, cleaned seeds whose vigour and germination had been carefully checked were sealed in aluminium-foil packets from which the air had been extracted (Huxley, 1969). Suttons was the first company to offer this system for the amateur gardener. By the early 1970s, the business had increased by 25%. This had been helped by not increasing seed prices. About the same time, Suttons became the first company in the seed trade to advertise on television when Douglas Collins promoted a plastic garden label, which was known from its shape as a T label. This was advertised on ITV in a 7-second advert.

Top left: This seed store held nearly half a million pounds worth of seed at the time this photograph was taken.

Top right: Germination and vigour tests in Suttons seed testing laboratory.

Bottom left: Old brass measures being used for hand packeting.

Bottom right: Using a small machine for sealing packets.

Top left: Packeting seed of a relatively uniform shape; the seed is placed in the hopper and fed through, packets are automatically sealed and it can handle 80 packets a minute.

Top right: A machine making packets from a large roll of laminated foil. The machine fills and seals in one operation.

Bottom left: Using the spiral vibrator (right) rather than the direct feed hopper (left) to pack irregular shaped seed such as scabious which tends to clog the direct feeding mechanism.

Bottom right: Checking the packets during the final stages of packeting.

# 5. On to Devon

Douglas Collins died in 1972, and the company passed to his family with his deputy, Frank Hunt, running the company. It was a decade of huge change for Reading. The M4 was extended beyond the town, and the three Bs (bulbs, beer and biscuits) which had been the mainstay of the Victorian town moved out of the centre: Courage's brewery to the edge of the town by the M4, biscuit production by Huntley and Palmers ceased, and Sutton Seeds moved to Torquay. Creeping urbanisation of Reading and Greater Reading, pollution and a shortage of part-time workers have all been suggested as reasons for its departure. Also the company wished to expand at a time when the Government was offering support to companies which moved outside of a 40-mile radius of London: the centre of Reading is exactly 40 miles from London. The preferred site of Wargrave was well within this magic circle. After Douglas Collins' death, his executors decided to put the company up for sale and agreed a two-part deal with Slough Estates plc. Slough Estates wanted 60 or so acres of the Earley site, but had no interest in the seed business. The Collins family sold the Earley site, which was then developed as a trading estate. The name is retained as Suttons Business Park, but the land is now owned by Standard Life.

Various relocation options were considered, and the company finally agreed a move to Torquay, which took place in 1976. The choice of the new location often gives rise to the question 'Why Torquay?' Of course it's a lovely part of the world, but not exactly the centre of the universe from a business and logistics perspective!

With these types of decision, there is rarely a simple or single reason. Frank Hunt, being a keen sailor and having spent many holidays sailing off the Devon coast, would have been aware of the area's potential, and the local council was indeed very receptive to a business like Suttons coming to 'The Bay'; secondly, and linked to the local council view, was the employment pattern of the company. Seasonal or temporary staff were employed in good numbers in the autumn/winter/early spring periods, which was a perfect match for the main seasonal employment in the area. This was, and still is, linked to tourism, which employed people mostly in late spring and summer.

So began a major uprooting of the business from its origins and home for 170 years to the south-west of England. That itself is now 30 years ago, and the company is today considered one of the older or long-established businesses in Torbay.

'No longer would railway passengers be delighted by the sight
of colourful beds of flowers at the Trial Grounds as they entered
Reading from the east. Even though that is at least 30 years ago, it
is amazing how many people 'of a certain age' still ask if the company has its land/premises beside the railway line at Reading!

'As might be imagined, the move of the whole company from
Reading to Torquay was quite an operation. It commenced in April
1976; the first departments to go were the seed packeting unit with
its specialist packing machines, followed by the seed warehouses
so that seed could be made available to start packeting for the next
season at the earliest opportunity. Fortunately the move was to an
empty purpose-built factory and office complex, so it wasn't too
long before the machinery was in place and work could recom-
mence.

'About 30 members of staff made the move over a period of 6
months as other departments were relocated, these being senior
and technical staff such as seed specialists and laboratory personnel. There was also a nucleus of new Torquay people who had been
recruited prior to the move; these had had the benefit of working in
Reading during the firm's last season there and became managers in
the new set-up in Torquay. One way or another the roads between
Reading and Torquay were very busy with Suttons' people that
summer: firstly to find new homes, with the relocation costs being
met by the company, and then to move house as near as possible to
the date of the departmental move, or face weekly commutes either
way.'

(Ron Butler, personal reminiscences)

There is a sad story concerning the magnificent main pavilion of the
greenhouses on the Earley site. A few days after Suttons had made the
move to Torquay in July 1976, Gerry Westall (who had helped set up
Suttons Seeds Market Growers Ltd) received a telephone call from a
gentleman in London. He was acting for a client wishing to purchase the
main pavilion of the Sutton glasshouse (a magnificent cast-iron structure
standing some 40 feet tall). Regretfully, Gerry had to inform him it had
been demolished by a bulldozer the previous week!

The new premises in Torquay were sited on Hele Road facing Newton
Road, and covered 70,000 square feet, of which 10,000 square feet was
office accommodation. In addition, 237 Hele Road (opposite the main
building) was purchased to house the publicity department.

'The 30 or so staff who moved from Reading were augmented by
a further 170 local people who had to be trained ready for the
new season, which commenced in October. The work-force was
further increased by 200 temporary staff recruited from the summer holiday trade and the Job Centre. The company was fortunate

to have the use of spare capacity on the Torbay Council computer to process the agents', and stockists', accounts. The mail-order business continued as the manual system that had developed over many years. Despite the size of the warehouse, extra storage space was required: this was located at Totnes and Heathfield, near Newton Abbot. Eventually this led to the development of a further 20,000-sq-ft facility close to the main building.

After the land in Earley had been sold, the company itself remained in the ownership of the trustees of Douglas Collins. Negotiations continued after the company's move to Torquay and, in May 1978, the business was sold to a Swedish seed company of long standing: W Weibull AB of Landskrona (situated on the west coast of Sweden, near Malmö). More changes occurred as, although Weibull was family-controlled, AB Cardo had a 25% stake in the company. Cardo was an investment company, and subsequently bought out the Weibull family. At that time it was fashionable to diversify, and Sweden's largest company, AB Volvo, acquired AB Cardo. Thus Suttons became a small wheel in the giant Volvo empire.

'Volvo reorganised its non-vehicle companies into their own group, Procordia AB. In the 1990s it divested itself of these non-vehicle activities, and sold Suttons to a French agriculture and horticulture group, Vilmorin SA, in June 1994.'

(David Chelley, personal reminiscences)

Hele Road, Torquay.

In the mid-1980s Reckitt and Coleman put up for sale a group of seed companies which it owned. These were Carter's Tested Seeds, a direct competitor to Suttons; R and G Cuthbert, which had exclusive rights to supply the Woolworth chain of stores; and Samuel Dobie and Son, a mail-order brand that mirrored Suttons' mail-order business, but differed from Suttons in that it did not supply shops or garden centres. In October 1985, Reckitt and Coleman accepted the Suttons' bid for these companies. Also hidden in the purchase were the rights to Samuel Ryder and Son (whose founder provided the famous golf trophy, the Ryder Cup).

All these new acquisitions were based in Llangollen in North Wales and, to achieve savings, the Dobie business moved to Torquay after two years, and a further building was leased to house this business. Eventually, all the administration was transferred to Torquay and later the computer section followed, as this technology became an essential tool of business. The Carter's brand held the Royal Warrant to HM the Queen and HM the Queen Mother; this continued until the reorganisation of the Suttons group.

In the mid-1990s, following the change in ownership, and some 20 years after the move to the area, the company started to consider once more the suitability of its premises and location. Leases were coming up to expiry so it was time once again to think about the future. What were the options? Was the existing configuration of four different buildings, plus outside storage, the most efficient for a modern-day business? By the end of 1997, a deal had been struck with all interested parties, which meant the company would leave Hele Road and its other premises, and move to a new purpose-built facility on the other side of Torbay, in Paignton.

Work on the green-field site of about 6 acres started in the spring of 1998. Horrendous weather caused all sorts of problems with the initial ground works, but by December 1998 a fabulous new facility of some 9,300 sq. m (100,000 sq. ft) all under one roof was completed on time and ready to move into. The move went smoothly, and the business was fully operational at its new location in January 1999.

2006 was a memorable year for the company with its bicentenary, and much had already been done as a lead-up to this, including a complete revamp and re-launch of the whole of the Suttons' range of packets and displays. In addition, a new propagation range was launched linked to the seed displays, and a new runner bean cultivar 'Celebration' and a surfinia petunia 'Double Red Celebration' were introduced.

On the occasion of the bicentenary, it is interesting to compare the company now with that of its counterpart in Reading 50–60 years ago.

The most obvious change is that it now occupies a building only seven years old and built to modern standards, with open-plan offices and a really large warehouse which is easily adaptable for seasonal work, unlike in Reading where they had worked for over a hundred years with very old-fashioned facilities.

The company now has a large design studio for the many catalogues produced 'in house'. These are designed and prepared right up to the printing stage by Suttons' own staff, whereas in previous times only the initial layout was done in Reading. The methods of ordering seeds and plants by customers has changed from being entirely by post to many telephone orders and now on-line: in the last year around 16% of the mail-order business has been conducted via the internet.

In the mid-1950s, there was no stockist trade; today a large part of the business is done through shops and garden centres. This entails the early packeting and pre-packing of designed collections to enable the autumn despatch of both seeds and stands (also supplied) to meet the demand. A large area of the warehouse is required for this purpose to enable the collections to be made up in good time.

Thanks to the recent move, the company has benefited from the newest technology in the control of temperature and humidity for seeds, and especially in seed packeting. The modern machines have both speed and accuracy, very necessary when the seed of hybrids is of such value and needs to be counted exactly. Also reel-feed machines of great speed are essential when very large quantities of a particular variety are required for promotional work. Before the 1960s, all the seed was packed in paper packets under normal conditions before being sent to the customer by post. Machines were much slower then and a considerable amount of hand work was involved, particularly with seeds of difficult shape like those of marigolds.

The staffing of the seed testing laboratory is now reduced, but it is still a very necessary part of the company. The germination and purity tests are still just as essential, but they do not now have to work with agricultural crop seed or get involved with soil testing and amenity grasses, as was the case in Reading.

The mail order side of the business has developed enormously under both the Suttons and Dobies brands, together with the new self developed brand of Ferndale Lodge, started in the late 1990s. The latter supplies an extensive range of practical garden tools and equipment to hobby gardeners throughout the UK. Each year some 25 catalogues of various brands, offerings, sizes and number of pages are produced – a far cry from the few mailed in earlier years under the Suttons brand only.

The biggest development area in mail order in the last 10–15 years has been the sale of young plants by post. Typically these are small packs of anything from 5 to 140 plants, the larger quantities being what is referred to as 'plug' plants in various sizes. Nowadays, this business has almost exactly the same percentage of sales as seed, so it is significant. The concept was started by Dobies in the 1980s and, when Suttons acquired that company in 1985, it effectively accepted the idea.

In 1997, recognising the wonderful array of old images it had in early catalogues – often in full colour – Suttons moved into the card and social stationery market with the 'Heritage' range. This business was built up over some 4 years, but eventually closed down due to the ongoing difficulties and quite different dynamics in that market place.

Export business has always been key to Suttons, and in 1993 a new era began with the opening up of the vast Russian market, following the collapse of communism. The sheer scale of the packet seed business in Russia, and former territories like the Ukraine has to be seen to be believed: there is no doubt it is by far the biggest in the world with an estimated 500–1000 million packets per annum!

In the early part of the century another new business area in promotions was being developed from relatively humble origins. Typically, packet seed is sold to other organisations, or newspapers and magazines, for them to use as a 'give away' product as an incentive, e.g. a cover mount on a gardening magazine. In the last 5 years, Suttons has sold over 20 million packets to one breakfast cereal manufacturer alone. Other promotional sales are by way of reader or special offers in the press, typically of plants, or garden tools/equipment.

Although the company is in a less central location in its new premises, modern transportation and communication links mean this is less of an issue, and it is hoped that the company will have a long and happy association with Paignton.

# 6. Seeds and Plants

There is no doubt that the attention to detail and the resolve to sell only the best seeds and plants available were important factors in making Suttons a household name and one to be respected worldwide. By providing a range of varieties for use in various climatic and soil conditions and with the constant search for new and better ones, the company gave its customers, whether buying in large or small quantities, a wonderful choice and even more importantly assurance and reliability. Over the years the company built up a great rapport with its suppliers, knowing full well the difficulties to be expected with crops which can all too easily be affected by the weather and other natural elements, but always insisting on accuracy and the best care of plants. In a business which relies so heavily on trust, no one can identify varieties from the examination of the seed, for example; honesty and straightforward dealing are essential. There is a strong tradition of business relations extending over many generations with seed-growers and others, which only enhances the quality and care taken.

## Seed Production

The trade in seeds has long been of national and international importance and, as the business in agricultural, vegetable and flower seed trade developed for Suttons in the mid-1800s, the firm started to produce seeds on its own farms and then to have seeds grown on contract by others. Having raised strains of seed of particular value to the business, it was natural to perpetuate these varieties carefully; this was done by sending basic (mother) seed to selected growers to produce the large quantities required for sale. All these crops would be visited by senior managers or the partners to ensure that no errors were made with the seed crops, and that they were properly placed for isolation purposes and made pure by rogueing (removing all off-types), so that after harvest the resultant seed sent to Reading was of top quality and could be guaranteed to all customers.

The principal growing area in England was the county of Essex, where there were many highly-qualified specialist seed-growers and farmers for flower, vegetable and farm crops. As well as their expertise, there was the fact that the weather conditions were usually drier, especially in late summer and autumn when the crops were harvested, which assisted quality and germination. In the early days, all the work from sowing to harvesting was done by hand, but as mechanization came in and the number of land workers decreased, machines were developed to handle most of the work, although some small crops still needed the personal touch.

Seed crops varied greatly in size, due to vastly different requirements as well as to the actual seed yield per given area. With agricultural crops, areas of 10 or more acres per variety were quite common, also for peas and beans; other vegetables were mostly between one and ten acres. For the majority of the flowers, smaller crops were required, with many grown in glasshouses or under other forms of protection. With many of the most important selling varieties, it was quite usual to split the seed crops into two or three separate areas, so that in the event of one crop failing at least some seed was available.

Average seed yields varied according to species e.g. peas 1 ton per acre, brassica crops 6 to 7 cwt per acre, onions 3 to 4 cwt per acre. However, often seed yield could be devastated by pest or disease, or even a hailstorm just before harvest. Also inclement weather at harvest time could result in sub-standard germination of the seed, so that extra cleaning was required to improve the seed lot. Occasionally bumper yields were obtained, and this caused problems with over-supply and price-cutting on the wholesale market. Fortunately over the years, methods were found to keep seed in improved conditions by cold storage. Then in the 1950s, thanks to pioneering work in California, seed held in controlled temperature and humidity conditions was found to maintain its viability over a longer period, levelling out the supply and demand position.

The price of agricultural and horticultural seed crops had to be above the return obtainable by the farmer for seed corn or potatoes, as the work and especially the hand labour to be undertaken was greater and the yields more variable. Also as the root crops and many vegetables were two-year crops (biennials), this had to be costed into the expected returns. A few crops were perennial, such as the grasses, and these yielded seed for several years. However, all these crops helped in providing a 'break crop' in the normal arable regime, which was always useful for the farmer.

The specialist staff required as fieldsmen and crop roguers were trained in-house, and it was usual for three or four men to walk the crops, removing 'off-type' plants and those which did not meet the variety specification. For example, in pea crops, all varieties tend to revert to the wild form, which is recognizable by plants with narrow leaves, small flowers and pods; these need to be kept to a minimum as they reduce yield. Some flower seeds are sold as mixed colours, especially the hardy annual sorts, and these are often grown as mixtures in the field. However, sometimes the species has a strong tendency to seed heavily from a dominant colour and in this case it is better to grow all the different colours separately in isolation and to manually mix the resultant seed to an agreed formula, thus giving the customer a good colour range when grown in the garden.

Many crops need to be grown in isolation. Any of the brassica crops readily cross-pollinate, so a minimum area of 1000 yards around the seed crop is necessary. This meant any other seeding crop or indeed any odd plants left in back gardens or on allotments had to be removed before flowering. Mangold and beet are wind-pollinated, so an even greater distance is necessary, and certain areas of East Anglia were zoned so that only similar varieties were near one another. However, there are a number of crops which are self-pollinating: these can be grown in close proximity providing no mechanical mixing takes place at harvest or threshing time. Crops such as lettuce, tomatoes, asters and sweet peas fall into this category.

The normal contract arrangement was for a given area of land to be sown or planted by the farmer, with all necessary labour done by him, including the harvesting and the pre-cleaning of the seed; then for the produce of the crop to be delivered to the seedsman. The farmer was paid, subject to satisfactory germination and purity.

As the range of subjects and the quantities of seed required increased, it was realised by the partners that Continental growers could be used; the first recorded visits to France started in 1883, to southern Italy in 1897 and to the Netherlands in 1898. These visits were continued every year and often several times a year, with the exception of the Second World War years, until Suttons left Reading in 1976.

## France

The first trip in July 1883 was undertaken by Arthur Sutton and J H Millard to see the standard of growing of both vegetable and grass seed crops in France, and also in Germany. Their journey took them from Reading to Paris, and then on to Tours and Angers in the Loire Valley where they saw many vegetable seed crops. On returning to Paris, they took the night train to Frankfurt and, after one day there, on to Erfurt to see the famous seed company Benary. Finally they had a long journey to the Hamburg area to inspect grass seed production, and then a 24-hour journey home: a total of 2,300 miles in nine days (Millard's diaries, MERL).

In 1887 two of the partners visited the area of Bruyères to the south of Paris. Later in 1900, Arthur Sutton and W F Giles also travelled there. As Arthur Sutton was a great enthusiast for cycling, they took their bicycles by the night train to Paris and while a horse-drawn cab took their luggage from the Gare du Nord to Austerlitz station they cycled across the city, which in those days was free of taxis and cars. As time progressed, the area of the Loire Valley around the town of Angers became the principal area and, right up to the First World War, many weeks were spent each year cycling to the various farms to inspect the crops. Seed crops continued to be grown there during the 1914–1918 War, and W F Giles was given special permits to continue the visits each year. He records that in 1915 the vines and most of the seed crops were destroyed by storms and, with the lack of able-bodied men, the other crops were in a deplorable condition. However, by some means, crops were planted in succeeding years and the produce shipped back safely to England. A large variety of flowers and vegetables continued to be grown around Angers until the 1970s, in an area also famous for its range of perennial plants and shrubs, which were sold worldwide. Another area which had developed over the years was near Avignon in the south, where the more sun-loving types did better.

## Italy

The main crops were originally all varieties of cauliflower, which required crop inspections in January and February. In the early 1900s the journey by train took two-and-a-half days to reach Naples, where the partners or managers would have arranged to meet an interpreter. Then the next few days were spent travelling north from the city, then to the foothills of Vesuvius and around Pompeii, with the grower to inspect all the crops. The travelling was done partly by train but mainly by horse-drawn carriage, which was often in a poor state of repair, and in the very cold weather conditions of late winter, it was certainly not a comfortable journey. In a letter between partners in 1908, it is recorded that the Italian production of cauliflower seed was almost one ton per annum over the 7 varieties being grown at that time. The cost of travelling there was about £30 for a Departmental Head or £62 if a partner went as well, so these visits were obviously cost-effective.

The next most important crop was onions, which were widely grown in the Puglia area by the Adriatic around Barletta. In 1909 W F Giles reported that the one and only hotel there had a dozen bedrooms with iron beds and washstands, stone floors and no carpets: not a lot of home comforts, and certainly not fit for any of the partners. Immediately after the war, in January 1919, Giles recommended his visits: the outgoing trip took four nights and three days of continuous travel with no food or water on the train all the way to Naples. The trip lasted three weeks, including visits to the Barletta area. He records many long slow train journeys, then travel by horse and cart over many miles of muddy tracks in appalling weather conditions, and finally getting away from Naples just before the whole area was put into quarantine because of smallpox. Food was in extremely short supply, and he only survived by

From photos taken by M' Arthur Sutton on visit January 1899

Sutton's Vegetable Seeds—Complete List for 1900—continued.

# CAULIFLOWER—continued.

Vesuvius in the background

from the Kennella

It may not be known to many of our customers that several of the Giant Autumn Cauliflowers can only be seeded successfully in the genial climate of Southern Italy. The above illustrations (from snapshots taken in January last when inspecting our crops) give some idea of the seed-plants in different stages of development.

Weeding the onion crop.

Inspecting a flower seed crop in Naples.

taking a good supply which lasted for the first 10 days, and then having to pay exorbitant prices for any that could be obtained locally. In many cases, the same growers and agents were used over the years; in fact one Neapolitan family looked after Suttons' interests there for five generations. It was not uncommon for young members of the family to come to Reading to work with Suttons' experts, both to gain instruction on the requirements of the seed trade and to help with the language.

There was also a thriving flower-seed business, particularly in the Naples area, where many annuals were successfully produced. To see the fields of such crops as mesembryanthemum and portulaca in full flower was really eye-catching in the summer sunshine. Some of the more tender ones were given the protection of poly-tunnels to ensure high-germinating seed. In consultation with Suttons' specialists, many hybrid flower-seed varieties were produced there, and have become firm favourites with British gardeners.

After the Second World War, vegetable seed production, and especially F1 hybrid seed production, tended to be centred on the Cesena district of northern Italy. Suttons also used farmers in the Marche area around Ancona. Onions were particularly successful there, with the bulbs being produced the first year in the fertile coastal land and then transported to the hills for replanting, where the air movement before ripening assisted in keeping down disease such as mildew.

Giles and Potter's visit to inspect cauliflowers, 1935.

1 – Carmine Mennella
2. Aniello    "
3 – Novara – *** guide for 40 years
4   W. F. Giles
5.  F. G. Potter
6 & 7  other sons of Mennella
8  Mennella's flower-seed foreman

On the top of Mennella's house. Vesuvius in background
1935.

## The Netherlands

Horticulture was and still is the mainstay of the Dutch trade, so it is not surprising that seed-growing was also very important. With the deep very fertile soils, a very wide range of vegetable and flower seed crops was produced there. The Dutch were expert at producing superb-quality runner beans, and are world-famous for their bulbs, onion sets and shallots.

There were two main areas for seed production in the Netherlands. In the south-west, the islands were ideal for many sorts of flower and vegetable seed production with good isolation and excellent soil conditions. Flakkee Island was almost completely covered with seed crops, in particular broad beans, peas, Californian poppy and nasturtiums. They had an interesting way of harvesting the nasturtiums, allowing the plants to wither and die so that all the ripe seed dropped onto the soil, and then they hoovered up the seed and debris before sending it to be cleaned by machine. Until the 1950s, travelling between crops meant island-hopping by ferry and the area felt really remote, but now it is just a question of road and bridge transport. Many of the Dutch seed-houses are centred around Enkhuizen in the north, another area widely used for seeds in the past. It was always quite a thrill to go from office to trial grounds by boat until the polders were filled in. In the 1950s they revolutionised the vegetable seed lists with the introduction of F1 hybrids in many subjects, particularly vegetables, and these have now become the standard. Originally the trip to the Netherlands was by train and overnight ferry from Harwich to the Hook of Holland but, with the advent of commercial flights, trips became much quicker; in fact due to the short distance between Reading and Heathrow airport, it was quite possible to go for the day by taking the first flight out. This was very useful not only for crop inspections, but also to see trials of new varieties at the optimum time.

## Other Areas

As transportation improved, the growing of horticultural seeds expanded worldwide. Huge quantities of garden peas were produced on the Canterbury Plains of New Zealand, and an area of Australia was used for the production of virus-free lettuce seed because it was aphid-free. Parts of America also became popular, with the Lompoc valley in California used for flower seeds, especially the half-hardy types and many F1 hybrids. Further north in Idaho many vegetable seeds were grown, especially green beans (*Phaseolus vulgaris*), and these were also produced extensively in East Africa. Many of the more exotic flowers such as impatiens were bred and produced in Costa Rica, and more recently vegetable seed production has been found to be economic in Chile.

Selecting plants for stock seed of Suttons Imperial Cabbage at their Trial Grounds Earley, 1930's.

## Quality Control

As all varieties of flowers and vegetables came originally from wild types, it is necessary to re-select constantly from the best plants to maintain a high quality. The most successful way for many years was by marking the most typical plants by staking at normal maturity time, known as 'stock in the crop', and all these plants were then harvested separately once the seed was ripe. Another method was to select plants of perfect quality, e.g. roots of carrot, and for these roots to be replanted in isolation for seed the next year. This is only possible with biennial crops (those running to seed in the second season), and applies mostly to vegetables and root crops. The majority of flowers, salad crops and herbs are annuals. A more recent method is by progeny testing, where seed of each individual selected plant is grown on separately, and only those of top quality are put together for further multiplication. In the early days, plant breeding was done on Mendelian lines, but by the 1940s much more sophisticated methods were introduced with the resultant large increase in varieties, especially F1 hybrids. In flowers, the main improvements were larger flowers over a longer period; in vegetables, uniformity of maturity time and disease-resistance.

New varieties for the catalogue were achieved in a number of ways. Suttons carried out considerable plant-breeding work to improve varieties and fill gaps in existing ranges. The company also took samples from foreign seed companies and individual plant-breeders, and compared these with known varieties in the trial grounds. When improvements were found, a marketing arrangement was made, sometimes on an exclusive basis, to sell these seeds through the catalogues. Local seed from some of the large private estates and individual gardeners was also taken, re-selected and built up into saleable quantities, often being given the name of the source, e.g. Blenheim Orange and Hero of Lockinge melons. Huge strides were made in the improvement in varieties of mangold, swede and turnip in the latter part of the 19th century. Not only were yields per acre increased, but the animal feeding value was improved, giving the farmer much better value for money.

Until the 1950s, varieties of vegetables and flowers tended to be similar for both the private gardeners and commercial growers. The advances made by plant-breeders in the use of F1 hybrids especially in vegetables, were quickly taken up by the market growers in spite of much higher seed costs, as the advantages in uniformity of harvest time and yield more than made up for the cost difference. For the amateur gardener, where the manual costs are of much less importance, they took much longer to gain a place. In flower plant production, the use of F1 hybrids for plug plants was essential, to get maximum germination and uniformity of seedlings. This wide divergence in varieties between the amateur and market garden catalogues eventually led to Suttons selling off the market-garden trade in 1975, to concentrate on marketing to private gardeners through the mail-order catalogue or via garden centres and other outlets.

The high cost of producing F1 hybrid seed is due to several factors. First, the initial research to find compatible parent plants and the trialling of probably hundreds of lines to find the ones most suitable is a costly process. Then seed has to be produced in isolation from both parent lines which often yield lightly, and then the full-scale crop to produce the seed for sale. With some subjects such as carrots and onions, genetically-controlled male sterile lines can be used; in other crops, like Brussels sprouts, self-incompatibility is a useful factor. For hybrid tomatoes, which are very popular, every flower on the female parent has to be emasculated by hand before the pollen from the male parent, grown separately, is brought in for cross-pollination. This obviously was very labour-intensive and costly, but the advantages of disease-resistance more than outweighed the extra premium.

### The Improvement in Seed Technology and Production of Plugs

By the 1970s, the demand for high-quality seeds to supply the professional market-garden growers was coming from the producers of vegetable plants. The company was looking for virtually 100% germination and seed of regular size and density i.e. seeds that could be readily handled by machines. Where seeds were of irregular shape and size, i.e. lettuce, carrot, parsnip etc., these were pelleted. This involved applying a clay-based coating to make the seeds perfectly round and of a similar size. A further advance was developed whereby seed was 'primed' in the laboratory; this meant that seed was pre-germinated and selected for uniformity and, importantly, plant vigour. Obviously at this stage, any non-viable seed could be discarded. This had great benefits to plant-raisers in that it shortened the time of production and ensured the very best healthy plants. Totally automated plant-raising was here to stay. Growers no longer purchased seed by weight: they would buy it by count.

In the case of flower seeds, plug production came later. Initially a trade began to develop for trays of seedlings. The first subject marketed was begonias, a difficult species to raise successfully. The first trays sold in this country were imported from Germany: these were grown under clinical conditions, with precise temperature and humidity control and the use of supplementary light. It was not long before a number of nurserymen started growing seedlings in this country, and the range of subjects was greatly increased. This created a demand for high-quality seeds and, as in the case of vegetable seed, improved the quality of flower production. Direct-sown plugs of ornamental plants appeared in the mid-1980s. High-performance flower seeds were coming on-stream from companies in the USA, Netherlands and Japan. Now the value of sales among retail companies has moved strongly towards plants and plant products, and every year the sale of seeds to the retail market decreases.

## Seed Testing and Soil and Plant Analysis

When John Sutton commenced his seed business in Reading, the testing of the seed he sold was conducted in greenhouses where he was able to simulate conditions similar to those his customers would employ when sowing their seeds. The company soon realised that greenhouse test conditions could not guarantee clinical accuracy and reliability of results; nevertheless efforts continued to improve methods of analysis year on year. By the mid-19th century Suttons had its first seed-testing laboratory, and from then on the company established its own critical standards of seed germination potential and purity. Stocks of seed that did not reach the set standards would not be sold. However, the company continued to test random samples of its seed stocks under trial-ground conditions, thereby giving a 'belt and braces' assurance about the high quality of its seeds. The seeds tested ranged from cereals, herbage and amenity grasses to vegetables and flowers.

There is no doubt that some seed companies were not averse to adulterating the seed they sold, so as to gain an advantage in price. In the 1850s and '60s, the practice of mixing cheap or old seed with new was commonplace, and was such a problem that in the 1861 catalogue Suttons included a page on the subject.

*Sutton's Spring Catalogue and Amateur's Guide for 1861.*   55

# THE ADULTERATION OF SEEDS.

So common is the practice of mixing old or dead Seeds with good Seeds for sale, that we who scrupulously abstain from conforming to this custom, experience, occasionally, considerable inconvenience when we have to compete with Seedsmen who are *not* so scrupulous.

**The Editor of the Gardeners' Chronicle and Agricultural Gazette,** so long ago as 23rd February, 1856, made the following observations on the comparative value of Genuine Seeds, and those which have been adulterated.

" No wonder that the public should wish to be enlightened on this matter. We are glad that our attention has been directed to it thus opportunely when gardeners are procuring their spring supplies.

" Everybody knows that after seeds have been kept a certain time they are incapable of growing. It is equally notorious that all seeds may be *killed* by hot water, or hot dry air. In neither case is there a change in their outward appearance, except in particular instances. It is also notorious that some seeds are undistinguishable by the eye although they produce totally different plants. No one, for instance, can tell the *varieties* of Carrot, Beet, Turnip, Cabbage, Radish, &c., from each other by their seeds. Red Beet, for instance, worth 8s. a pound, is not to be known by its seeds from Mangel Wurzel, nor Cauliflower worth *half-a-crown an ounce*, from Cabbage seed worth 5s. a pound. These data furnish the clue to the great mystery before us.

" A sells all his seed *as he bought it* ; but B knows better ; he perfectly understands the love of the public for what is cheap, and he complies with the popular taste and *prepares a cheap article.* Instead of acting like his simple competitor, he buys for a shilling a pound of Cabbage seed which has either died a natural death, or been killed for the occasion. This is carefully mixed with the Cauliflower seed, and makes as nice and clean a sample as can be desired. In this way he obtains 2lbs. of seed for 17s. instead of 1lb. for 16s.

" If we are to judge from the endless complaints which reach us there must be a good deal of such ingenuity at work. It is therefore desirable, in the interest of the fair trader no less than in that of the public, that the manner of detecting such practices should be explained. ' Trying' seeds reveals the secret.

" Gardeners are not the only persons interested in the operation. When we look at the low prices at which *Agricultural Seeds* are sometimes sold, we cannot doubt that a ' trial' of such against very high priced seeds would be advantageous. *The subject indeed is of more importance to Farmers than to Gardeners, when we consider how much greater is the stake which the former have in their crops. They may discover that very cheap Agricultural Seeds are as expensive as very cheap Manures.*"

**The following Circular Letter, sent to us and other seedsmen, will throw additional light upon the subject :—**

"———— ————, *London, 24th January,* 1859. 

" Gentlemen,—I have sold this day some Indian Rape Seed, for mixing with Turnip Seed. I enclose a sample. If you will have some at 56s. per quarter, in the Docks, you can. I have sold some East India Radish Seed at 9s. the Bushel. If you want some Seeds for mixing, I shall be very happy to serve you."

*The above was the first communication we had ever received from the writer, and we need scarcely add that it was never replied to.*

The following also was received more recently, and is further indicative of the prevailing custom :—

**Copy of Letter, the original of which, as also the one quoted above, with name and address in full, may be seen at our office.**

*No. —, ———— Street, Southampton, 27th April, 1860.*

" Messrs. Sutton and Sons,

" Gentlemen,—Being in possession of a new and improved method of killing seeds without the use of any chemicals so that the seed when in an 000 state has not that unpleasant smell it has when killed by the old method and does not look perished if it be crushed. A man by the new process may kill ten or twelve quarters per day, and the apparatus is so constructed that it is impossible for a single seed to leave it alive ; and one great advantage is, that if you want a sack of 000 seed in a hurry you may kill a sack of Rape or Turnip, or any seed, and have it fit for use in an hour. Seed in the process of killing increases in measure and weight, and when you *send it out* to be killed of course the seed killers keep the extra weight and measure. If you think it worth your attention I will send you a small working model so that you may kill a few pounds of Kale for Cauliflower, or any small seeds, in a few minutes, and instructions for making a large one on receipt of a post office order for £2.—Yours truly ———— ————."

The writer of the above also being unknown to us, we had the curiosity to call at the address given, and ascertained that it was no " hoax," but was assured by the " Inventor" that he had supplied several seedsmen with the apparatus, and that he was *formerly* in the seed trade himself. We may add that we have since heard from the same individual at another seaport town to which he has removed.

We give this information, not from any desire to shake the confidence of the public in their Seedsmen generally, but merely to caution them against purchasing Seeds which are offered at unreasonably low prices ; and we take the opportunity of asserting distinctly that we never do mix bad Seeds with good, —that we never have conformed to this practice during the many years we have been in business, *nor do we intend to do so, whatever competition in prices may occur.*

LONDON: PRINTED BY SPOTTISWOODE & CO. NEW-STREET SQUARE.

Article taken from the Sutton's Spring Catalogue concerning the adulteration of seeds, this includes a letter from a company offering to sell a special oven designed to kill seed.

## The Agricultural Gazette.

### SATURDAY, APRIL 18, 1868.

WHAT IS "NETT SEED?" The term is, we find, well known to people in the seed trade. This we have on the best possible authority. But they have generally managed very cleverly to keep it to themselves; for though, as growers of farm crops, we have been buyers of farm seeds for 20 or 30 years, we do not remember having heard it till the other day.

We lose no time in announcing our discovery; for it is right, especially at this season of the year, that those who are now spending their annual 20*l.* to 100*l.* with the seedsman for Grass seeds, Turnip, Mangel Wurzel, Carrot, Cabbage seed, &c., should know that there are seeds and *seeds*—that the retail men who offer seeds in the country, if they do not grow these seeds themselves, are at the mercy of "the trade" —and that "nett seed" is not a very easy thing for them to get, and therefore not an easy thing for them to supply. But "nett seed" is just honest seed. It is the seed which was grown last harvest time. And the existence of a special designation for it, like the difficulty of obtaining it, indicates wide-spread dishonesty.

If you go into the manure market you may buy nitrate of soda or saltpetre of a certain per-centage value, guaranteed as genuine up to 80, 90, or 95 in every 100 parts by weight; but the discount here is a natural defect. When you buy "nett seed" you have a certain per-centage in like manner of risk and failure, dependent on natural causes. But go into the seed trade as a wholesale buyer, and you are offered seed of which only a certain per-centage is warranted to grow, not because last harvest was a bad one, but because the worthless remainder has been *added*. And go into a shop as a retail customer, where the seedsman does not grow his seeds himself, and you will inevitably be offered that same villainously doctored seed, professing to be the natural produce of the season, and to present only such natural faults as cannot be avoided.

And this is the way in which farmers are every day defrauded. And the fine gentlemen, who arrange among themselves every spring-time what per-centage of admixture shall be sent out with the season's produce—whatever care they may profess to take that there shall always be sufficient living seed to produce a crop—are simply rogues. And their conduct, when it shall have been brought home to them before the judge, must end in their conviction as common felons.

Let us hope that the conscience of some of them may be startled into life by an ugly phrase of this kind coming thus abruptly into collision with the every-day employment of their phrase —"nett seed,"—from which the whole rascality is necessarily inferred.

An article describing 'Nett Seed'.

In the 18th April 1868 edition of the *Agricultural Gazette*, there is further comment on what at that stage was known as the selling of 'Nett Seed' and the admixtures made with it.

The first official seed-testing station in Europe was set up in Denmark in 1871, and this was followed by several other countries in the next few years. However, in spite of the 1869 Seed Adulteration Act in the United Kingdom, it was never enforced satisfactorily here. A few of the major seed companies, including Suttons, had their own laboratories by 1871 but, if they required seed to be tested for export, samples were usually sent for official testing to Zurich for clearance. Further attempts at producing a statutory system here were again thwarted in 1901 by the opposition of the trade in general, although a seed committee including M J Sutton worked hard to push it through.

In 1900 a meeting was held to consider the testing of sprouting seed by chemical processes and the action of $CO_2$ on the growth of plants, but nothing appears to have come of this.

Together with seed testing, Suttons' laboratories carried out analytical work on the root crops grown on the trial grounds, testing for sugar by means of a saccharimeter, and fibre content of the roots, particularly mangold and swede, to ensure a high percentage of feeding matter and a greater palatability for the animals. The work was linked with the plant-breeding programme at a time when root crops were of great economic importance. The analytical work quickly expanded to include the analysis of soil samples from farmers and market-growers who were anxious to know if their soils were deficient in one or more of the major elements, i.e. calcium, nitrogen, phosphorus and potassium. Soil samples would also be examined for the presence of eel-worm cysts, a pernicious pest that attacks potato crops. Nutrient analysis of soils and the microscopic examinations for eel-worm infestation continued at Reading up to 1976.

In the years immediately following WWI there was no Seeds Act to control the marketing of economic seeds, i.e. vegetable, grass, herbage and cereals. The sale of flower seeds (non-economic) has never been subject to legislation and is still not covered, but nevertheless the company had its own in-house standards for every subject, which were carefully adhered to. The sale of economic seeds to farmers and commercial growers was becoming big business and, regrettably, attracted a number of rogue traders who were selling very poor-quality seed of low-to-nil germination potential. Furthermore, such traders were selling seed stocks adulterated with other seed kinds, which was beginning to have an adverse impact on the economy. A typical example of the folly of buying cheap seed is well illustrated in the 1913 catalogue: Prizewinner mangold seed bought from Suttons cost 11s 1d to sow an acre, whereas cheap seed from elsewhere could cost as little as 3s 4d per acre. But the difference in weight of the crop could easily be 5 or 10 tons per acre, so the advantage would be at least £3 15s 0d per acre. It was the food crisis following WWI that persuaded Parliament in 1918 to make the Seed Adulteration Act enforceable by law, with consequent penalties for infringements. The Government determined to bring in new legislation embodied in the new Seeds Act. At the time, Suttons was the premier seed house in the country and was held in high esteem throughout the industry. Being a reputable company, Suttons was involved with Government officials in drafting new legislation, which was eventually passed as the 1920 Seeds Act. The Act remained in force up to 1973, when it was replaced by the EEC Seeds and Plant Varieties Act, which itself has been amended several times since.

The Official Seed Testing Station was set up by the Government in 1917 in London, moving in 1920 to Cambridge, which was to become the home of all agricultural and horticultural regulations up to the present time. The head of testing at Suttons at this time was Miss Evershed. In 1924, a law was passed that all testing-station superintendents were required to pass an examination at Cambridge, following a 6-week course, to which Suttons sent its head man, Mr Louch.

The Seeds Act laid down minimum standards of germination potential and purity below which seed could not be sold to the public. The following are examples of the minimum germination figures at which seed could be sold at that time.

| | |
|---|---|
| Italian Ryegrass | 80% |
| Rye | 80% |
| Tares and Vetches | 90% |
| Turnip and Swede | 80% |
| Mangold | 60% |
| Peas | 70% |
| Runner Beans | 60% |
| Cauliflower | 60% |
| Parsnip | 45% |
| Onion | 60% |

The Act included a list of noxious weeds which, if present in a seed sample above a given percentage, could not be sold, on penalty of heavy fines for anyone breaching the law. Seed companies are required by law to keep detailed records of seed-test results on all economic seed stocks marketed; such records have to be available for inspection by ministry inspectors.

The Seeds Act legislation covering the whole of the United Kingdom required seed companies to invest in modern seed-testing equipment, and to test seeds in accordance with the rules laid down by the Official Seed Testing Station of the Institute of Botany, Cambridge. Furthermore, such analytical work had to be carried out under the strict supervision of qualified personnel. In order to test the range of economic seeds covered by legislation, a company's seed-testing laboratory had to carry a licence in the name of a qualified individual employed by the company. Before leaving Reading in 1976, Suttons would have tested upwards of 30,000 samples of seed each year.

Under controlled laboratory conditions, the majority of seeds germinate best under full light conditions, rather than being buried. Most seed kinds are tested under transparent cloches on top of heated water tanks, and usually involve 4 replicates of 100 seeds per test. There are of course some seeds that will only germinate in the dark, and for these, purpose-built cabinet incubators are employed. The hundreds of different cultivars that have to be tested require a range of temperature environments such as alternating 30°–20°C, or 20°C constant, or conditions below room temperature. A few species germinate best in a refrigerator at 5°C. The duration of a test may vary from a few days to a few months, depending on the species. If a seed sample is found to be dormant (quiescent, not ready to germinate) the dormancy is broken by a process known as vernalisation. The purity test involves inspecting samples in great detail under magnification. If samples contained impurities (foreign seeds, soil and plant fragments) greater than the minimum percentage allowed under law it meant that the parcel of seed represented by the sample tested couldn't be sold in its existing condition. From the laboratory report, it was possible to advise the warehouse manager on an appropriate method of re-cleaning by machinery or by hand, and then a fresh sample was taken from the bulk and subjected to a full analytical test. At Suttons, all flower-seed stocks were sampled and tested under the same rigorous regime as for economic seeds.

Seeds come in all shapes and sizes from almost dust in some flower seeds to large vegetable seeds such as peas and beans, with some like the beet family having a cluster of seeds. For example, while a single timothy grass seed may weigh 0.5 mg and a carrot seed 1.3 mg, a cabbage seed averages 4 mg and a pea seed 400 mg.

To assist the technicians in the identification of the impurities likely to be found, the company had assembled a collection of over 3000 samples of cultivated and weed seeds from around the world. A selection of the more unusual ones includes banana (*Musa ensete*), Chinese water chestnut (*Eleocharis dulcis*), devil's claw or unicorn plant (*Ibicella*), strychnine (*Nux vomica*), tea (*Thea bohea*) and cotton (*Gossypium sp*). This whole collection is of special use when seed crops which have been grown abroad are scrutinised and unusual impurities are found. The collection was put together over many decades by laboratory staff, with the assistance of friends and colleagues interested in the improvement of seed lots, and is still used in Suttons' seed-testing laboratory even today.

Suttons' seed-testing laboratory was also used for conducting courses in turf management. Each year, candidates from throughout the UK who were responsible for, or required training in the skills of, maintaining golf courses, bowling greens, sports fields, parks and open spaces would descend on Suttons for a week of intensive study. The course concluded with a written examination. Candidates who attained a predetermined standard received a 'Suttons Certificate of Competence in General Turf Management'.

In 1915 Martin Hubert Sutton carried out a series of experiments with ore containing radium to establish claims made for crop improvements. He varied the proportion added to the soil and, with controls, grew various vegetables, grasses and flowers. The results showed overall a benefit for rape, clovers, radish and lettuce, but little or no effect on peas, tomatoes, nasturtiums and other flowers. In the same year an American company in Pittsburgh was offering radium fertiliser at $0.50 per 2 lb can or $3.75 per 25 lb can. The recommended dose was 1 lb per 50 sq. ft. In the 1950s, in collaboration with the Atomic Energy Authority at Harwell, various seeds were irradiated to see if any breakdown in varietal make-up could be obtained, but trials especially with tomatoes were inconclusive.

Various methods of assistance in sowing seeds have been tried over the years. Incorporating seeds in a degradable tape was first introduced in 1916, and has been re-offered over the years with very limited success. Pelleting small seeds to enable them to be more easily handled was widely used in the 1960s, especially for the commercial trade where seed drills were built to handle individual pellets for spaced sowing. This worked well under optimum ground conditions and with very high-germinating seed; otherwise gappy rows resulted. With multi-germ seeds like beet and mangold, methods were evolved to rub the seed down to a single germ, so that the farmer gained in reduced labour for singling the crop.

For many years, paper packets had been adequate for the home trade; seeds sent abroad were subject to many changes in temperature and humidity, so for this reason export orders had to be sent to a special packing room. Metal inner envelopes were used, sealed against moisture, with the name and a colour picture on the outer packet. The picture was particularly important where foreign languages were spoken, so as to identify the contents.

The maintenance of high germination right up to the point of sowing became of great importance and, for this reason, Suttons pioneered ways of so doing. By drying the seed down to predetermined levels of moisture and then storing them in special chambers at constant humidity and temperature levels, the seed was kept in a state of semi-dormancy. In 1965 the company introduced its 'Harvest Fresh' foil packets consisting of layers of kraft paper, polythene, foil and an inner polythene sachet. Following very extensive laboratory trials of their own, confirmed by the Official Seed Testing Station, Suttons was given a special licence by the Ministry of Agriculture guaranteeing germination over a 3-year period in unopened foil packets. This covered all flower and vegetable subjects, with the exception of peas and beans, sweet peas and a few others.

## Trial Grounds

With the increase in business activity, the partners realised the need for land for the production of seeds and garden plants, so that by the mid-1830s nursery land was obtained and some of their own estate land was being used for this purpose.

One of the principal purposes of the trial grounds was to ensure that all seed lots sold by the company were true to type and variety. As this was not possible by examination of the seed, a sample of every delivery to the warehouse was taken; this was grown on to full maturity and recorded by the staff from the vegetable or flower departments, and only

Suttons Earley trial grounds, looking towards the Great Western Railway, showing part of the main glasshouse complex and a crop of Soya Bean (taken in the mid-1930's).

This decorative Victorian barn could be seen from the London road, but it was demolished in 1976 when Suttons moved to Torquay. Note the old fashioned bell cloches. (They were part of a display for a show at Warley Park, Birmingham in 1910).

then was it passed for sale. There were many thousands of trials each year and, in addition to their main use, they also proved to be colourful and interesting to visitors.

Another use for the land was for basic or mother-seed crops, where small quantities of seed were saved for the future production of large-scale crops, grown on contract for Suttons by specialist growers in the UK and abroad. For example, a patch of several thousand roots of one variety of parsnip would be grown, from which only a hundred or so of the most perfect roots were selected for re-planting for a seed crop the following year. Similarly, an area of spring cabbage was grown and only the best left for seed, with all the poorer plants destroyed. With mangold, several tons of typical specimen roots were chosen, and then laid out for inspection and further selection. These had to be free from side roots, show hardiness and true colour and above all density, which means high feeding quality. These large roots were then stored in the mangold shed through the winter months, and were replanted in early spring in an isolated spot away from any other flowering root crops, so that there was no chance of cross-pollination at flowering time. The seed collected would be trialled and then used for future seed crops, so that it was probably 5 or 6 years before the results of this work reached the customer. It was only in this way that the high quality could be maintained and pedigree lines established for each variety.

It is recorded that in 1837 Martin Hope Sutton had obtained land in Queens Road, Reading, and had bought his first greenhouse for £48, and the following year he was selling greenhouse plants (Corley, 1991–3).

By the 1860s, the company had a nursery near the centre of Reading at Portland Place, and there was also a trial ground in the large garden of Martin Hope Sutton's residence in Christchurch Road.

In the 1870s, land was leased in Earley on the eastern outskirts of Reading. Eventually this and other plots were purchased, covering an area of some 75 acres. This land between the two railway lines cost £600 for the piece previously used by Fidlers (a local nurseryman) and £750 for land from Lord Sidmouth's estate; he did not include any of his London Road frontage as he wanted to build a housing estate there. Over the years this became a well-known landmark for passengers travelling on the Great Western and South Eastern Railways, and also on the main A4 London Road.

In the late 1880s, Martin John Sutton resided at Dysons Wood, some 4 miles north of Reading. The following is a report by the Agricultural Gazette of 16th January 1888.

'Leaving the seed ground I was driven to Dysons Wood. The day was unfortunately not propitious. A dense fog hid everything, and I could not see ten yards ahead. There are here nearly 150 acres around a very handsome residence. Woodland – pasture of various dates – a certain proportion of arable land – and good homesteads – extent enough and variety enough to give scope for any agricultural experiment the tenant might desire to make. A herd of Dexter Kerry breed cultivated here has already made its mark in the show-yard. And a more perfect display of multum in parvo than one of these compact and substantial little Kerries of this particular strain does not exist.

'Mr Sutton has, in conjunction with Dr J A Voelcker, conducted here a series of manure experiments on several of his grass fields – old pasture five years old and permanent pastures containing and excluding perennial rye grass, also three years ley, containing and excluding rye grass. There are thus in each of six such fields, eighteen plots, each of 100th part of an acre in size contiguous, the whole surrounded by a fence and each plot by a wire fence. The manure is supplied in such doses as would be used in ordinary farming practice, and such variety, according to a number of different formulae, as may indicate by results the effect of a dressing with ammoniacal and mineral manures. Basic cinder (basic slag), nitrate of soda, Kainite, sulphate of ammonia, Peruvian guano, ground coprolites, superphosphate of lime, boiled bones, dissolved bones, raw bone meal – all of these have a place; and the results which are published in a pamphlet, will have a growing agricultural value as the years go on. The produce of each plot is cut and weighed twice a year; and the value in excess of that which received no manure, as well as from the outside grass, is placed against the cost of dressing. The experiments which began in 1886, already illustrate the special value of nitrogenous manure for grass growth; and it is satisfac-

*tory to find [in] how many cases the money value of the excess of produce has largely exceeded expenditure. These experiments have been already fully reported and commented on in the* Agricultural Gazette *by Mr H Evershed and they have been widely published in other journals. The inspection here was, however, a mere episode in my day's work last Wednesday.'*

Plans were discussed in April 1901 for new buildings on the western corner of the main trial grounds, which were not to cost more than £5000. To celebrate the official opening of the new glasshouses in January 1903, representatives from all the national and horticultural press were invited to a tour of the new buildings (particular interest was shown in the new primula house) where they were entertained to lunch in the new glass pavilion. The previous day, 22nd January, all nursery and farm staff were invited to a supper.

The following account is based on extracts from a booklet entitled *Suttons at Reading* written at that time, and gives a good insight into the work carried out then and as it continued for many decades.

*'The new and extensive range of houses has been erected for the purpose of saving seeds from stocks of such high-class flowers as can only be successfully grown under glass. The latest heating methods have been adopted and all the houses are inter-connected. Autumn and winter are especially colourful with the cyclamen showing their charms from October until the seed pods form. In December and January the primulas are at their best. From pure white through various shades of rose and pink to full rich crimson*

Glasshouse with a crop of *Primula malacoides* for a seed crop.

*are the colours which have been achieved and come true from seed. The double primulas offer additional attraction with their different shades of colour and even the foliage is now more elegant so that the plants are interesting long before a flower is visible. As many as 15,000 plants of primula covering a quarter of an acre of glasshouse space were grown for seed in one year.*

*'Cinerarias succeed the primulas and are at their prime in March and April and are now easily grown from seed with a rich diversity of colours. Calceolarias and gloxinias continue the flowering sequence with the seed-raised varieties giving a wider range of colours and types. A relatively new subject grown from seed at that time was tuberous rooted begonias with its rich range of colours giving beautiful blooms from June to September, only six months from seed sowing.*

*'The seed production of each of these flower types is under the personal supervision of a 'Grower'. It is his responsibility to obtain the optimum temperature and watering regime required and to watch over the plants from sowing to planting out and to control growth during pollination and through to seed collection.'*

Due to the considerable increase in water usage, the windmill pump was found to be inadequate, so in July 1904 the town's water supply was connected to a tank in the grounds. Later that year, some more land became available at Southcote Manor, an ancient estate on the western outskirts of Reading. The directors visited the site and decided it would

Suttons rented land at Southcote Manor. This picture shows cabbages being grown around the moat. The house looks a little dilapidated. It was demolished in about 1920.

Trial grounds at Langley with a seed crop of 'Continuity' Broccoli. July 1948.

A general view of the trial grounds at Langley, showing patches of various flowers for selection and seed production. 1929.

be suitable for growing and breeding potatoes, as well as other seed crops and experimental trials, at a rent of £150 per annum. In October 1906, between 200 and 300 important horticulturalists from all over the UK were invited to an open day to see a large demonstration on the cultivation of potatoes. This event was also well supported by the horticultural press. By 1908 it was decided to stop growing potatoes at Southcote, but to continue with trials and seed crops of vegetables and flowers, and by 1912 the annual cost of maintaining this area was £522.

At the outbreak of war in 1914, reports from the military authorities indicated they were considering the commandeering of Southcote Manor, but this did not happen. At the end of December, a great storm in the evening destroyed a portion of the wall in the garden, some of which fell into the moat. The manor was demolished in the early 1920s, and the site is now part of a large housing complex.

Another big step forward was in the autumn of 1913, when the company purchased the seed business of Messrs J Veitch & Sons Ltd which had been carried out at Chelsea for the previous 60 years. In addition, Suttons also procured an extensive area of land at Langley, east of Slough, which had previously grown many thousands of apple, pear and other fruit trees for that firm. To commemorate this acquisition, Suttons presented all their staff with an extra week's wages just before Christmas. This land of some 50 acres was used continuously for flower and vegetable seed production, and also for a while for the raising of young fruit trees and shrubs. Being of a much heavier soil structure than the gravelly soil at Reading, it was most useful for moisture-loving crops. In the summer months it was just as colourful as Earley with many flower crops, and it was often said the railway passengers from Paddington alighted at Slough station in the mistaken idea that they were already at Reading. Also in the summer, a van went daily from Reading to Slough taking warehouse staff to work on the land, as well as technical staff to rogue the crops, and the van was then used to make deliveries in that area. These trial grounds were sold by Suttons in the 1960s and '70s to Slough Corporation.

Plans were approved in 1920 for a plant-breeding station to be constructed on the Earley trial grounds. This was situated quite close to the Great Western Railway, and brought together the work previously done in various locations. From here numerous new varieties came into existence from controlled crosses based on Mendelian principles, and later by more modern techniques. As the potential new varieties progressed, they would be tested alongside existing types in the trials to prove their value.

To give some idea of the scope of the work undertaken at the trial grounds, the following gives the average number of trials of individual subjects grown each year.

|  | 1900s | 1920s |
|---|---|---|
| Asters | 746 | 2000 |
| Primula (under glass) | 161 | 575 |
| Stocks | 256 | 900 |
| Sweet Peas | 388 | 1200 |
| Garden Peas | 728 | 1158 |
| Garden Beans | 370 | 496 |
| Beet | 172 | 204 |
| Carrot | 160 | 215 |
| Lettuce | 350 | 350 |
| Onion | 360 | 360 |
| Tomato | 250 | 351 |
| Brassicas | 1351 | 1450 |
| Mangold | 257 | 288 |
| Swede | 206 | 299 |
| Turnip | 234 | 335 |

As well as all the important data these trials gave the company, they were obviously of great interest to other agriculturalists and horticulturalists, and the following are some of the thousands of visitors who made the trip to the Earley or Slough trial grounds.

1867  A reporter from the *Gardeners' Chronicle*

1882  Many visitors from the Royal Agricultural Show. This was held in Reading in the area which is now Palmer Park, some 300 yards from Suttons' trial grounds

1899  A party of Siamese students

1900  250 members of the Institute of Journalists

1901  100 members of the British Dairy Farmers' Association

1903  The Hungarian Commission of Agriculture
      The national and horticultural press

1904  His Highness Ran Rana of Talawar

1913  The Kabaka (King) of Uganda

1914  Staff from the *Journal of Horticulture*

1920  The Genetics Society
      The Berks, Bucks and Oxon Branch of the Land Agents' Society

1921  The Director of the Danish Seed Testing Laboratory, Copenhagen
      Davis Tannoch, Balance Gardens, Dunedin, New Zealand
      S Gsharngafaoni, Government Farm, Bengal
      S M Stewart, missionary to the Cree Indians and Eskimos, Labrador
      W J Dowson, Agricultural Department, Nairobi, Kenya

| 1922 | Komanoske Taniguchi, Kagoshima Imperial College, Satsama, Japan |
| | Arno H Nelisberg, Cornell University, Ithaca, USA |
| | Arnold Caddy, R.S.O., Victoria, Australia |
| | Florence York, Pasadena, California, USA |
| | T J Pemberton, Christchurch, New Zealand |
| 1930 | Empire Farmers |
| 1931 | International Horticultural Conference. |

In 1921 much thought was given to Readel's patent gassing of plants with carbon dioxide, which claimed wonderful results by transmitting carbon dioxide to plants by smoke from boiler furnaces! It appeared to be very cheap to install at £100. However, later in the month, it was decided not to proceed with this. In the same year, Harold Fowles was appointed to be outside foreman. The company had a detached house built for him, near the edge of the grounds and facing London Road, where he stayed until his retirement in 1960.

In September 1938 approval was given by the Air Ministry in London for Suttons to set up its own meteorological station. This was situated on the area of Suttons' grass advisory station, which contained many hundreds of agricultural and amenity grass trials. Readings of rainfall and temperature were recorded at 9 a.m. each day and forwarded monthly to the Air Ministry. The equipment also included a sunshine recording instrument on a brick pillar some three feet tall. The data were published in the Monthly Weather Reports with a general summary of weather in an annual report. This service was continued until the early 1960s; after this the information was still recorded for the benefit of the company until 1975, just a year before the move to Torquay.

A view of the main drive and experimental lawn grass plots and the crop drying building, looking towards the Great Western Railway. 1909.

The origins of the grass advisory station go back to 1863 when Martin Hope Sutton founded a grass garden containing a large number of species and varieties from all parts of the world. Many of the plants had an important use in agriculture, while others were employed solely in the production of lawns and sports turf. While some of the grasses were notable as injurious weeds, others were grown for their decorative purpose, but all were of interest to the botanist. Wide-ranging research was carried out here in all respects of grass growth and usage, originally with regard to mixtures required for new pastures and later in connection with turf maintenance, such as the comparative value of varieties from seed; root development on differing soil types; the fertilizing of grass for various purposes; the effects of herbicides on grass varieties; fungus control and other chemical experiments.

The role of trial-ground manager was highly respected. In addition to the day-to-day running of the glasshouses and outdoor land, which required wide knowledge of the normal growing methods and the more demanding needs of crops for seed, he was expected to produce and display thousands of first-class plants for agricultural and horticultural shows throughout the year. One such man, E R Janes, was so highly regarded for this expertise in the period 1930–1950, winning many gold medals at the Chelsea Flower Show and elsewhere, even to the extent of displaying produce in North America, that he was presented with the highest award of the Royal Horticultural Society, the Victoria Medal of Honour, for his services to horticultural exhibitions. Others to receive this prestigious award were A W Sutton, E P F Sutton, W F Giles and F G Potter for services to horticulture throughout their lifetime. For well over 100 years, the company has been involved in working with the RHS both at council and various committee levels. Very many varieties of flowers, vegetables and potatoes bred or introduced by Suttons have received awards after being grown under trial conditions at Wisley.

Due to the specialist nature of vegetable crops grown by market gardeners, field-scale trials were run in the principal areas to measure results under local conditions. One unique area was Cornwall, for growing winter-heading Roscoff cauliflowers. This business was of so great a significance to Suttons that a trial ground was set up at Gulval, just outside Penzance, for trialling and selection purposes. This land had been used previously by the Ministry of Agriculture as an experimental station, and was taken over by Suttons after WWII. Later it was also used for flower trials, and it was interesting to see the varietal variations due to climatic conditions between this area and Reading. In the Scottish border country, trials and selections were made by Suttons' experts until the 1950s of turnips and swedes for the agricultural trade; the selected roots were des-

patched by rail to Reading and, after further careful selection for trueness
to type, were replanted in isolation for basic seed.

Finally, after 100 years of fine service, the trial grounds at Earley
grew their last flower and vegetable plants when the company made the
move to Torquay in 1976. All the buildings were demolished, including
the glasshouse complex built in 1903.

The front of the Conservatory; this faced the Great Western Railway line, large glass houses ran at right angles from both sides of the large centre piece, with small glass houses coming off at right angles from those.

Once the company was organised in Torquay, the next requirement
was for a new trial ground. As there was no suitable land around the
company headquarters, arrangements were made with a nurseryman at
Stoke Gabriel to rent a neighbouring field. All the plants that required
raising under glass were grown at the nursery, and the whole field was
planted up so that, by the summer, it was a sea of colour with the flowers, and also producing many fine vegetables. This situation continued
successfully for some years until a new site was found at Ipplepen in
1989. A new large glasshouse was erected there and the field divided
into long beds for the planting out or direct sowing of all the flowers
and vegetables. As has always been the case, copious notes were taken
of each trial, from sowing and planting times to flower or maturity, so
that a profile of each variety was established; in this way, potential new
varieties could be measured to ensure they were an advance in some way.
Many, however, were not satisfactory, and were discarded.

On a glorious July day in 1990, the trial grounds received an official
Royal opening when the Duchess of York performed the ritual tree-plant-
ing ceremony and showed very great interest in the purpose of plant-test-
ing. In addition to trials, an area was developed as a show garden where
all new varieties were on display. Every year a Press Day is held where
the major garden journalists assemble, so that they can see and hopefully

write about or broadcast on the new varieties. Throughout the summer, the trial grounds became a most popular place to visit, with many thousands of holidaymakers walking round and taking notes.

## Notable varieties of flowers and vegetables

Over the years Suttons has produced and introduced many hundreds of new varieties: the following are some of the more outstanding ones.

*Chrysanthemum, Charm.* This originated from a single plant in a seed crop of the cascade type which Suttons was growing in Kenya, and it was probably a mutation. It was isolated and much to everyone's surprise the seed of the next generation bred true, and further selection work was carried out. Dwarf-growing plants with ball-shaped heads measuring up to 3 ft across and carrying 2000 blooms were regularly produced in a wide range of colours, and there is no doubt that this was a major introduction in 1947. It received a gold medal from the National Chrysanthemum Society.

*Greenhouse flowers.* In the days of the large private estates, greenhouse flowers were extremely important to supply the large house for dinner parties etc. Suttons specialised in a wide range of calceolaria, primula and gloxinia, with its Triumph strain being outstanding, and for this purpose the company maintained high quality by growing beautiful plants in its own greenhouses for seed. Suttons can well claim to have been the originators of a large number of varieties of *Primula malacoides* and *Primula sinensis*, giving growers a wonderful colour range from which to choose.

*Nemesia suttonii.* This was introduced in 1888 from crosses made between *N. strumosa* and *N. bicolor* and awarded a first-class certificate in 1892. The original colour was orange with somewhat insignificant flowers, but the strain now includes a wide range of colours, all of which are exceedingly striking. *The Gardeners' Chronicle* of 13th April 1892 commented: 'Few annuals have created such widespread interest as the handsome N. suttonii.'

*Venidio arctotis.* This plant was bred at the Slough trial grounds from numerous crosses between *Venidium* and *Arctotis grandis*. The brilliantly-coloured flowers are carried on long stiff stems, making it ideal for cutting and as a pot plant. Unfortunately, in spite of the best endeavours of Suttons' plant breeders, all efforts to produce fertile seed were unproductive; it therefore had to be grown entirely from cuttings, but nevertheless was still a great success and was introduced in 1953.

*Wallflower, Persian Carpet.* Introduced in 1956, this very popular pastel-shade mixture was an immediate success, and continues to be so to this day.

*Pea, Little Marvel.* Introduced in 1900 this variety is still available today. Over the years it has won many awards, including an award of merit from the RHS. It is noted for its dwarf habit and dark green seeds.

*Pea, Show Perfection.* Bred at Reading in the 1950s from a cross between Evergreen and Achievement, this tall pea was popular in gardens until space became a problem. It is still the main prize-winner on the show-bench at local and national shows with its long, curved, dark green pods.

*Broad bean, The Sutton.* Bred from a cross between Exhibition Longpod and Becks Green Gem, this is the finest dwarf-growing variety, making it ideal for the small garden. Introduced in 1923, the freely-branching plants carry a heavy crop of 5- or 6-seeded pods.

*Runner beans, Suttons Prizewinner.* Bred and introduced in the 1880s, this outstanding variety received a first-class certificate at the RHS in 1892. For very many years it was recognised as the outstanding long-podded variety of the finest quality.

*Cucumber, King George.* First offered in 1911 from a cross between Matchless and Telegraph, this fine greenhouse variety is still available today, and is often seen on the show-bench. The fruits are of good length, very dark green in skin colour with a small handle.

*Tomato, Alicante.* Introduced in 1966, this is a very popular non-hybrid variety. It crops well under a wide range of growing conditions, and is most useful for the amateur gardener.

*Rhubarb, The Sutton.* First offered in 1894, this variety resembles Victoria, being quite large with a more upright habit and much earlier to crop in the open ground. It has a beautiful colour, a rich bright red which remains after cooking, with large, exceedingly tender, sticks. It was a leading variety for well over half a century, and is still found in collections to this day. It was twice given the RHS award of merit.

## Victorian Vegetables

Looking back through old Suttons' catalogues, it is interesting to find that many varieties from the 19th century still survive and are quite widely grown, in spite of the many advances in plant-breeding in the last 50 years. Very few of those listed in 1837 lasted throughout Queen Victoria's reign, so it is important to remember those men and companies which made such strides in improving quality and yield in the latter part of the 1800s.

*Peas.* One of the finest for many years was Ne Plus Ultra, a tall-growing sort with wrinkled seed making it much sweeter and more succulent than the old hard, round-seeded varieties grown previously. In 1881 Suttons introduced American Wonder, a sweet early pea growing only 18 inches tall. Gradus, a second early with good sweet flavour, has stood the test of time.

*Broad beans.* The Aquadulce and Seville types first appeared here from the Continent in the late 1850s, being of special use for autumn sowing outdoors for the earliest crops. The Windsor type, both green- and white-seeded, come from the same period.

*Dwarf beans.* The variety Canadian Wonder is about the only one to survive but, with its flat-shaped pods which quickly become stringy, it has become outclassed.

*Runner beans.* Painted Lady, with its scarlet and white flowers (grown mostly for its decorative value) is still seen in gardens. The long-podded varieties are of a more modern introduction, Suttons' Prizewinner being one of the first in the 1880s.

*Beetroot.* The Globe or Detroit type was introduced in the 1890s as was the long-rooted Cheltenham Greentop, but it is the round-rooted types which are the most popular.

*Carrot.* James Scarlet Intermediate, a main crop with long tapering roots, has lasted for well over 100 years, as have the Nantes types, which are early and short-rooted, and were introduced from France in the 1870s.

*Parsnip.* The Student was a huge step forward when it was bred by Professor Buckman in the 1860s from the wild parsnip, and has been the mainstay of this subject for a long time.

*Turnip.* Two old varieties are still with us: Snowball, with its smooth white round roots, and Veitch's Red Globe, a main-crop variety with a purple crown.

*Cabbage.* The main improvement was with the introduction of the non-bolting spring cabbages such as Early Offenham and Flower of Spring. The Large Blood Red pickling cabbage has been available for well over 100 years.

*Cauliflower.* Veitch's Self-Protecting was for a long time the leading variety for autumn heading, and Early Snowball is an excellent summer-heading type of Continental origin.

*Broccoli.* Probably one of the longest surviving varieties is Purple Sprouting, which was already well established in the early 1800s.

*Celery.* Solid White has stood the test of time, although more recently the self-blanching types have become popular.

*Cucumber.* For greenhouse use, Telegraph and the variety The Rochford, raised by the famous growers of the same name, both reigned supreme for many years. The latter was a great favourite with commercial growers.

*Leek.* Musselburgh and The Lyon, both originating from Scotland, have been widely grown since Victorian times.

*Onion.* James Keeping is one of the oldest varieties still around. Ailsa Craig has also been with us for 100 years or more, and is still a favourite when grown for the show-bench.

*Lettuce*. Always a popular subject for gardeners, with All The Year Round and Tom Thumb being widely offered through the years. In the cos types, Paris White is another that has stood the test of time.

*Melon*. Although not so widely grown now, Blenheim Orange and Hero of Lockinge were most popular in the days before the import of fruit became normal practice.

*Tomatoes*. It was only in the latter part of the 19th century that these became popular. Best of All and the yellow-fruited Golden Queen are two varieties from that era.

## Bush Tomatoes

Much excitement was aroused during the latter part of World War II when frost-resistant varieties of tomatoes were brought in from Russia by the Ministry of Agriculture. Many trials were carried out by research centres, market growers and seedsmen, including Suttons, to evaluate them, as well as others of Canadian origin. The results showed that Stambovoi was a good early type with round regular-shaped fruits, but Bison was later-fruiting and a poor cropper, with large irregular-shaped fruits. Although they did not need staking, the plants required some pruning, and the trusses needed support to keep the fruit clean, so they were still labour-intensive. All these varieties proved to be more resistant to adverse weather conditions but no more resistant to frost than English varieties, either early or late.

Bush types have existed on the Continent and in the USA for many decades. In fact, in Suttons' 1862 catalogue, a variety called Upright or De Laye was offered, and many others were trialled in the early part of the 20th century. They have never proved to be successful as a commercial crop, and the main use today with modern hybrids is as patio or hanging-basket plants.

## Mummy Peas

This is one of the perennial myths of the vegetable world. As far back as 1849, a pea was advertised under the name of Grimstone's Egyptian Pea or Mummy Pea; it was said to have come from the pyramids, and was sent out in 5/- packets of 10 seeds. In 1873 it re-appeared in the press; the *Gardeners' Chronicle* of 11th January 1873 said it was synonymous with buck pea, cluster pea, crown-podded and possibly others. Again through the 20th century this story has re-appeared and many articles were written about it. Suttons was often asked to evaluate such claims, but they were all quite spurious, and in the 1920s during a business trip to Egypt, Mr Sutton enquired of museum authorities there and was assured there was no foundation to the story. Imperial College of Science and Technology, London, agreed that any seeds would be powder after 4,000 years, whether they came from the pyramids or elsewhere. Until the 1960s Suttons had a collection of the old crown-podded types kept for scientific purposes only, and these were eventually sent to a seed bank for preservation. The mummy pea myth refuses to die, with new claims coming to light from time to time. For example, James Witchell from Arlingham, Gloucestershire, donated the 'Tutankhamen pea' to the Heritage Seed Library at the Henry Doubleday Research Association in 2001. He said that the pea came originally from Highclere Gardens, Lord Caernarvon's estate.

## Seed Potatoes

Over the years Suttons introduced many outstanding new potato varieties. Most of the crosses were grown and the development work was done in Scotland, as was the large-scale bulk production for sale, for reasons of disease resistance. Seed potatoes have always had a great problem with diseases, most notably at the time of the Irish famine. From the 1870s, Suttons was involved in breeding varieties with resistance or immunity to disease. First of all in 1876 came the introduction of Magnum Bonum, which was the pioneer of all blight-resistant varieties and which yielded well in all parts of the country. It was so popular that it outlasted many later-bred varieties. In the early 1900s, another disease threatened the potato crop, wart disease, but fortunately immune varieties were found and improved ones developed from them. Suttons had great success with varieties such as Ben Lomond and Ben Cruachen, which in 1924 was awarded the Lord Derby gold medal for the finest variety immune from wart disease.

A tercentenary potato conference was held at The Rotunda in Dublin in December 1896 under the auspices of the Irish Gardeners' Association. Suttons put up an exhibit of 209 varieties made up as follows: 35 varieties introduced by Suttons; 32 seedlings (potential new varieties); 136 standard varieties in general commerce; 6 botanical species, which have a scientific interest only and included *Solanum etuberosum*, *Papa amarilla* from Peru, African potato and *Solanum maglia* from the Chinos archipelago. Suttons was awarded a gold medal, the fourth for potatoes for the company; the others were awarded at York in 1895, the International Potato Exhibition in 1892 and Ceylon in 1891. Many further awards were made: 1906 was a particularly good year with 4 gold medals, the last one in February where the exhibit of 267 baskets of different potatoes was acknowledged to be the finest collection ever presented.

In 1903, a year remembered for its record rainfall and disastrous potato harvest, Suttons introduced a new variety named Discovery. The result of a cross between Reliance and the Suttons Flourball, this main-crop variety proved to have exceptional yields as well as being disease-resistant. From reports around the country where a limited amount of this variety had been grown, it obviously had a great future. Originally offered in the catalogue at 10/- per lb with a limit of 3 lb per customer, tubers from the once-grown seed were being sold after harvest at 15/- per lb for next season's crop.

During 1904 Suttons offered 4 varieties of potato from seed, all at 1/- per packet. These were Early Regent, Reading Russet, Myatt's Ashleaf and Suttons Flourball. In an earlier catalogue, it was stated that 'cultivating potatoes from the seed or berry is recommended as one of the best preventatives against the potato disease. It is also very convenient for sending abroad by post and is easily raised in almost all climates'.

Inspecting the potato trials at Southcote Manor, Reading in 1906.

In 1906 the company conducted a very wide-ranging potato trial at Reading. This compared such things as yields from various sizes of seed sets. A comparison between 8 varieties from 4 different areas showed Scottish and Irish tubers giving the highest yields, followed by Lincolnshire and the south of England, which was decidedly poor. A trial was made of 6 early and 12 main-crop standard varieties for yield by ware, seed and chats. Another trial compared earthed-up plants with those grown on the flat; the highest yield was from the earthed-up plants, especially for ware potatoes. On the completion of the trials in October, over 100 people were present by invitation to examine the results and discuss the yields. These included Government and other scientists, farmers, and head gardeners from the large estates.

Suttons grew over 1000 lines of potatoes in 1907, made up of 672 trials of commercial lots, 135 nursery grafts and 234 seedlings, which gives some indication of the importance of this crop, both to Suttons and farmers and gardeners. In 1926, Suttons had 30 seedlings of potential new varieties, far too many for one company to offer, and some of these were presented to the Ministry of Agriculture for further development.

Staff would journey north three times a year to supervise the planting, rogueing and finally the lifting of the crops. The October/November journey also covered the lifting and boxing for export to South Africa of anything up to 800 tons of the variety Up to Date. This trade started before the Boer War, and went on without a break through two world wars until about 1964. For the domestic market, many hundreds of tons of tubers were bagged and sent to Reading by rail, then transported by Suttons' own lorries to the warehouse. As required, the tubers were then riddled for size and hand-picked to remove any damaged ones before being repacked into the appropriate-sized bag for despatch to the customer. It was not at all unusual for delays to occur due to very frosty weather when it was unsafe to have them in transit.

## Nursery trade

In the years between the wars, Suttons issued a seasonal catalogue listing many thousands of plants which were delivered to customers by post or by rail; these were despatched carriage-free to the nearest railway station. Customers in the Reading area were offered free delivery by the company's own motors. A large proportion of this business was the sale of hardy flowering perennials offered singly and per dozen, with chrysanthemums, carnations and delphiniums being the most numerous. Also popular were greenhouse plants, flowering and ornamental plants, roses, and fruit trees and bushes, together with kitchen garden plants such as asparagus, sea kale and rhubarb. During the 1960s, herbs were becoming very popular and Suttons offered a range of plants at 3/- each or 33/- per dozen; also listed was a kitchen collection of dried, rubbed herbs for 7/6d.

This business continued into the 1960s, by which time garden centres took over, except for small items which could be posted. At the same time, the sale of young bedding plants for commercial use was established and, once postal and packaging difficulties had been sorted out, it proved to be an excellent way for gardeners to produce their half-hardy annuals, rather than to grow them from seed. These plug plants are now established as an ideal mail-order subject, and sales continue at a high level.

## Bulbs

The first separate bulb catalogue was issued in 1871, although they had been sold previously by mail order. Except for periods of war, the majority of the bulbs were obtained from the Netherlands, and Suttons' experts would make annual visits at flowering time to ensure that only high-quality bulbs were sent. It was also possible at that time to see potential new varieties there and to compare them with those grown on the trial grounds, so as to offer customers the very best available. Once the bulbs had been harvested, cleaned and sorted for size, they were despatched by lorry and ferry. First came the hyacinths, daffodils and tulips from early August, and then later gladioli and dahlia tubers for planting in the spring. For the latter, despatch from Holland had to be carefully timed so as to avoid periods of severe frost during the winter. In more modern times, insulated lorries were well worth the extra expense to ensure safe arrival in the warehouse, and even then despatch to customers sometimes had to be delayed in periods of bad winter weather.

At the beginning of the 20th century, a very wide range of bulbs was listed, from forcing varieties to large quantities of outdoor types for the big estates. These were offered at prices per 1,000 bulbs of narcissi, tulips and crocus, with special reduced prices for orders over 10,000 bulbs of one variety, so obviously the demand was very great. In hyacinths, over 200 varieties were offered and nearly 100 single tulip varieties, so the customer was really spoilt for choice at that time. In the 1950s, the sales of flowering bulbs represented some 10% of the total sales value of the home garden market, and still today bulbs by mail order are of great importance.

## Grass seed

The success of the company for many of the early years was due to the sale of grass seed for agricultural purposes. By the identification of useful types and the rejection of poor strains, mixtures suitable for farmers were made up on a scientific basis for the first time. In 1882, 54 separate mixtures were offered in the catalogue.

A quotation for grass seed dated 1845 has survived for the Great Western Railway at Paddington for the following areas:

> 'the slopes in front of the station, on the north side of the yard and for those half a mile back from the terminus'.

Other quotes were received for the supply of grass seed for Wallingford Road, Didcot, and Swindon.

Customers for grass seed in 1857 included :

The Royal Farm near Windsor
The Royal Horticultural Society in London
The Crystal Palace Company
Aldershot Army Camp.

*'The success of their (Suttons) prescriptions for permanent and
temporary pastures is well known and the strict science of their
methods as opposed to mere comparisons was emphasised by the
publication in 1871 of the first geological map of England especially designed for the use of agriculturists. Having by experiment and
observation prepared mixtures of grasses to suit not only each particular strata, but also each variety of surface soil, Messrs Suttons'
map enabled the farmer to see for himself the varying conditions of
land which necessitated such differentiations, and to avail himself
to the full in ordering seed, of the latest geological and scientific
knowledge.'*

The Times, *10th March 1906*

Pedigree Herefords on pasture grown from
Suttons agricultural grass seed at Aston
Rowant, the estate of Charles V Sale Esq.,
(Estate Agent Captain E W Joslin).

All the seed produced for Suttons was grown as a specific variety
and as well as UK production, much was imported from New Zealand,
Canada and the USA as well as European countries. Only after completely successful germination and purity checks was it made available
for sale. If it was required as mixtures for either pasture land or amenity
use, it was extremely important to obtain a thorough mix, and this is
where all the machinery and skill of the staff at Suttons could guarantee
a perfectly even distribution of each variety in the mixture.

The importance of this trade, both domestic and for export, can be
imagined from the fact that the sale of grass seed was consistently above
60% of the total sales value of agricultural seed sales between 1862 and
1926, with the exception of the WWI years, when root seed sales took

over and the export of grass seed was drastically reduced. In the period 1875–1890, Suttons made up sufficient grass-seed mixtures to sow 30,000 acres per annum.

The Golf Greenkeepers' Association was formed in May 1912, with Martin Hubert Sutton as one of its vice-presidents. A report in *Golf Illustrated* stated: 'Mr Sutton together with Mr Beale of Carters Seeds, the other vice-president, have done more in the interest of golf and to produce improved modern golf courses than any other men living. Mr Sutton has given both time and money by donating prizes for essays on greenkeeping.'

Through the 20th century, much more emphasis was put on the sale of grass seed for sports grounds, bowling greens, lawns etc, and this is where the use of finer-leaved types became so important. When one considers that, for one acre of sports ground, turf could cost at least 15 times as much as seed, plus the fact that the seed mixture could be specially made up according to soil and climate needs, it is not surprising that the slight delay in waiting for a playing area to be usable was worthwhile. The huge increase in the number of golf courses in Spain and Portugal in the 1960s and '70s resulted in massive deliveries of grass seed there, as well as expert staff to advise on and oversee the work.

Grass seed export order for a golf course in Portugal, being loaded on to wagons in the GWR goods yard. July 1959. Bob Bradbook on lorry, Bill Andrews in doorway.

# 7. Nineteenth-Century Suttons

In Victorian times Suttons was a massive six-acre labyrinth of offices, warehouses and storerooms. It is difficult to imagine what it would have been like to work for such a company at this time. The office workers would, by 2006 standards, be dressed in very prim and proper attire, and the manual workers in waistcoats, collar and tie.

The scale of the buildings was huge; there was a colossal number of sacks and packets of seeds, and there was a whole kaleidoscope of sights, sounds and smells.

It is lucky that the following snapshots of the company have survived, so that people today are able to glimpse the world of Victorian business.

The first account is from the 27th November 1852 edition of the *Gardeners' Chronicle*.

'*Messrs Sutton & Sons of Reading Berkshire. This important seed establishment is situated in the Market Place of the fine old town of Reading, which is easily and speedily reached from London by the Great Western Railway. The shop is fitted up with all the appliances and conveniences for dispatch, which an extensive business demands. Bulbs with which it is chiefly furnished at present, are all labelled with printed labels, as are also the seeds, which are put in packets ready for placing in collections at the shortest possible notice. The excellent mode of labelling everything with printed labels is worthy of special remark, as by this plan the possibility of committing mistakes must be greatly diminished. Behind the shop is an extensive double range of warehouses, which are occupied by garden and agricultural seeds, more especially Turnip and Grass seeds, both of which Messrs Sutton have one of the best collections in the country. In the saving of these, as well as all other seeds, the greatest possible care is taken, in order that they may be all found true to name. Beyond the warehouses is a small garden in two compartments, both furnished with glasshouses and pits. Here the vitality of the different kinds of seeds is tested, and the gayer kinds of plants kept for decorating the shop and for sale in pots. In the first compartment we remarked two pits full of nice Pelargoniums and Cinerarias which were set on a sparred stage, with a chamber below, in which the air circulates freely, being admitted under the trellis work, both at the front and back, through apertures opened and closed by sliding shutters. Bulbs in pots plunged in old tan were coming forward in a frame covered with calico, which has stood the wear and tear of 10 years, and still it answers the purpose, although it is now beginning to give way. It was not oiled or dressed with any composition whatever, that having been found to rot the calico, causing it (although it throws off the water a little better) to last a much shorter time than that to which no glazing composition has been applied. In the second department was a neat half span roofed Pelargonium house, well ventilated at the front and back, and filled with promising plants in 8 inch pots. The front shelf was covered with beautiful examples of Lee's Flower of the Day, whose handsomely variegated foliage renders it attractive at all seasons. In front of this house are numerous pits filled with Crimson, China, Fairy and other Roses; Mignonette, Calceolarias, Carnations and plants of that description. Some of these pits had only recently been erected, and were glazed with panes at least a foot in length, which have the advantage of permitting more light to pass through them than smaller ones. The borders here, as well as in the other compartments, were filled with the better kinds of Conifers, both in pots and planted out, and which looked exceedingly healthy, considering they were grown in a town. Ivies are much wanted, and therefore cultivated in pots here, both walls of a passage connecting the two gardens just mentioned being covered with them. The principal nursery, however, belonging to this establishment lies on the south side of the town, in a fine level situation where there is good soil six feet deep on gravel, so that notwithstanding, all the rains we have lately experienced, when the whole valley of the Thames is one sheet of water, this ground is comparatively dry, and can be worked with facility. Here Roses, fruit trees, evergreens and Conifers are chiefly cultivated, together with here and there patches of the most choice vegetables for trial. Forest 'stuff' is not encouraged, the ground being too valuable to be occupied by that kind of cropping, which can be cheaply 'bought in' from other quarters. This firm has also given up the saving of Rye, Vetches and Clover, in order that undivided attention may be given to the finer seeds, such as those of Turnip and Grass. Of the latter, examples of all that are valuable to the farmer, or for forming permanent pastures, are collected here, and correctly labelled, so that an opportunity is afforded of inspecting their different characters while growing in the same soil, and under precisely the same treatment. In the Horticultural portion of a piece of land set apart as 'sample ground', we remarked rows of Broccoli, Cabbage, Lettuce etc., all growing side by side, and labelled with their names in full; also beds of choice Beetroot, Carrots & etc; for transplanting for seed. Upwards of 30 varieties of Peas had been grown here, but they were cleared off, with exception of Suttons Goliath, which is still producing pods and blossom, although it was sown on the 22nd August. It is therefore a good Pea for a late crop, and it appears to be very productive; its flavour resembles that of Knights Marrowfat. Many sorts of Potatoes had been cultivated here, but were now stored away. Messrs Sutton stated that from notes made at the time of digging up Sodens Early Oxford and the Early Walnut-leaf Kidney were the earliest, and that the Red Ash-leaf, Doctor Nelson's Favourite and British Queen were the most productive second-early varieties.*

'Of agricultural crops a compartment was allotted to Turnips, containing about 40 varieties of Swedish, hybrid and other kinds. Of the former, the best appeared to be Sutton's Purple-top and River's Stubble Swede. Among hybrids, Sutton's, Skirving's, Dales, and River's Yellow Stone are all especially worth a mention. Chivas's Orange Jelly was particularly fine, both as regards smoothness and colour; and Ballantine's Yellow is likewise a promising kind. The largest Turnip in the grounds was the new Lincolnshire Red, so called from its being brought originally from that county by Philip Pusey Esq, who presented the stock to Messrs Sutton. Of Mangolds and Beet (which were of a great size), we noticed a large red variety called the Elvetham Long Red, a new sort introduced by Messrs Sutton; also very finely formed Yellow Globe Mangold, besides the large Crimson Beet and the white Silesia Sugar Beet. There were also Kohl Rabi, Drumhead and other Cabbages, White Belgian Carrots, and a very large new red variety, which seemed likely to vie with the White Belgian itself for size.'

The next description is again taken from the *Gardeners' Chronicle*, this time from the 9th February 1867 issue.

'On approaching the Company in the Market Place at Reading, one sees an unostentatious building, but on entering it is obviously one of the most unique, but also one of the most extensive and best managed seed stores in the Kingdom.

'This must contribute to the brilliant success of the firm. The entire establishment is divided and sub-divided into numerous departments, each of which has a skilled foreman presiding. The number of Warehousemen, Clerks and others, employed during the busy season (December to April) is upwards of 100. Among other advantages (which in this 'pushing' age are too often forgotten), they have their Saturday half day holidays, and shorter hours in the summer, and, what is by no means unimportant, commodious and well ventilated offices for the numerous Clerks and others employed. There is also a large reading-room, which is open during meal times, and after business hours, supplied with the Daily Papers and other Periodicals, and to which is attached a well furnished Library.

'The principal 'Order Room', which is nearly 100 feet long and more than 30 feet wide, is completely fitted up with several long rows of counters, and some thousands of seed drawers, bins, and pigeon holes, all distinctly labelled and every other convenience that experience could suggest. This is exclusively for the execution of Garden Seed Orders, and from the extent and good arrangement which characterizes everything, we were not surprised to hear how large a number of orders are safely executed and packed in a day.

'We now come into the packing areas and the Agricultural Seed Order Department. There was a separate division for every article, with a large ticket at the head of each sub-division; the sacks also had a label fixed to each, and a memorandum showing the particular parcel or lot number sent to each customer is duly entered in the Warehouse Book for future reference.

'We were taken to an extensive block of buildings in the King's Road, which was a store for Grass Seeds, Mangel Wurzel, and Turnip Seeds. If at the Market Place premises we were struck with the minutiae of detail, the magnitude of the operations here are not less remarkable. Entering the three storied building, we find it really possesses the advantages of a five or six storied building without its concomitant drawbacks. For instance, after passing down a long avenue of sacks of Grass Seeds, stacked high above the head on each side, and coming, as we supposed to the end of that particular class of seeds, it was only to find ourselves entering another compartment on the same level but with a current of air passing directly through that portion of the building, and where might be seen the same kind of seeds undergoing the process of cleaning, by means of various machines found by experience to be most adapted to the particular type of seeds going through at the time. In this way there is one floor, in its two compartments, occupied chiefly with Grass Seeds both home and foreign grown; in another Turnip Seeds and in a third Mangel Wurzel; and these stack after stack in such large quantities.

'In this part of the establishment, the more extensive of the Export orders are executed, and we find a large quantity of Grass Seeds just now packed in stout hogsheads and zinc lined cases for exportation to New Zealand by the next vessel.

'In the Plant Nursery is an additional house recently erected, and heated with hot water, expressly for the purpose of testing the germinating power of the new seeds, immediately they are received from the contract Growers employed by Messrs Sutton. We are informed upwards of 8,000 acres are in this way occupied every year with seeds for that great Reading firm; their practice being to select roots perfectly true to their type, from which the seed is saved. This choice seed is subsequently distributed among the growers employed by them to grow the required quantities. At the time of our visit, (early in November) we notice numerous kinds of Broccoli, Cabbage, Winter Greens, Brussels Sprouts & etc, planted in their rank for trial at the ground in Kendrick Road [their Portland Place Nursery]; but perhaps the most important was a collection of about 200 species of Grasses in their allotted plots. We next drove to Manor Farm at Whitley, where we found many acres of Mangel (Mangold) Wurzel, Swedes, Turnips, Kohl Rabi, Drumhead Cabbage & etc, all growing in one large field, one 'land' or a portion of land being devoted to each variety. All of these having been sown under similar conditions of soil, manure and treatment, by which means respective merits are subsequently determined. To this department Mr Martin Sutton pays special attention *and his practised eye readily enables him to detect in existing varieties any improvements or deviations. Here we particularly notice Sutton's Selected Yellow Globe Mangel, beautiful in shape and small top, but of extraordinary size; also their New Yellow Globe Intermediate Mangel of very fine flesh, remarkably free from coarse roots and a sort which we think will become generally cultivated; Sutton's Champion Swede, one of the finest sorts known, of excellent shape, said to be very hardy; and Purple-top Mammoth Turnip, very large producing a great weight per acre - this is apparently a selection from their Grey Stone variety.*

*'We next visit a large field at the back of Cintra Lodge (the residence of Mr Martin Hope Sutton), sown with a number of different parcels (lots) of Swedes and Turnips, the seed being of the current year's harvest (1866) for sale during the ensuing season. These trials are made immediately the new seed is ripe, for the purpose of thoroughly testing the correctness of the various sorts before sending them out to the public. On the opposite side of the high road are traditional Trial Grounds, where the now celebrated early pea 'Ringleader' was first tested in conjunction with its several competitors. Here also the choice dark red Beetroot known as 'Suttons' and other new and distinct vegetables and flowers have, from time to time been raised. Near this sample ground is a plot of Italian Rye Grass and Alsike Clover, sown six years ago and occasionally renovated, which is still very vigorous and several plots of Bromus Schraederi sown at different times during the past twelve months. This latter plant grows here very vigorously on very poor gravelly soil, and Messrs Sutton have discovered that the great secret of success in its cultivation is constant cutting or grazing. If allowed to stand more than three or four weeks it runs to seed and then ceases to grow, but on being cut it immediately sprouts again and continues growing throughout the winter – a great advantage in a forage plant.*

*'Nearer the town, at Portland Place, is a considerable piece of nursery ground, on which is grown a good stock of Fruit Trees and Roses, Conifers & etc, furnishing sufficient supply for good local business, which is all that is sought; the chief trade of the firm being in seeds, of which their choice stocks are in great repute in nearly all parts of the civilized world.'*

15 years later, the *Farmer and the Chamber of Agriculture Journal* of 22nd May 1882 comments in 'Souvenir of a visit to Messrs Sutton's seed establishment':

*'Reading today owes a great measure of that prosperity which causes it to rank among the most prosperous of our provincial towns, renowned as it is for both biscuits and sauce, yet we suppose our agricultural visitors connect the town of Reading rather with seeds than with any article of diet. Here was compiled the first priced*

*descriptive Seed Catalogue ever issued. In Reading printed labels were first attached to packets of seeds; and from Reading seeds were despatched, carriage free, years before any other firm followed the example set by Mr M H Sutton, the present head of the Reading Firm. He also introduced complete collections of seeds, which are at present the recognized method for the supply of amateurs' gardens, and which are now sold by tens of thousands. In fact it may be said that the system of the seed trade as now known was formed at Reading, and that most other seed businesses throughout the world are imitations of the great Reading establishment.*

*'The Proprietors of this great business – the largest of its kind in the world – can look back upon a rapid growth from comparatively small beginnings. Half a century since the father and grandfather of the present Partners were engaged in a corn-dealing and milling trade; but the founder of the firm, so far as the seed business is concerned, was Mr Martin Hope Sutton, the present senior partner. Amongst the causes which have contributed in a little more than a generation to raise this immense commercial fabric, none has been more powerful than the crusade waged by Messrs Sutton & Sons against the abominable practice of seed adulteration. The firm of Sutton, however, always made it a rule not only to send out unadulterated seeds, but only those of proved growth; and so rapidly has the business increased, that the remark we once heard fall from a New Zealand Colonist, 'If you want good seeds go to Sutton's of Reading', is to be found practically realised not only in every part of the United Kingdom, but in all parts of the civilized world.'*

By the time the nineteenth century came to an end, Suttons had developed into a large prosperous company with a set of offices, stores and order rooms that covered about six acres of ground. The workforce was large, mostly male and smartly dressed, regardless of whether they were doing office or manual work. The following account is based on *Suttons Seeds,* a promotional book produced by Suttons at the time.

While it will take the reader only a short period of time to read about Suttons' Market Place premises, according to the writer of the above book 'to obtain a comprehensive idea of the several departments, a visit of not less than two hours is necessary'.

Suttons' handsome Market Place entrance gives the visitor little idea of the scale of the labyrinth of buildings that lie beyond. Above this entrance is the private office of Suttons' senior partner, Martin F Sutton. This room is the hub of the business, where the partners' meetings are held and all of the company's important decisions are made.

Visitors sign the Visitor's Book which includes the names of ministers of agriculture from foreign parts, ambassadors of the principal powers of Europe and colonists from distant lands.

Inside the main entrance from Market Place; the double door on the left led into the garden shop.

## Post Office and Letter Opening

Within the vestibule, the company has a well-equipped post office.
The amount of post arriving at Suttons is of course very variable. Large
amounts of correspondence are dealt with daily throughout the year, but
in the horticultural and agricultural seed season the throughput could
rise to very large numbers indeed, with 15,000 letters and parcels having
been recorded as passing through this private post office to correspond-
ents and customers on just one day alone. The employees within this
integral post office wear smart uniforms with a double row of brass buttons down the front.

Incoming post is opened in Leonard G. Sutton's spacious private
office. At just after 7 a.m. a Suttons mail cart is despatched to the
Reading Post Office to collect the day's letters. As with all the activities at
Suttons, the partners are heavily involved, and Leonard personally super-
vises the opening of the mail. After opening, the contents of the envelopes
are divided into various groups such as order forms, requests for catalogues and railway and shipping communications.

The lower parts of the walls have attractive wooden panelling, the
light fittings are ornate works of art and the room is heated by an open
fire, surrounded by a beautiful mantelpiece. The correspondence itself is
moved around in large wicker baskets.

The various departments open at 9 o'clock when each one receives
its share of the morning post, i.e. the foreign letters and orders go to the
export trade partner etc. In order to ensure that all correspondence is
dealt with promptly, each letter and order is stamped with the date and
the particular mail by which it arrived. Any letter containing money is
sent to a private room where the nature and amount of the remittance
is marked on it. As further security, all of the notes, cheques, drafts and
postal and money orders are stamped. The whole process is repeated as
later mail batches are received.

## The Ledger Office

Keeping track of orders, invoices and payments is a mammoth task, and
the size of the Ledger Office matches the scale of the job. At 148 feet
long by 37 feet wide at its widest point, it accommodates 75 clerks for
the UK accounts alone (the foreign and export accounts are managed
in a different department).

The United Kingdom accounts are entered into 26 huge volumes,
each of which contain the details of several thousand customers. In
addition, there are 46 cash journals; day books containing names,
addresses and invoice totals; a double set of press-copying books; and

The Order Office: Here the orders were processed before being passed to the seed rooms.

26 enormous registers of customer files. These customer registers are particularly important as they are used for addressing catalogues. Suttons claim that 'the method of reference is so arranged that any account can be found in a few seconds'. The many thousands of customers render the counting-house work naturally complicated and laborious. In some cases there are hundreds of accounts open to different people of one and the same name; for instance, the surname 'Smith' has between 600 and 700 accounts. Other names which readily occur to the reader also have

Below: Ledger Office 1920s.
Right: Invoice Office 1920s.

accounts open by the hundred, so that some little exercise of ingenuity and skill is necessary to keep all things straight.

Great importance is placed on the filing away of orders and correspondence, as customers frequently ask for repeat orders from year to year, even when they themselves cannot remember what they have ordered previously. To accommodate all this paperwork, an immense record office has been constructed from which any paper can be retrieved 'within thirty seconds'. Each day hundreds of orders are found and returned within hours. In addition, it is not unusual to file nearly 2,000 new orders or letters in a day. To accommodate all this paper, an enormous amount of shelving is required. In fact, 'were the shelves on which the papers are placed, with the standards supporting them, stood end on end, they would far exceed the height of Snowdon'.

All the cheques, money orders, postal orders and even stamps are kept and processed within the Cash Department. In order to detect any errors, a return from the cash journals in the Ledger Office is made to one of the partners for comparison with the bank passbook.

As this paperwork is so important to the company, at the close of business each day, all the books are put on to trolleys which are then lowered into a fireproof room via a hydraulic lift. This room is accessed from above by a self-closing steel trap-door.

As well as this army of clerks in the main offices, many more can be found within the departments.

## Despatch Office

As the business is very varied and complex, orders might need to pass through many departments before being completed. Conversely, a simple order for a couple of packets of flower seeds might only have to go to the flower-seed department before being sent to the customer. It is because of this logistic variability that all orders have to pass first through the Order Office, where they are recorded, and the most efficient route through the company is determined for each order.

Generally the order starts to be compiled in the department with the least bulky items that are required, and ends up at the department where the greatest quantity is needed to complete the order. The orders are closely clocked and monitored during their journey through the departments and, once completed, they are returned to the Despatch Office. To ensure accuracy and accountability, the assistants involved in compiling the order adds his initials.

The Despatch Office then adds the address labels and advises customers of the type and number of packages they are being sent and the route by which it will be sent.

### *Flower Seed Department and Flower Seed Order Room*

The sheer number of varieties of flower seed sold by Suttons, and the large number of customers who give their custom, ensures that the flower-seed department is a highly complex and intricate business. Overseeing the logistics of this important department is Leonard G Sutton.

The Flower Seed Room, pre 1914. Note the gas lighting.

The Flower Seed Order Room is the hub of the operation. This room not only assembles the almost infinite variety of flower-seed orders to the needs of individual customers, but is the focal point of tours designed to impress visitors to the firm. The view given to visitors is indeed impressive, as the Order Room is a vast open space filled with row after row of table-high cabinets of finely-crafted drawers and the walls are lined with orderly rows of thousands of smaller drawers. These drawers are

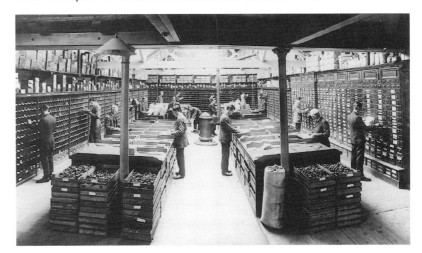

The Flower Seed Room in the 1930s. The Boxes in the foreground contain Gladioli corms.

in turn re-supplied daily from an adjacent warehouse. The seed in this warehouse is stored in rows of sacks before being transferred to packets of various sizes ready for the ordering season rush.

The seeds supplied by Suttons are highly valuable and precious. For example, the cost of producing the calceolaria seed exceeds ten times the weight of the seed in gold. The high value of the seed can be seen from the fact that a pack of double begonia seed costs 5/-, which is a lot of money by any standard, and only contains enough seed to fill a shallow metal spoon with an outside diameter of three-sixteenths of an inch!

Obviously, such highly valuable seed must be handled with great care, with every effort being taken to avoid draughts. In order to try and ensure this level of care continues right up until the time of sowing, the very small seeds are first packed in very small white envelopes before being placed in a larger paper packet labelled with the name of the variety and a brief cultural note, in order to impress on the sower the high level of care the seeds require and deserve.

The sheer complexity of the Flower Seed Order Room is illustrated by the fact that there are nearly 200 varieties of asters, nearly as many stocks, over 100 sweet peas etc. With hundreds of orders coming in every day and a single order comprising anything up to 300 cultivars, many thousands of packets need to be packed, and collated and completed orders checked daily.

Those orders which consist of just flower seeds are returned to the Despatch Office, with those also requiring vegetable or farm seeds moving on to the appropriate department.

## Vegetable Seed Order Room

If the flower seed department was a hive of industry, the Vegetable Seed Order Room can only be described as literally teeming with life. It is 159 feet long, 30 feet wide, and 20 feet high. Standing at the extreme end, one can see a small army of assistants flitting hither and thither, intent upon the execution of the particular order each has. The centre of the room is occupied by rows of counters, upon which the assistants arrange the packets required by each order, as they bring them from the innumerable drawers which, each distinctly labelled after its kind, occupy a large proportion of the wall space. The millions of packets of seeds necessary for the requirements of this department were all made ready prior to the commencement of the busy season. As an illustration of the extent of the business transacted in this room, on one day in January it had contained more than 2 million packets of seed. Within three months, this immense stock had dwindled to a few hundred packets, and some staff then would have been engaged in preparing documents for the next season.

Right: A view of the Vegetable Seed Room. The man standing fourth in the second row, looking at the camera was M Bowery, head of the department.

Below: The Vegetable Seed Room. A general view showing the old gas pipes for lighting protruding through the work counters.

Right: The Vegetable and Flower Seed Rooms combined in 1952.

In many ways the Vegetable Seed Order Room mirrors the Flower Seed Order Room; however, it differs in a couple of main ways. First, vegetable seeds tend to be much larger than flower seeds, and the Vegetable Seed Order Room is much larger and serviced by several warehouses, instead of just one. Adjoining this large room are several small ones. One contains the stock of vegetable seeds used to replenish stocks in the main room. Immediately underneath is a great storeroom for peas and beans, and adjoining this store is another for carrot and parsnip. Secondly, while the flower seeds are supplied in just one or two packet sizes, many of the varieties of vegetable seeds are supplied by weight, in quantities ranging from half an ounce to several pounds, or by volume from a pint to many bushels.

Arthur W Sutton is in charge of the Growers' Department, and the initial selection, harvesting and threshing is done before the seed arrives in this department. Having arrived in the Vegetable Seed Department, the seeds are further processed before packaging. First, the undersized seeds which will only produce weak plants are sifted out before the rest of the seed is forwarded to a specially-constructed room which is designed to provide the level of light required for all the seeds to be closely scrutinised in order to remove any defective seeds. To avoid possible confusion, only one variety of seed is allowed in this room at any one time. Finally, the remaining seeds are packed into the sizes of packet that are most commonly required, and then sent on to the Order Room.

The biggest challenge of managing the Vegetable Seed Order Room stems from the fact that each type of vegetable seed is not required in a steady stream throughout the year, but is required to be supplied in large quantities within a comparatively short period of time.

Having received the required complement of flower seeds and vegetable seeds, each order is then sent on to the Packing Department, where any seed potatoes and farm seeds are added. The customer's original order is then returned to the Despatch Office, so that the required labels can be produced, and then on to the Ledger Office for booking.

Below: The Pea Granary, packaging peas and beans, c.1900.

Right: The Pea Granary. Women sorting peas, c.1910.

## *Seed Potato Room*

Now at the end of the nineteenth century, Suttons has become an important player in the seed potato market. The demand for the company's seed potatoes in this country grows year by year, but this is dwarfed by the demand from abroad, with immense consignments being despatched annually to South Africa and other colonies.

Cygnets rescued from the Holy Brook. The brook flowed by the side of the Potato Department which is now the site of the Reading (town) Library, and the brook flows in a culvert under it. The photo was taken by the staff entrance in Abbey Square. The doorway at the back of the picture was the entrance to Suttons Abbey Hall. The man with the crook was Mr Bowsher, the local Swan Master. Ted Young on the right worked in the pea and bean stores. He also designed, and made equipment for drying vegetable seed crops, eventually becoming foreman of the department.

Suttons has revolutionised the potato trade by the introduction of its successful variety Magnum Bonum. This has been followed by a series of original seedlings that combine productivity with excellent table qualities and, most important of all, resistance to the dreaded potato-blight disease.

The Seed Potato Room is reminiscent of a well-lit schoolroom, with the supervisor sitting at a high desk and up to 30 men dressed in waist-

coats, aprons and cloth caps picking over the seed tubers to ensure that
Suttons' reputation for excellence is maintained.

Men sorting seed potatoes, c.1930's. The
man standing second from the right in the
second row is thought to be Bill Monger,
who became foreman of the potato
department.

## The Stock-Rooms

The heart of the Suttons' empire is its large stock-rooms. These rooms
store the precious seed that is used to restock the Farm, Flower and
Vegetable Seed Order Rooms. The stock-rooms contain large shelving
units storing long rows of sacks and bags of many shapes and sizes, containing the vast array of horticultural seeds supplied by Suttons. Visitors
to these rooms are often surprised by the smallness of many of the bags
in these storerooms, but when one considers that an ounce of some of
the varieties stored here contains about three-quarters of a million seeds,
these small containers still represented bulk storage. Although all parts
of the Suttons' business are busy and often frantic, by comparison the
stock-rooms are relatively quiet.

As well as seeds for sale, Suttons also stores seed for its own use, for
instance seeds of more than 350 kinds of new peas, none of which has
as yet been offered to the public.

In order to ensure the maintenance of its reputation in the United
Kingdom, Suttons sells all of its seeds direct to the sower and does not
supply any agents or seed dealers for re-sale in Great Britain or Ireland.

## Seed Trial House

Here a sample from every parcel of seed received on the premises is carefully tested. 50 or 100 seeds are taken out of each bag indiscriminately and sown. A record is kept of the percentage of growth, and nothing is allowed to leave the firm unless it is satisfied the seed will give a good result.

## The Bulb Department

At this time Suttons has a flourishing trade in the supply of bulbs. As with everything the company does, quality is its marketing edge over competitors. In order to ensure that Suttons has the pick of the Dutch bulbs, Martin Hubert Sutton or one of his staff makes a visit to Holland each year to inspect the bulbs while they are flowering.

Two large stores are dedicated to the Bulb Department and, as the demand for flower seeds is low in the autumn, the Flower Seed Order Room is taken over then for the collating of bulb orders. The hundreds of large cases used to transport the bulbs from Holland are opened, and their contents transferred to the counters and bins, so that they can be examined, brushed and labelled in readiness for the compilation of the orders.

The men who compile the orders are highly skilled and although, to the untrained eye, the different cultivars of tulips, hyacinths and narcissi appear identical, these workers can readily identify and separate them if they become mixed.

## The Agricultural Seed Store and Farm Seed Order Room

The largest room on the Suttons' premises is the Farm Seed Order Room. At 250 feet long by 60 feet wide, it was more than sufficient to accommodate the great Masonic gathering of 1890. While Reading Town Hall could not hold the assembled diners, only a fraction of Suttons' Farm Seed Order Room was required to seat the Most Worshipful Grand Master, the members of Grand Lodge, Provincial Grand Lodge and hundreds of members from Lodges all over the country.

Despite its great size, the Farm Seed Order Room is not a warehouse, but an assembling area. The huge stocks needed to compile the orders come from neighbouring buildings such as the Grass, Clover and Root Seed Stores, via connecting bridges.

With a capacity of 304,704 cubic feet, the Agricultural Seed Store is a sight to behold. Turnip, swede, and other round seeds are stored in the basement, where the cooler temperatures help control mites

A busy scene in the Farm Seed Order Room in the late 1890's preparing orders, note the container for New Zealand.

that would otherwise infest the stored seed. The first floor stores the clovers, the second the mangel seed and above that are the much lighter grasses. As the bulky seeds of rye grass are required in such large quantities, they are stored in a separate building that is capable of storing thousands of quarters. Natural grass seeds, grown in the best districts of the Rhine and the Moselle; Scotch rye grass seeds from the fertile lands of Midlothian; clover seeds from almost every county in England and country in Europe; mangel seed, grown on the fertile fens of Cambridgeshire; swede and turnip seeds from Essex and Kent, give some idea of the extraordinary magnitude of the quantities required for Suttons' immense agriculture trade. 'Pointing to a great stack of Grass Seeds, we posed the question: about how many acres would these seeds sow? After a few moments calculation, the reply was 53,000 acres. Another bulk of Clover Seeds is sufficient for 75,500 acres; one of Mangel Seeds, 32,000 acres; and another of Turnip seeds 102,000 acres.'

Another view of the Farm Seed Order Room, showing the number of men employed to cope with the volume of trade from December to April. Mid 1930's.

A similar scene in the late 1950's. The man weighing seed on the scales, in the left foreground, is Percy Hayward; he was still riding his bicycle when he was in his late 80's. Arthur Guest, in the white apron, by the scales on the right, excelled at growing large show chrysanthemums.

The Farm Seed Stores, a section of various grass seed cleaning machines, late 1950's.

No matter how clean the seed appears to be when it arrives from its source farm, it is cleaned again on Suttons' own machines. A powerful engine drives this machinery, with a second engine to power the lift. Despite a wide range of cleaning machines now being available, the seeds of some species still have to be cleaned by hand, possibly requiring two or even three methods to ensure purity.

Suttons is the market leader in the supply of grass seed for the restoration of pasture. Much of the pioneering work in the development of grass mixtures was done by Martin Hope Sutton, whose studies determined which species are best for fattening animals, and the proportion of each species required for a particular soil type. This important work is being carried on by his son, Martin J Sutton, who with the help of chemists measured the feeding value of the different grasses and clovers. The culmination of this work was the publication of the standard work *Permanent and Temporary Pastures* in 1886. In addition, he has carried out an extensive series of trials on the comparative influence of various manures on grass crops.

Until now, the standard method of improving meadows and pasture has been to sow them with the sweepings of hay-lofts. Obviously, this product is full of dead and damaged seed and seed of undesirable species, and its composition is entirely hit-and-miss. The work of Martin Hope Sutton and Martin J Sutton has allowed Martin J Sutton's son, Martin Hubert Sutton, to develop a wide range of grass and clover mixtures for both permanent and temporary pastures.

In the essay on *Permanent Pastures* and its *Farmers' Year Book*, the company gave lists of no less than 54 different mixtures, and all of these were prepared separately; the prescription for each was recorded in a book, together with those for special purposes, such as for sowing down the grounds of the International Exhibitions of Paris, Vienna, Philadelphia and Melbourne, the race course at Gibraltar, the cricket ground at Malta, or the extensive sheep-runs of New Zealand.

The Farm Seed Order Room has become very adept at packing large and varied orders from overseas customers at short notice in a manner that ensures that they can be despatched to any part of the world without losing their vitality. Some of these orders can be huge: one government order included nearly a quarter of a million packets of horticultural seeds, another order filled 39 400-gallon iron tanks, and a single South African customer ordered 325 tons of seed potatoes! The export trade has proven to be big business for Suttons, and over a period of just 4 years the shipping of seed potatoes alone has increased thirty-fold.

## The Packing and Loading Floors

Down one side of the large square room that is used to pack the goods that arrive from many parts of the Suttons' site is a range of benches set at heights to allow the packaging of a variety of different-sized packages. This side of the room is used to pack orders that contain only seeds, and for which boxes are used. These boxes are made in the nearby carpenters' shop.

The Packing Department. Note the number of hampers being used. Pre 1914.

The other side of the room is used for the packing of mixed orders, which contain more bulky items such as seed potatoes, bulbs or plants. Each order is packed in the container that is deemed to be most suitable, but on this side of the room, hampers are more commonly used than boxes.

The middle of the room is occupied by four seed potato bins. When small quantities are required, ranging from one gallon to one bushel, they are weighed out from these bins; but when large quantities are needed, they are brought direct from the potato store in sacks or bags.

The loading floor at 8,100 square feet might seem large, but it is frequently tightly packed with sacks, hampers and containers ranging from small boxes to 400-gallon iron tanks weighing over 30 cwt. To ensure the containers cannot be tampered with once they have left Suttons' premises, they are sealed with protective lead seals bearing the firm's trade mark. The packages are then given address labels and weighed for shipping. Trolley and sack carts bring goods in from other departments at ground level, while two special slides bring in goods from above.

A road running around the building allows the loading of 10 horse-drawn vans at a time, and effectively separates outgoing and incoming vehicles. Areas within the building are allocated to all the great railway companies, and Suttons owns sufficient horses and vans to allow the daily shipment of between 75 and 100 tons.

Suttons' pre-railway era choice of Reading as a base has been a good one, as by now it is served by all the great trunk lines, either directly or by connection, and several goods stations.

## The Carpenters' Shop

The carpenters' shop is a hive of activity all year round. It was originally set up to produce boxes for the delivery of seeds, but the skilled workers can turn their hands to anything, from making and laying new floors to repairing broken springs on the site's many swing doors.

At the very busy periods of the year, the packing boxes are required at a rate faster than they can be produced, so a large stock of the more commonly-used sizes was made and stored to ensure their availability at periods of peak demand. While the production of standardised sizes works well for delivery to customers in the United Kingdom, those for the export trade need to be custom-made. Having determined the cubic measurement of the various packages to be despatched, a case of the exact size is constructed using strong materials to ensure that, having left the careful handling of the Suttons' employees, the container can withstand the rougher treatment it might have to endure on its long sea

The Carpenters' workshop, making wooden boxes for the packing of seeds. *c.*1914.

voyage and subsequent inland journey. Although hampers are sometimes used for seed potatoes, generally these export cases are lined with zinc to protect the seeds from the vagaries of tropical climates.

Although construction of packing containers is the majority of the workload, Suttons' skilled carpenters are just as happy to produce desks, cabinets or counters complete with intricate drawers and fittings. Indeed, all the mahogany desks in the Ledger Office were the work of the carpenters' shop.

## Suttons Fire Brigade

The large volume of wooden packaging, paper packets, sacking, dried plant material, straw and dust mean that fire is a constant danger. Suttons, therefore, took the sensible precaution of maintaining its own fire brigade. The captain of this fire brigade is Martin H F Sutton, with the professional expertise being provided by his engineer, who gained his experience while working for the London Fire Brigade.

The equipment consists of a small but powerful horse-drawn fire engine, many hand-pumps, dozens of filled buckets and scores of grenades (these originated in the USA in about 1871, and were manufactured in this country from 1877. They were ball-shaped glass containers consisting of 1-1½ pints of a solution of sodium bicarbonate or salt water, which were thrown at the base of the fire). These portable appliances, each bearing the name of the person responsible for its use, are distributed throughout all the departments.

To ensure an adequate water supply, a 3-inch main connected to the Reading Waterworks has been laid through the complex of buildings. At intervals along this pipe are lengths of hose, complete with nozzles, ready for immediate use. At night, stand-pipes are connected to the mains. In addition to the engineer in charge, two watchmen are employed to guard the premises.

## Stabling

Operating a large company such as Suttons requires the movement of a large volume of materials. To facilitate the movement of these goods, Suttons has its own stables to house the large number of horses required to pull the heavy carts. The entrance is a grand, semi-circular roofed building proudly bearing the name Sutton & Sons on a large curved sign that matches the line of the roof. The airy, cathedral-like interior contains an area for washing vans and trolleys under cover. [As with many

Three wheeled 'Scammel' lorry outside Suttons old stables, 1950's.

A Suttons lorry of the 1920's, with Robert Horne and Bert Harding.

Victorian edifices, the Suttons' stables were a grander and more elaborate affair than was necessary merely to house the horses or would be provided in the modern era of dull, utilitarian architecture]. The head groom lives in a residence attached to the main building, and the carters who work under him take enormous pride in polishing their harnesses and vehicles.

## Abbey Hall

This large and well-appointed building can accommodate nearly 1,000 people. Its main function is for holding daily morning prayers. These brief 10-minute services are conducted by the chaplain of the firm, who is also vicar of one of the Reading parishes. While attendance at these services is not compulsory, they are well attended and they already have a 50-year history. As well as these services, the Abbey Hall is also used for business meetings, popular lectures and company entertainment events, as well as local charitable use. On flower show days, Suttons' Abbey Hall becomes the focal point. [On 27th June 1903, the Abbey Hall was discussed by the board in connection with various organizations. It was decided not to allow some organizations to use the hall, in particular the Philharmonic & Literary and Debating Societies. The Board preferred that its use should be confined as much as possible to meetings of an evangelical character, not for political meetings].

This completes the tour of the main buildings on the Suttons' site.

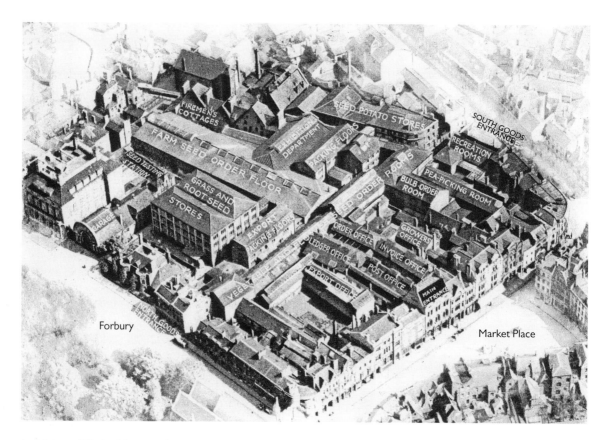

Aeriel view of Market Place premises
1923.

Staff leaving work from the Abbey
Square entrance. Dick Gilkerson and
George Maynard are in front on the
extreme right, late 1920's.

# 8. Royal Associations

The Suttons were passionate royalists. Many companies have used connections with the Royal Family as a powerful marketing tool, and Martin Hope Sutton was quick to see the potential of using his close connections with the Royal family to promote the good name of the company to his customers. Since its early days Suttons has had strong royal associations and from the 1850s began to refer to the company as the Royal Berkshire Seed Establishment; in 1889 it shortened the title to the Royal Seed Establishment. In Macaulay's *Reading Directory* of 1859, Suttons' advertisement refers to the Royal Berkshire Seed Establishment and shows a Royal coat of arms. There is no mention of a Royal appointment, but it goes on to say 'Under the Distinguished Patronage of Her Most Gracious Majesty the Queen, and HRH the Prince of Wales'. The first mention in a catalogue was in 1862, which stated that the company was 'Under the patronage of Her Most Gracious Majesty the Queen, His Royal Highness Prince Albert and His Royal Highness the Prince of Wales'.

In 1858, at the request of the Prince Consort, the company supplied a complete botanical collection of growing specimens of grasses to Osborne House for use by the royal princes and princesses, and they have continued to supply seeds to the Royal Households ever since. Hodder (1956) wrote: 'For Martin Hope Sutton there were frequent commands to go to Windsor to advise on the Royal Gardens of the castle, and after Queen Victoria herself would drive round in her little pony chaise pointing out what she desired to be done. On several occasions too he was called to Osborne to meet Her Majesty and plan improvements to the grounds of her maritime summer residence'.

In 1871 Suttons received a Royal Warrant as Seed Merchants to His Royal Highness the Prince of Wales, and in 1882 the Prince of Wales visited the Suttons' seed trial grounds. In this year the Royal Agricultural Society of England held a show in Reading on land which is now Palmer Park. In the 1883 *Farm Seed Catalogue*, Suttons wrote: 'We look back with very sincere pleasure on that successful and agreeable meeting. We were glad of the opportunity it afforded of becoming personally acquainted with a large number of our customers who had previously been known to us by correspondence only.

'To those who were prevented from coming by any cause we wish to extend a cordial invitation to favour us with a call on any convenient occasion. We feel sure that a visit to our Stores and Trial Grounds will prove interesting to all who are engaged in agriculture or horticulture.

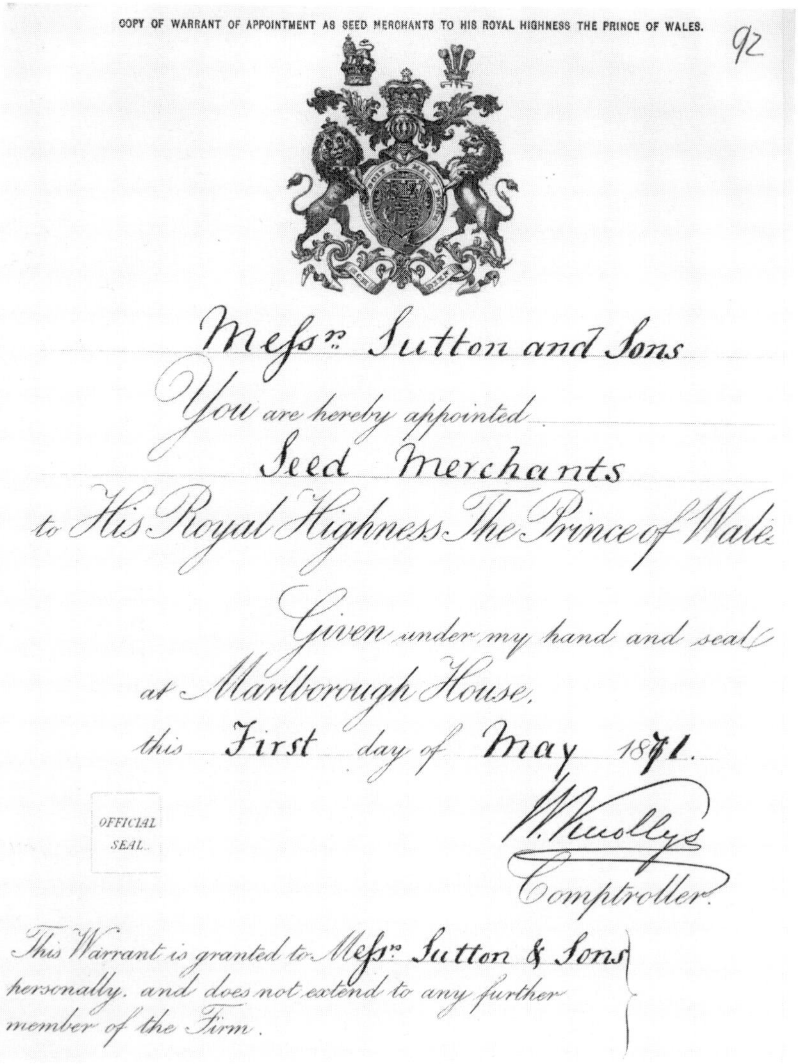

COPY OF WARRANT OF APPOINTMENT AS SEED MERCHANTS TO HIS ROYAL HIGHNESS THE PRINCE OF WALES.

*Messrs. Sutton and Sons*

*You are hereby appointed*

*Seed Merchants*

*to His Royal Highness The Prince of Wales*

*Given under my hand and seal at Marlborough House,*

*this First day of May 1871.*

*W. Knollys*
*Comptroller.*

OFFICIAL SEAL.

*This Warrant is granted to Messrs Sutton & Sons personally, and does not extend to any further member of the Firm.*

Royal Warrant from HRH the Prince of Wales, 1st May 1871.

'Our Stand was honoured with a visit from HRH the Prince of Wales after which he was driven about 300 yards to our Trial Grounds on the main London Road.'

The Times (13th July 1882) wrote: 'A select party entertained the Prince at luncheon in a special pavilion, after which His Royal Highness made a tour of the show, and on leaving was driven a short distance on the main London Road to Suttons Seeds Trial Grounds. This firm possesses the largest retail seed business in the world, exceeding even that of Messrs Vick at Rochester in the United States'.

The front cover of an early edition of the publication *Sutton's at Reading*.

*The Standard* (7th July 1882) reported: 'At 3 p.m. the Prince left the show yard and drove a short distance to the trial grounds of Messrs Sutton & Sons, which just now are a scene of beauty and a centre of fragrance from the large area of flowers, now in full bloom. The Prince was accompanied during his visit by the venerable gentleman Mr Martin Hope Sutton, who established the seed business, and from whom he heard with evident interest a description of the magnificent floral display by which he was surrounded.'

In 1884, the company received the Royal Warrant as Seed Merchants to Her Majesty Queen Victoria.

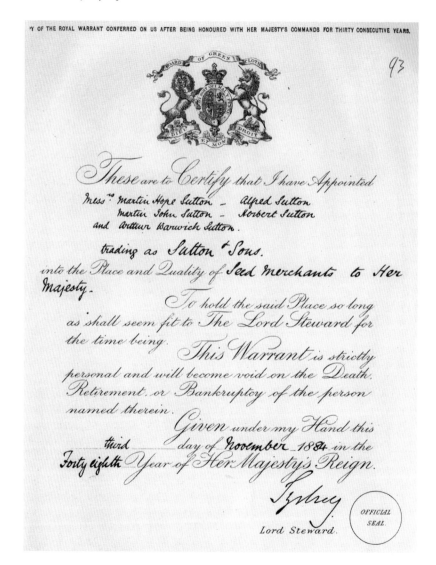

Royal Warrant from HRH Queen Victoria,
3rd November 1884.

The *Journal of the Royal Agricultural Society of England* (second series, vol. xxv, Part II, No. L, October 1889), describing the Royal Agricultural Societys' Show at Windsor on 23rd June 1889, wrote: 'Messrs Sutton & Sons of Reading were entrusted with the important task of carrying out the whole of the floral decorations. On all sides the Pavilion was draped with appropriate climbing plants, the virginia creeper, ivies green leaved and variegated, the Mexican Cobaea scandens with its large purple goblet-shaped blossoms, the yellow-flowered canary creeper and others. At the principal entrance were seen vines, bearing clusters of purple grapes, entwining the pillars which supported the roof of the porch. On the north, south, and west sides of the garden were straight borders, having a background of coniferous plants, green, golden and silvered. Below were the beds of foliaged or flowering plants, and in places specimens of the beautiful cut-leaved Japanese maple; an edging of blue compact lobelia, alternating with the elegant grass-like isolpeis, completed the border on three sides. The velvet lawns, produced from Suttons fine lawn grass seeds, were so exquisitely close, fine and green, that they might have been growing many months, but as a matter of fact were only the production of a few weeks. In the centre of each lawn was a fine specimen of Japanese retinosporas, one of the handsomest of the smaller growing coniferous plants; and on the north and south sides of the garden the initials V.R. were formed in the grass with blue lobelia, creating a very charming effect'.

In its 1890 catalogue, Suttons proudly stated: 'Her Majesty the Queen graciously honoured us by accepting the Pavilion Garden and other Floral Decorations for removal to Osborne; and we have received the following letter of acknowledgement: "Windsor Castle, June 30th 1889 – Sir Henry Ponsonby is commanded by the Queen to thank Messrs Sutton for the Floral Decorations and Miniature Garden surrounding the Pavilion, which they have had the kindness to present to her Majesty."'

1890 saw another visit by the Prince of Wales, this time to Suttons' Reading premises in Market Place. *The Times* wrote: 'His Royal Highness the Prince of Wales, together with His Royal Highness the Duke of Connaught and Strathearn, and the various officers of Grand Lodge and Provincial Grand Lodge, were received by Mr Martin Sutton, who conducted the Prince of Wales and the distinguished company to the banqueting hall. The room, which is usually used for executing orders for farm seeds, had been most artistically decorated.'

A more detailed account of this visit, which appeared in the 20th December 1890 edition of the *Reading Mercury*, is reproduced in the following box.

Various Suttons
publications and seed
tins.

Suttons trial ground at Gulval, near Penzance, with St Michaels Mount in the background. Various flower trials were conducted, but the main trials in the area were of winter cauliflower.

The Duchess of York at the opening of the Ipplepen trial grounds in Devon, assisted by John Rowe, the Trial Grounds manager, July 1990.

## Royal Visit to Reading 16 December 1890
## Grand Masonic Ceremony and Banquet
## H R H The Prince of Wales
## The Duke of Connaught & the
## Duke of Clarence

The main purpose of the visit was for HRH the Prince of Wales to install his eldest son HRH the Duke of Clarence of Avondale as Provincial Grand Master of the newly constituted province of Berkshire. The ceremony was enhanced by the presence of HRH the Duke of Connaught Grand Master of England and Provincial Grand Master of Sussex and Lord Carrington, Grand Master of the United Grand Lodge of New South Wales, together with a considerable number of distinguished Masons.

A special train of six saloon carriages left Paddington at 10.30 a.m., conveying about 200 of the Grand Lodge Masons, stopping at Slough and Maidenhead where more Masonic brethren embarked, arriving at Reading at 11.10 a.m. After the introduction of many dignitaries the Royal Party were driven in carriages, some loaned by local gentry, to the Town Hall which had been lavishly decorated for the occasion. Other delegates had arrived by train from all over the U K. At about 1.15 p.m. the party made their way to the Market Place. Snow was falling, and the roads and pavements were slippery.

For some time before the arrival of the Royal visitors at 1.30 p.m., a large crowd had congregated in the Market Place. Men of the Royal Berkshire Regiment had lined the streets and mounted police had no problem in keeping roadways clear from the Town Hall to the Market Place. The Mayor and Corporation attended the Royal Party to the vestibule at Messrs Suttons. They were met by Mr Martin John Sutton, the managing partner of the firm, who in turn introduced the Prince to Mr Martin Hope Sutton and Mr Alfred Sutton as the founders of the firm, and then Mr Herbert Sutton, Mr Arthur Sutton and Mr Leonard Sutton as the present partners in the business. They immediately conducted the Royal party to the Royal retiring room adjacent to the banqueting hall. On their passage through the brilliantly lighted corridors, the Princes noticed with evident interest some of the large photographic pictures on the walls. The visitors' book had been placed in a convenient position, where the three Princes duly signed. Gatherings of privileged spectators, including many ladies, witnessed the arrival from different locations within the company.

The principal features of the floral decorations displayed consisted of cyclamen and primulas. The entrance lobby was surrounded by tall palms, the graceful foliage of which was seen to the best advantage by the illumination of electric light. Along either side of the long corridor running through the cash and post offices was an unbroken line of white primulas, overhung with ferns and dracenas. Moving on, the party passed through another corridor between the partners' private offices and the Growers' Office, this is normally an open area, but for the occasion had been roofed over and lit by three arc electric lights. The floral displays gave it an appearance of a conservatory or winter garden. Shrubs were grouped on either side, and the beds surrounding them were planted with dwarf palms and dracenas and the most beautiful of all scarlet Van Thol tulips and white Roman hyacinths, reminding the visitors of spring, and leading them to forget for the time the snowy December morning outside. From this corridor the way led us through the potato and pea floors. On either side were cases of models of Sutton's vegetables and beautiful coloured plates of their flowers, as well as a number of primula, cyclamen and solanum and other ornamental plants. From the despatch floor a staircase led to the very large Farm Seed Room, which had been transformed into the banqueting hall. The corridors throughout were laid with crimson baize. The Royal Arms of England, Prince of Wales's feathers, trophies of flags and other devices were placed in effective positions throughout the route.

The Royal retiring room consisted of two apartments; the first laid with a luxurious Persian carpet and the inner apartment a Persian rug. Handsome tapestry hangings covered the walls. The room was furnished with the most elegant furniture of Queen Anne style, consisting of cabinets, occasional tables, and other articles in rosewood inlaid with ivory. A number of divans and other chairs were richly upholstered in silk and Genoa velvet. The smaller apartment contained furniture in Spanish mahogany, and the walls were draped in Madras lace. Red baize carpeted all the way from the retiring room to the banqueting room, and handsome floor lamps heightened the effect of the decorations in this part of the premises.

### The Masonic Banquet

With the art of the upholsterer and decorator the spacious room, which is normally the Farm Seed Order Department, was converted into a banqueting hall decorated throughout

Farm Seed Order Room. Transformed into a banqueting-hall for visit of HRH the Prince of Wales, December 1890.

in pleasant and harmonious styles. The use of the Masonic emblems, giving an especially appropriate character to the ornamentation, while the room was well lighted and comfortably warmed. The size of the room formed for the banquet was 150 x 60 feet and was chosen for the venue as it was the largest covered area in Reading without roof supports to obstruct the view. A large amount of additional space, which could have been utilized to cope with an even larger assemblage, was devoted to cloakrooms and other purposes.

This department, it will be remembered, before this occasion had been the scene of festivity, namely, on the occasion of the Queen's Jubilee. The high table was on the east side, and was covered with crimson felt. Over the seats of the Princes was an elegant canopy of silk damask in blue and gold, and bearing the Masonic device appropriate to the rank of the Prince of Wales. Just in front of the Grand Master was a margin of fern-leaved primulas, not in flower and an attractive band of red and white cyclamen in full bloom; and similar plants were grouped on the tables. At the extreme end of the building a platform had been arranged for the band of the Royal Marines (Portsmouth Division). Exotic plants formed a pretty screen and the back was hung with crimson baize with festoons of gold plush. Some very handsome floor lamps formed an attractive addition to the illumination of this part of the room. An immense quantity of art drapery was needed for the adornment of the sides and roof. The roof throughout was hung with striped Belgian cloth in soft artistic colours, and the walls were draped with Oriental curtains. Trophies composed of shields and banners decorated the walls at intervals. The supports to the roof were hung with bunting and various Masonic symbols.

The Royal party on leaving the company were greeted by many hundreds of cheering people. At Reading station they re-boarded the special train which departed at 3.10 p.m.

## Luncheon for the Mayor and Corporation in Suttons Abbey Hall

Directly the Royal party had passed through Suttons to the banqueting hall, the Mayor and Corporation and a large number of local business men were entertained to lunch in the firm's Abbey Hall, where everyone enjoyed a sumptuous lunch, followed by a number of speeches. The guests started to depart at 2.50 p.m. to see the Royal party leave from the main entrance at the front of the building. The festive mood continued until 5.30 p.m., when the public were admitted to the corridors and the banqueting hall, and for some time a steady stream of several hundred people were directed out by the north entrance opposite the Forbury.

*Reading Mercury,* 20 December 1890.

Suttons flower seed measures which were
used when the seed packets were hand
filled. The size and value of the seed dictated
which measure was used.

Victorian grass
display cabinet
acquired by MERL.

Acknowledgement of a customer order.

Acknowledgement card (reverse).

High speed seed packaging machine at Paignton.

The Seed Store at Paignton.

1898 saw another example of Royal patronage of Suttons' show stands. The Temple Flower Show held on 21st May 1898 in London (a forerunner of the Chelsea Flower Show) was attended by the Princess of Wales, the Duke of York, Prince Charles of Denmark and Princess Victoria. HRH the Duke and Duchess of York visited Suttons' stand and admired their massed display of gloxinias, which won a gold medal. A Daily Telegraph report at the time records the Princess of Wales was so impressed, that she commanded Mr Sutton to send some of his gloxinias to her at Marlborough House. Mr Sutton presented the Princess with a crystal and silver casket containing photographs of the greenhouses in which the gloxinias had been grown. Of course, as exhibitors of the highest class Suttons' show stands were often visited by members of the Royal family, such as on the 21st May 1900 when Her Royal Highness attended the Temple Show.

During the Royal Counties Agricultural Society's Show at Reading in 1902, the Royal Party did not visit Suttons' premises, but Suttons were involved in several aspects of the show. Martin John Sutton and Leonard Sutton were among many distinguished people who were at the opening ceremony. *The Reading Observer* of 11th June 1902 wrote: 'The Mayor's pavilion, Council Offices and the Royal Box were tastefully decorated with the season's most popular flowers. The work was undertaken by Messrs Sutton & Sons who generously furnished the whole of the floral adornments of the Show. The flower beds surrounding the Mayor's pavilion are certainly the feature and look exceedingly charming, being filled with the South African annual (Sutton's Nemesia strumosa), Sutton's Giant Mignonette and their tuberous begonias, petunias, Lilium harrisii, lobelia, pansies, saxifrage pyramidalis, calceolarias etc. The interior of the pavilion was beautifully decorated with well-flowered plants of Sutton's Gold Medal strain of Gloxinias 'Her Majesty' (pure white) 'Duke of York' (scarlet with white edge) and 'Duchess of York' (dark blue with white edge). All were greatly admired. Many streets in Reading were decorated for the Royal visit and Suttons' premises in the Market Place were adorned with decorations and illuminations. A canopy was erected from the kerb to the main entrance and decked out in red, white and blue. The illuminations consisted of the Royal Arms with a star on each side; the effect at night was quite spectacular.'

The next royal visit to Suttons' Market Place premises came in 1918, when King George V and Queen Mary were the honoured guests. Mid-February 1918 brought the news of the possibility of an impending visit by HRH King George V and HRH Queen Mary. This was discussed with Mr Bryant and Colonel Wygram. It was understood the visit would probably occupy about an hour and a half. Messrs Brown Snr, Leaver and Plumer were consulted and they all considered such a visit possible, and notwithstanding the pressure of work during this period, it would be highly desirable.

Early in March, arrangements for the royal visit proceeded. Mr Blaxill was to order the canopy for the front entrance and a cluster of flags for the centre window of the first floor. It was decided Martin Hubert's daughter Ena would present a bouquet to Her Majesty the Queen in the museum, and that his other children should occupy Leonard Sutton's office. On the same day a meeting was held with all the Heads of Department, who requested that they wished their wives to be present on the day of the visit. It was agreed that Mr Shorter's office would be available for them as well as Mr and Mrs Farmer, Mr Deane, The Revd C D F Walters and others.

Royal Visit. King George V in the Vegetable Seed Room, March 1918.

To commemorate the royal visit, all staff were given an extra week's wages. Prior to the visit the question arose regarding the correct procedure for cheering the royal party. The Heads were informed that this would be left to their discretion, but where it took place, it should be when the King was leaving the department, not when he was entering. It was agreed that the lunch hour would be delayed until the bell rang at about 1.15, after the King's departure. Arrangements were made for Mr Brown Snr to accompany the King's party and Mr Grant the Queen's party.

The day of the royal visit, the 12th March 1918, proved to be a great success. The front corridor was decorated on both sides with banks of cyclamen and other flowers from the nursery and a red drugget [a

An attractive bed of Salvias in the Sutton's
trial grounds; photo looking towards the
Great Western Railway line.
*(Scanned from a glass slide)*

Vegetables at Southport Show 1959.
*(Scanned from a glass slide)*

Suttons Charm Chrysanthemums
*(Scanned from a glass slide)*

Suttons exhibit at Chelsea Flower Show.
Early 1960's.
*(Scanned from a glass slide)*

coarsely-woven fabric used as a floor or table cover] was used from the entrance up to the Museum Reception Room. The partners received the King and Queen at the entrance, Arthur Sutton introducing Leonard Sutton and Martin Hubert Sutton after being himself introduced by the Mayor. Also present were the Earl of Cromer, the Dowager Countess of Airlie, the Commissioner for the South Midlands (C K Butler) and the Director of Supplies from the Food Production Department (Lawrence Weaver). The ladies present were Mrs Martin Hubert Sutton and Mrs Phil Sutton; Mr Phil Sutton was in France on active service. The company instructed Walton Adams, a local photographer, to prepare an album of pictures for inspection, and a similar request was made to the London photographers who were in attendance.

Four royal events were recorded in 1926. The first on the 8th May, when the new Caversham Bridge over the river Thames was opened by HRH the Prince of Wales, accompanied by Leonard Sutton; the Prince visited the trial grounds on the 25th June; on 6th July 1926 King George V and Queen Mary admired Suttons' display garden at the Royal Agricultural Societies Show at Crawshay's Estate in Caversham, Reading; and on 8th July HRH The Prince of Wales attended the same show (Crawshay Estate is now the BBC Monitoring Station and Caversham Park Village).

The Royal Agricultural Show at Caversham, Reading. King George V and Queen Mary visiting Suttons' stand. July 1926.

An account of the visit of the Prince of Wales (later King Edward VIII), which appeared in the *Reading Mercury*, is reproduced in the box overleaf.

## The visit of HRH the Prince of Wales
## To Reading 25 June 1926

His Royal Highness arrived by train at 10.30 a.m., dressed in a single-breasted grey suit and a bowler hat. He was met by several local dignitaries and a party of 150 ex-service men, employed at the Great Western Railway Station. After acknowledging the cheers His Royal Highness proceeded to inspect the guard of honour furnished by the Depot of the Royal Berkshire Regiment under the command of Captain Furlong.

The Royal Party were then driven in procession through cheering crowds to Suttons Trial Grounds, where they were greeted by groups of employees standing at vantage points; on reaching the glass pavilion, the centre of the glasshouse complex, he was cheered by a guard of honour of 177 ex-servicemen employees. The Mayor then introduced the Prince to Messrs Martin Hubert Sutton, Phil Sutton, Noel Sutton, W J Brown and A H M Salmon. His Royal Highness signed the visitors' book. He showed keen interest in examples of seeds in the process of germination, and also of a large model of the firm's premises. He passed from the pavilion into the range of glasshouses and was particularly interested in the fertilization of gloxinias and the fine specimens of antirrhinums and salpiglossis.

A short ride along an avenue from the glasshouses brought the Prince to an area near the Experimental Station, where he planted an acer tree. From there he proceeded to Suttons Plant Breeding Garden, which featured some new cultivars of vegetable and agricultural plants which attracted his attention; an outstanding one was V.C. pea noted for its length and size of pea. Alongside it was a tiny wild pea from which, over many years, it had been bred. He handled several of the freak vegetables and asked many questions.

The famous putting green on Suttons experimental grass plots appealed to him immensely. He then tried a mashie shot, which caused some amusement as a piece of turf was dislodged which resulted in some bantering comments from the army of photographers.

Passing along an avenue of sweet peas being grown for exhibition, the Prince re-entered his car, wearing a buttonhole of pink sweet peas. Noticing the ex-servicemen had again formed a guard of honour; he had the car pull up and walked through the ranks. He enquired to a number of the men if they were employed in these gardens before the war. Noticing the ribbon of the Military Medal worn by ex-Corporal A V Withers (who served with the 1/4th Royal Berkshire Regiment), the Prince enquired where it was he received the award; on being informed of a place in Italy, he remarked that he was there at the same time, in 1918. He also shook hands with ex-Sergeant Major Livingstone, of the Duke of Connaught's Regiment who was wearing the Indian Frontier Medal and the Long Service Medal in addition to those relating to the Great War. Another ex-soldier with whom the Prince shook hands was Mr O J Quickendon, wearing the Territorial Long Service Medal, who served with the Royal Berkshire RHA in Egypt and Palestine and the Prince made special enquiries of Mr A Swallow, with whom he also shook hands, as to how he received the war injury to his arm.

These were the closing incidents in a memorable half an hour, and the Prince was loudly cheered as he motored away.

*Reading Mercury, 30th June 1926*

Royal occasions also had beneficial spin-offs for the staff. The Royal Show was held at Prospect Park between the 10th and 13th June 1902, and the staff were given a half-day holiday after 2 p.m. on the occasion of the visit of King Edward VII and the Prince of Wales. In December that same year the following notice was posted: 'Re the unveiling of King Edward's statue next Wednesday. The firm will close to enable anyone who wishes to attend the Ceremony.' An extra week's wages was given to all staff to commemorate the coronation of King Edward VII, and on 5th July 1893, Suttons announced all employees would have an extra week's wages and the company would be closed on the following day, giving staff the opportunity to celebrate the wedding of HRH the Duke of York to Her Serene Highness Princess Victoria Mary of Teck. Holidays were

Suttons trial grounds. A fine show of fibrous rooted Begonias.
*(Scanned from a glass slide)*

Suttons trial grounds. A seed crop of Calceolarias
*(Scanned from a glass slide)*

given for Queen Victoria's Diamond Jubilee (22nd June 1897), two days for the coronation of Edward VII (26th and 27th June 1902; unfortunately the King was too ill to be crowned that day and the coronation was postponed until 9th August). The death of King Edward is recorded on 6th May 1910. Three days later all departments closed at 11.50 a.m. and resumed at 2.15 p.m. (a concession of 15 minutes) so that they could attend the proclamation of His Majesty King George V, which was to be read by the mayor at noon. In 1911 the employees were given the 22nd and 23rd June off as holidays for the coronation of George V.

Suttons Seeds has continued to receive the Royal Warrant from each reigning monarch, being Seedsmen by Appointment to Her Majesty the Queen Mother, and continuing as Seedsmen by Appointment to Her Majesty the Queen.

# 9. Suttons at War

Periods of war had a great effect on the company's abilities to carry on its business as usual. Minor skirmishes abroad had an impact on the growing of seed crops, their transport back to Suttons and out again to customers, and indeed the volume of the export trade. Wars involving Great Britain directly had an even bigger effect. Many of Suttons' staff enlisted or were conscripted, leaving those who were left to maintain the business as best they could; and tragically many of these men never returned to take up their positions, creating many years of labour shortages. During and after wars, the market requirements changed. Those who were away fighting had no need for garden seeds; there were periods when the nation's gardeners switched from growing flowers to growing vegetables (and back again), such as during the Dig for Victory campaign in WWII. The loss of staff from the large houses and estates during WWI instigated social change that caused the permanent collapse of some markets and the expansion of others.

War also saw personal tragedy for the Sutton family. During WWI Leonard G Sutton lost four of his five sons, and almost lost the fifth.

## *Boer War*

Martin Herbert Sutton was in South Africa in 1899 and wrote back that he was 'concerned with the situation with the Boer War, in particular the effect it was having on the Company's potato trade.' (MERL)

Packing boxes of seeds for the blockhouses in South Africa, *c.*1902.

The five men who signed up for the Boer War (29th January 1900) were given £5 each by the partners and, on their return, they organised a welcome home party by taking the men by boat from Reading to Henley-on-Thames and having supper at Martin John's boathouse (June 1901). Mr Early received £5 for his suggestion of sending parcels of seed for the gardens of the blockhouses in South Africa.

## World War I

At the commencement of World War I, the government issued guide-lines to UK companies which had traded with Germany and Austria up to this time, regarding a blacklist of those based in neutral countries but still covered by the prohibition by the Board of Trade. Suttons was affected, as the company had several contacts in Germany who supplied them with flower seed. They sought advice about a German living in Switzerland who supplied them and were advised that, since his business was transacted through an agent, he was likely to be blacklisted.

War commenced on the 4th August 1914 at 7 p.m., and by the 5th November Leonard Sutton was already worrying about insurance cover for aircraft damage. The Drill Club had been started by some of the staff; the directors did not mind other employees joining in with the special attractions such as route marches, but they insisted that those who used the ranges must be members of the Drill Club. Initially the members did not wish to amalgamate with the Reading Citizen Defence Force, owing to the pressure of work during the busy season, but reconsidered some three months later (19th April 1915), as there were advantages in drilling in larger numbers and sharing the greater facilities that were available. This patriotic gesture was approved by the board.

On 9th August 1914, a notice was put up stating 'owing to Abbey Hall being used as a recreation room for soldiers, prayers will be held in the new museum. Hope all will attend'. On 29th October another notice stated: 'As all our employees know it is our determined wish to maintain full time, full pay during the war, but if this is to be possible strict economies must be practiced in every department. With [this] object in view and with the hearty concurrence of our Heads of Depts, we have decided that beginning on Friday next October 30th, the hours of work will be from 8.30 a.m. to 1 p.m. and 2.15 to 5 p.m. By this means a very considerable saving in the cost of electric lighting will be effected' (Baskett's diaries, MERL).

By the 5th December 1914, 75 employees were serving at the front or in the UK, and each was sent a present of £1. At this time it was not necessary to encourage enlisting, but neither was it discouraged. In May 1915, Walter Giles, head of vegetable and agricultural seed production,

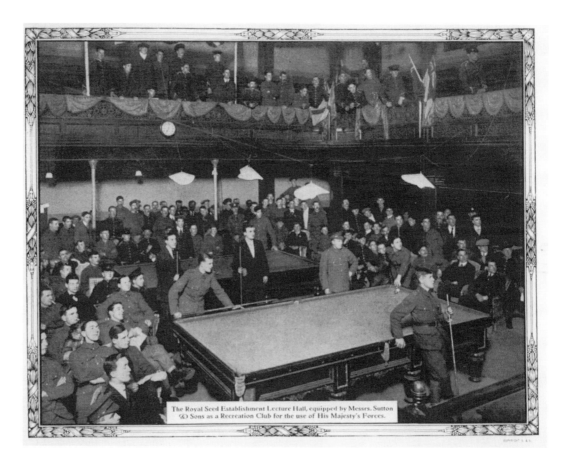

The Royal Seed Establishment Lecture Hall, equipped by Messrs. Sutton & Sons as a Recreation Club for the use of His Majesty's Forces.

Abbey Hall WWI Social Club for His Majesty's Armed Forces.

wrote to Arthur W Sutton suggesting it might be desirable for him to enlist, as an example to others who were holding back. The directors met with him and congratulated him on his public spirit, but said it was distinctly a matter which he must decide for himself. It was then decided to contact the War Office for information on the position in relation to experts in seed companies (the continuance of which was necessary for food production in horticulture and agriculture) enlisting in the army, and to consult Mr Giles later.

A notice put up by the company on 19th January 1915 stated: 'In order to encourage recruiting, it is still our intention to keep situations open for those who enlist. We wish however to make it clearly understood that this does not apply in any case where a recruit makes a false return as to his age.'

Another on 17th May said: 'We have never had any intention of modifying the promise made last autumn, to married men who enlist, viz … to make up their families' separation allowance, to the wages they were receiving from us. In the case of unmarried men who have dependents, we shall be glad to give special consideration to individual circumstances.' (Baskett's diaries, MERL)

Married men who enlisted were given an allowance. In July 1915 Medlicott who had been engaged for two years was shortly expecting to go to the front and, wishing to be married before leaving, was anxious to know if they would award a marriage allowance even though he had enlisted as a single man. The directors agreed to treat him as a married man from the time of his marriage. Arthur Sutton agreed to see Mr Palmer (September 1915), one of the company firemen, to express his sympathy at the loss of his son at Gallipoli.

A statement from *The Times* of 20th October 1915 on recruiting and Lord Derby's scheme was recorded in the minutes: 'Starred men who enlist will be attested, to be called on if wanted, but will be sent back at once to their employment. Unstarred men found to be indispensable in their employment may also be sent back.'

Suttons then prepared a list of men who were indispensable to the company. Martin Sutton told the men not to enlist as their work was so valuable; also the company would use its influence to secure their exemption. But the position changed by 22nd November as no application could be made for the retention of a man doing important work unless he had been attested (enrolled by military service). Neither could a man get the official brassard (armband) until he had enrolled. This situation was rectified by 30th December when the seed-growing industry, including heads of departments, was included on the list of reserved occupations.

Between the 24th and the 29th January 1916, blinds were put over the windows and lights shaded on account of Zeppelin airship raids and on 11th February the vegetable seed room worked through the night. The shiny tiles on the potato warehouse were painted to prevent them being targets for Zeppelin raids. Buildings being used at night had to be blacked-out under the Darkening Order. In February 1916, the local police reported to the firm that too much light was being emitted from various departments, in spite of the precautions taken. A local builder was asked to paint the windows on several of the ground-floor offices, and the following notice was sent to all departments: 'In the case of all departments working after tea, blinds and curtains etc must be drawn and screens put up before resumption of work and anyone causing light to appear through an open window, or by any other means, will be held personally liable for any penalty imposed by the authorities.'

Problems were encountered with processing the orders for the customers (this was also a problem for Sutton's competitors). During the war and immediately afterwards, the numbers of outstanding orders early in the year were as follows:

| | |
|---|---|
| *12th January 1915* | 700 |
| *12th January 1916* | 2,000 |

The staff were processing 400–500 orders a day and receiving 600–700 a day. It was suggested that perhaps the staff could work all through one night to ease the pressure. Volunteers were asked for and everyone agreed. On the day, staff worked until 9 p.m., with one hour's break, then from 10 p.m. to 6 a.m. with a break at 2 a.m. By 9 February there were more delays due to staff shortages.

| | | |
|---|---|---|
| *2nd February 1917* | 9,000 | *(processing 750 orders a day)* |
| *14th February 1918* | 22,000 | |
| *27th January 1919* | 7,000 | |

There was a shortage of men to execute the orders, and the firm was considering a change from using drawers to using open pigeon-holes for packets which would be built upon the counters, leaving sufficient room for each employee to process the order into a wire tray which would move along the counter as he went.

| | |
|---|---|
| *28th January 1920* | 11,000 |

It was decided that, in future, receipts for cash should be acknowledged the same day, and not in 3 days as at present.

These problems continued until 1923 when, on 21st February, it was noted that they were receiving 50 complaints a day due to delays in sending out orders.

Suttons continued to attend shows during the war: Chelsea, Smithfield, Birmingham and Edinburgh Dairy Shows, Dublin Fat-stock Show and the Royal Agricultural Show.

In December 1917 the following notice was posted: 'Suggestions have occasionally been made by employees, which we have been glad to acknowledge as distinctly useful in business. We have therefore thought it well to give every employee an opportunity of offering any suggestions, which may seem to him or her likely to tend to greater efficiency in the conduct of the business as a whole or of the department in which the employee is engaged. The box will be opened by a Partner once a week, every suggestion must be signed: but it will be treated as confidential.'

'Though the suggestions box has only been in use for about a week, several suggestions have already been received, and they are of such character as to clearly indicate this new departure will prove useful. Full particulars will be found in the Employees' Suggestion Book.'

5th January 1918

In order to encourage employees to help the war effort by growing vegetables, the company put up a notice on the 22nd February 1918 stating: 'We have made provisions for supplying our employees this season, with seed potatoes of the following varieties: British Queen, Langworthy and Arran Chief. Not more than one cwt of any one variety can be supplied to one person, and the charge will be a uniform price of 4/6 per bushel. Order together with payment should be given to the Deputy Head of Dept.'

A notice of the 9th March 1918 stated: 'His Majesty the King, accompanied by Her Majesty the Queen, has been graciously pleased to express his intention of paying a visit to the Royal Seed Establishment on Tuesday next March 12th, in order to inspect the work that is being done in connection with the food supply of the Country. It is our particular wish that all employees, on the entry of the King and Queen into their department, should at once stand up for a moment and then return to their usual work, as Their Majesties' wish is to see the work going on exactly as in the ordinary course. Their Majesties will arrive at 12 o'clock and visit the principal departments in separate parties and leave again at 1.10 p.m. In consequence, morning business hours will be extended until the bell rings at about 1.15, and work will be resumed at 3 p.m.'

A following notice of the 12th March said: 'As a memento of Their Majesties' Visit, and as a mark of our appreciation of the strenuous effort being made to cope with the demand for Food Production and Seeds, we intend to ask the acceptance by all our employees of one week's extra wages on Friday next. We hope that part of the amount will be invested in War Savings Certificates and to help to hasten a victorious peace.'

A national paper shortage persuaded the company to erect the following notice on 6th June: 'New postal rates and paper restrictions order. Need for increased economy. Postcards should be used whenever possible for brief correspondence. Stamped reply envelopes should not be enclosed, except when necessary, and postcards should generally be used for this purpose. The paper shortage is so acute that paper and envelopes must be used sparingly. Small envelopes and memorandum paper are provided, which can be obtained from the stationery room, and these should be made the best use of.' (Baskett's diaries, MERL)

On 11th November 1918, hostilities ceased on the German western front. The armistice was signed a few days later. A W Sutton led the thanksgiving service for the end of the war with special prayers, and a half-day's holiday was granted on 13th November 1918 especially for peace celebrations.

With the signing of the armistice, demobilization became a big issue. Suttons decided: 'In re-absorbing our men, they should come back with the old wage, plus necessary War Bonus. Every care should be taken to keep departmental expenses within existing bounds. The case of boys who are now men needs special treatment.'

On the 26th June 1919, a victory flower show was held at the firm, and all the staff were served with a sit-down tea supplied by the local caterer, Mr Allnutt of Earley. Arrangements were made at this time to send monetary gifts to the pensioners.

In 1919, in response to the King's suggestion that there should be a cessation of all normal activities and that every person in the Empire should remain silent for two minutes at 11 o'clock on the 11th November (Armistice Day), a special memorial and thanksgiving service was held in the Abbey Hall from 10.45 to 11.15 a.m.

A year later, on the 25th November 1920, a memorial tablet was unveiled in the firm's Abbey Hall listing all those employees who had given their lives in the war, including four members of the Sutton family and 15 members of staff.

This memorial tablet was removed by Vic Walton, an employee, just prior to the demolition of the building in 1962. He looked after it until early in the 1990s, when it was presented to Brock Barracks, Reading, the former headquarters of the Royal Berkshire Regiment. Unfortunately, over recent years it has deteriorated, and the cost of replacing it would be prohibitive. Luckily, there is a framed scroll of all the names and their regiments.

## World War II

As early as May 1938, the probability of war in Europe was being discussed, and the directors looked into air-raid precautions and fire drill.

Risk assurance for war would not be undertaken by Lloyds (29th September 1938). The Property Owners' Protection Association Ltd opened a War Risk mutual fund in which subscribers contributed yearly in relation to the value of their property. Initially the company decided against joining, as no compensation would be paid until the end of the war, and the amount might be quite a small percentage of the total loss. Two weeks later, it was agreed to subscribe at an annual subscription of £50 with £100,000 cover. Further discussions were recorded with regard to the membership of this organisation, which was not insurance in the ordinary sense, but a mutual fund to which the company would contribute for 10 successive years. If there was no war, the fund would be redistributed to subscribers. In the event of war, those whose property was damaged would receive payment for the whole or a portion of the damage done.

At the end of September seed potatoes, peas, and fertilizer were ordered for immediate delivery. This was earlier than usual, but the direc-

tors reasoned that the prices were bound to increase and availability
would be a problem.

On 10th December 1938, it was noted: 'Following a letter received
from the Reading Gas Company dated 5th December we decided to
grant leave of absence to any member of the staff in the Territorial Forces
to enable them to attend special courses of instruction, provided [that,] in
the opinion of the Head of Dept concerned, the applicant could be spared
from his duties. During the period of this special leave, the Company
will make up any difference there may be between the man's wages and
the amount he is receiving for Territorial Pay and Army Allowances. The
special leave is over and above the extra week's holiday on full pay granted to those in the Territorial Forces who attend a fortnight Camp.'

Former employee John Cox recalls:

> 'In the 1930s staff were entitled to one week's paid holiday. I had to
> ask permission if I could join the Territorial Army, and was told that
> the extra week's absence was approved, but would not be paid for by
> the company. We were in camp on the Wiltshire Downs in July 1939.
> We knew that war was imminent but were shocked when the War
> Office issued a directive to say, that for any TA unit which was mobi-
> lised the troops would not be allowed to return to civilian life. This
> was not too much of a problem for single men or those who were
> employed by a firm, but many had their own business or were mar-
> ried, and there was much heart-searching amongst these men.

> 'I was not discharged from the army until May 1946. I had not vis-
> ited Suttons but once during that 6 years. Upon my return, I found
> that my old desk had remained untouched; even the pens were in
> the pen tray! I left in July 1939 as an office boy and returned May
> 1946 as a married man, child on the way, no money, no home!'

Air-raid precautions were discussed in June 1938. Certain locations
in the premises were designated as shelters, and sand-bags were to be
filled for protection of the windows in these areas. These were the potato
store basement, pea store basement, loading floor and the basement
under the front office.

Further contingencies for the running of the company were discussed:

- To close down the London office and shop
- Not to have coloured plates in the catalogues, and to put vegetable
  seeds in the front of the catalogue and emphasise the importance
  of growing vegetables
- To make arrangements for darkening or covering all windows
- Hours of business to be altered to 8.30 a.m. to 4.30 p.m. instead
  of 9 a.m. to 5 p.m., thus reducing the use of artificial light. A
  number of torches would be purchased for use if the power was
  cut.

By May 1939, classes had been held on the jobs of the air-raid wardens, gas and decontamination and first aid, and the firm's fire brigade had been increased so that there were 24 in the fire brigade, 16 air-raid wardens, 8 decontamination officials and 16 first-aiders. By late July it became apparent that a state of emergency might exist at any moment, and the Government urged, and indeed later ordered, the provision of shelters for the whole of the staff. This was commenced by mid-August, and was practically complete by the declaration of war. Test evacuation of the buildings showed that all employees could be under cover in 3½ minutes. On the outbreak of war, it was arranged to have part of the fire brigade always on duty. For this purpose, a room was set aside for sleeping accommodation and a rota of duty arranged.

| | |
|---|---|
| *31st August 1939* | Germany invaded Poland |
| *2nd September 1939* | Germany having invaded Poland, it was evident that the country would be involved with war with Germany, and Suttons' business would be greatly affected |
| *3rd September 1939* | War declared with Germany at 11 a.m. |

Suttons played its part in the war effort. In July 1940 a request was received from the Ministry of Labour for men to work on urgent military defences at Pangbourne: a team of 12 men was supplied. Later, in August 1940, a request was received from the local Fuel Overseer, a Mr O'Kean, asking if the firm would grant permission for the storage of 1,000 tons of coal on part of the company's sports ground at Cintra Avenue on the southern side of Reading. The company secretary met a representative at the grounds, and selected a piece of ground lying between the south end of the bowling green and the allotments. It was agreed to let the site to the Department of Mines, but in view of the fact that the area would have to be restored to its present condition after the war, a restoration cost would be charged. A charge of *6d* per ton stored was also levied. In September 1941, flour stored in the seed-potato store for the Ministry of Food during the summer months caused subsidence!

## Fire Watchers

The Fire Watchers' Order (8th October 1940) saw the company complying with orders, with members of the company fire brigade being on duty 24 hours a day. Two young men with good eyesight and hearing were selected to act as spotters on the roof; binoculars would be provided.

During the war years, in addition to their day-time jobs, civilians were expected to join one of the following: Home Guard, first aid, blackout patrols, fire-watching.

Pictures from the 1941 catalogue 'The Home Front'.

A few of the Home Guard, ARP Wardens and Special Constables.

The Fire Brigade.

The Decontamination Squad.

The First Aid Detachment.

Suttons' premises had expanded over a hundred years or so by acquiring the adjacent buildings, and so consisted of a warren of corridors, passages, rooms etc, all with a high proportion of inflammable wood flooring, partitions etc. A fire-watching group was called for. Extra payment for this duty ensured sufficient volunteers.

'The assembly point was Abbey Hall, Kings Road. An employee warehouseman/fireman living locally was appointed to be in charge of the company's manual fire engine, complete with hose reels, buckets of water, hydrants etc. Sand buckets were filled, water *buckets were filled, stirrup pumps and shovels which staff had been trained to use were placed at strategic points around the firm and where accessible on roofs. A small shed was erected on the roof overlooking the Market Place, which gave the fire-watchers some protection from the weather and a commanding view over the town. It was also a good vantage-point for the aircraft spotters.*

*Their duties were to patrol around the firm by arranged routes during the blackout using dimmed torches; when the sirens sounded, all points had to be manned. A director of the firm was to be in charge, but living half a mile away had to be alerted when the sirens sounded. He arrived at the firm to do his duty on a bicycle, tin helmet over his shoulder, still in pyjamas. At the control point, there was a direct telephone line to the Reading fire station.*

*When all was clear, the lady fire-watchers might be observed enjoying a cigarette outside the premises in Kings Road and, on occasion, chatting to passing Yanks, while the male staff managed a quick dash around the corner to the local for a pint.*

*The firm is in safe hands, the ware potatoes that fell from the sack of seed potatoes are cooking nicely in the oven, bring your fat – Good night girls. Thank goodness the Luftwaffe didn't drop incendiary bombs!'*

John Cox, personal reminiscences

If an alert came during the busy season when the staff were working after 5 p.m., it was decided they would go home or into one of the shelters, and that any lost time would be made up on subsequent nights when there was no alert.

In spite of the war, the directors had to keep the company running. By 13th March 1941, women were the mainstay of the workforce; even so it was difficult because the Government required all available women to be employed in work of national importance. The ladies who had been taken on for the season and worked well were retained. It was hoped that the seeds would be tested as early as the 1st June so that they could be packeted earlier, provided that a further test, in early to mid-November, was done to prove that the germination was above the firm's standards and so they could be sold for the 1942 season.

Advanced purchases of grass and clover seeds were made. Normally 40 tons of red clover (*Trifolium pratense*) were purchased annually, but in view of the high germination this year, 10 tons were bought earlier than usual. As cargo space in ships crossing the Atlantic was in short supply, the price of timothy grass (*Phleum pratense*) of American and Canadian origin was expected to be high. Normally 8 tons of alsike clover (*Trifolium hybridum*) were bought from abroad each year; this year, 5 tons had already been acquired.

The war even had an effect on everyday matters such as the printing of catalogues. A minute of 24th December 1941 stated: 'Owing to the paper shortage we are no longer allowed to send out catalogues gratuitously, so we are supplying our Reps with postcards instructing them to obtain written requests from their customers, in accordance with the Ministry of Agriculture.'

Another edict in August 1945 gave permission to firms to distribute their catalogues to all their existing customers, provided that it was predominantly a food production catalogue. A reasonable number of pages of flower seeds would be permitted. It was decided to print 130,000 complete catalogues, for which the company had paper, and to apply for paper for a further 20,000.

On the 1st May 1941, it was recorded that duplicate records were going to be stored at the trial grounds. Shelving had to be installed, and the building reinforced against a bomb blast.

The first week in March 1942 was Warship week in Reading. Everyone was encouraged to contribute money or invest in War Saving Certificates and/or National War Defence Bonds. The company set aside £1,000 to buy these bonds and to help motivate the staff; it also gave £25 towards a warship. June 1943 was Wings for Victory week, and the company decided to invest £10,000 in 2½% War Bonds.

The company was unable to complete all orders. On 12th March 1942, acknowledgements of orders stated it had sold out of runner beans, onions, leeks and cress, and orders could not be delivered in under 3 weeks; it was also pointed out that the middle of April would be too late for sowing broad beans, parsnips and tomatoes, and that unfortunately it had also run out of early potatoes.

It was decided that the alphabetical price code on seed packets should be replaced by the price. Later that year, on 8th October, the Ministry of Food fixed the prices of one-ton and half-ton lots of seed potatoes which did not allow the company to make a profit, therefore it was decided only to accept orders of half-ton lots of a cultivar for delivery from Reading. Orders of 6 tons and over were to be accepted for delivery direct from Scotland.

On 1st December 1942, plans for a new cold-storage unit for storing and preserving special stocks of seed used in the production of seed crops were approved, and the order was placed with Pulsometer Engineering Company, Reading, at a cost of £725.

*'On the afternoon of 10th February 1943, Reading town centre was bombed by a lone German plane, causing considerable casualties and damage. At this time Reading was, as were many other areas, home for one of the groups of secret radio stations constructed between 1940 and 1942. For security reasons, the transmitters were*

*secreted in many different locations in the town. Unfortunately, during an air raid one was put out of action.*

*Nevertheless service was resumed some 10 days later in a small room within the glasshouse complex of Suttons' trial grounds. Apparently the aerial was visible from the Great Western Railway until the 1970s. This story was confirmed by the son of a former resident foreman, but he could not recall any more information.'*

Gerry Westall, personal reminiscences

Owen Sutton joined the Royal Navy in June 1943. His company responsibilities were shared between Phil Sutton and Noel Sutton.

In November 1943, the Ministry of Works took over the Recreation Club rooms in Abbey Hall on behalf of the American Red Cross, and agreed to meet the £100 cost of transferring its existing equipment to new accommodation in the Show Department. This was de-requisitioned in May 1946.

In May 1945, hostilities in Europe ceased and restrictions on purchasing many items were now slightly improved so that, by 5th September, the Government allowed the Dutch to export 5000 tons of bulbs for distribution in the UK, which allowed Suttons to fulfil its bulb orders.

# 10. The Art of Selling

While the name of Suttons is best known now for the supply of flower and vegetable seeds and plants to gardeners around the country, over the whole 200 years of the company's existence, there have been many other customers such as farmers and market gardeners, both at home and abroad.

Throughout this time, the company has pioneered many advertising techniques, for instance, by seeing the combined potential of the penny post and the expanding railway network, Suttons became one of the first mail-order companies in the world. Martin Hope's marketing strategy appears to have been to create a marketing edge by offering a more customer-focussed service than his competitors, and to be the first to understand the business value of new technologies. He sent out free broadsheets the year the uniform penny post started on the 10th January 1840, he used the railways to send out goods efficiently and had Suttons paying for the cost of transport, and he stole a march on his competitors by being the first seed company to sell high-quality germination-tested seed as standard. By 1856, the company had illustrated seed catalogues giving not only the full range of seeds available but also sowing and growing hints, as well as testimonials from satisfied customers. These became so useful to gardeners that they quickly became known as *Amateur's Guides* rather than catalogues once the farm seeds had been separated into a separate catalogue. For those customers requiring larger quantities of seeds, bulbs or sundries, they instigated another first: the sending of goods free of charge, delivered to the nearest railway station.

Thanks to the careful methods employed from the earliest days, Suttons was always able to sell and guarantee that its seeds were true to variety and of high germination. In the 19th century, this was far from normal practice in the trade, and doubtless led to the steady increase in sales over a long period.

Being an astute businessman, Martin Hope knew that merely offering the finest product available was not enough: customers must first know that you have a product available. To this end, he put a great deal of effort and money into many forms of advertising. In one year alone (1869–70), he spent £2,300 on advertising in journals and at agricultural shows, and £2,200 on printing catalogues. Over the years, many forms of marketing were used, but it was the catalogues for amateurs that eventually came to define Suttons as a company in most of its customers' eyes.

Suttons began advertising its seeds and bulbs in broadsheets (1833–1855) and catalogues (1856), and at stands at agricultural and horti-

The oldest surviving Sutton's seed list, a broadsheet for 1833.

cultural shows throughout the UK and from 1862 on the continent; in 1863, the first catalogue was sent to the Empire, with seed selected for these different conditions. Seed was being sent to New Zealand by 1841.

As well as merely advertising its products, Suttons used its catalogues and other publications to create and expand the market by educating its customers: by including instructions for cultivation, they increased their confidence to try growing species new to them.

Originally in the early 1800s, the clientele was entirely farmers in and around the Berkshire area, and this gradually spread throughout the country as the company became more famous. Until 1883, the sale of farm seeds represented half the value of total sales for the company; of this, 80% was grass seed, but even so the sale of root seeds was sufficient to sow 90,000 acres per annum. Export of all types of seed was very important, especially to those emigrating to the Empire.

Suttons West of England Globe Mangold, 1920's.

Fine roots of Suttons Prizewinner Mangold in clamp, 23rd March 1922.

Slowly and surely the interest in flowers and vegetable increased, with the large Victorian stately homes leading the way by having bedding plants in their borders and vegetables in the walled gardens. Also flowering bulbs were widely used, and special mixtures of grass seed were made available for the wide expanse of lawns, which could now be cut with the new-fangled mowers, also obtainable from Suttons.

By the start of the 20th century, growing flowers from seed became popular with home gardeners who, with the use of greenhouses, were able to produce fine displays of a wide range of plants, and the production of home-grown vegetables in back gardens and allotments became popular and even essential in times of war. Large-scale vegetable production also increased in the UK, and Suttons sold seed in bulk to market gardeners, producing its first annual catalogue in 1923. Other users of vegetable seeds in bulk were hospitals, prisons, schools and colleges, where vast quantities of staple subjects like cabbage and onion were grown on site. There was also a demand for flower seeds in quantity for parks departments for their display areas, and they also required amenity grasses for sports grounds, golf courses etc: these were met by using catalogues and representatives specialising in this work.

To improve the image of flowers grown from seed, a new international organisation for ornamental plants was set up in 1970. Fleuroselect conducts trials around Europe and, from these, awards are made to the best new varieties. Suttons has been a member since its inception and frequently offers Gold Medal-winning varieties in the catalogue. In addition, the company has assisted in giving trial ground space for variety testing, and also by providing qualified staff to act as judges.

## Catalogues and Advertising

Suttons has used a variety of methods to advertise its seeds, bulbs, plants, sundries and services. The first advertisements that have survived are the following.

---

## Mr R Webb's GENUINE
## Early White Warwick Peas

### John Sutton

*Begs to announce that these jointly celebrated peas may be had at his Corn and Seed Warehouses*

### 13 King Street, Reading

**and may be depended upon (as all other Seeds sold by him) as being new and true.**

John Sutton takes this opportunity of returning his sincere thanks to his numerous friends for the very liberal support he has received at this Establishment for upwards of 25 years and inform them that he has just received his Second Supply of Bulbous Flower Roots From Holland, Italy, Jersey, Guernsey etc, Which proves to be equally as fine as those received in August and assures them that all orders shall be executed with the greatest attention and dispatch.

---

*Reading Mercury,* 4th November 1833

# General Seed Warehouse
## 13 King Street, Reading

John Sutton (the original agent for the sale of Early White Warwick Peas) begs most respectfully to announce, that his extensive Collection of Garden Seeds for the ensuing season is now completed, and having been particularly careful in the selection of them assures friends they may depend upon having them of the best quality. The collection of PEAS consists of nearly thirty sorts, among which are the

## Early White Warwick

*Particularly recommended for the early crops, they having been repeatedly proved and universally allowed to be earlier than any other sort.*

The VEGETABLE and FLOWER SEEDS consist of many hundreds of different sorts, Catalogues of which may be had at the Seeds Warehouse. – Every kind of AGRICULTURAL SEEDS on sale at the proper season.

**N.B. The Trade supplied very advantageously**

*Reading Mercury*, 3rd February 1834

Regular small adverts were placed in the *Gardeners' Chronicle* of 1844, but by the 1850s these had increased considerably in size.

The oldest Suttons' farm seed catalogue which has survived is for 1858. It includes seed of furze or gorse (*Ulex europaeus*) at 2/6d per pound which, if cut young, could be fed to horses. Under the heading of Feeding Lettuces, Suttons Superb White Cos and Superb Green Cos were offered at 2/6d per ounce or 10/- per pound.

Another unusual item was a new yam from China (*Dioscorea batatas*, or *japonica*). The large roots were offered at 5/- per dozen. A testimonial for these roots from a customer in the Stourbridge area which had been published in the *Gardeners' Chronicle* of 14th November 1857 was quoted as reporting excellent results with this species.

The first Suttons' catalogue dedicated to bulbs appeared in 1871. Some of the covers for the 1880s, 1890s and early 1900s are works of art. 10,000 miniature seed catalogues were sent out in 1875 to the most prominent people in the directories. In 1895, the *Amateur's Guide* consisted of 158 pages, and had a print run of 85,000 at a cost of £4,900 to produce and despatch.

In August 1898, it was decided to obtain new floral tin plates to hang in hotels and railway station waiting-rooms. In June 1901 the railway companies were asked if the station plates could be replaced three times per year, with suitable advertisements of goods for sale. Later (1903) 520 new iron-plate adverts for stations were ordered at 11/6d each; 50 were to be used in the Cape Colony.

## Stewards, Bailiffs, and Gardeners.

We keep a list of Stewards, Bailiffs, and Gardeners who are seeking situations, and shall be pleased to render assistance to any of our Customers who may require a thoroughly reliable and practical man in either of these capacities.

## Cottage Allotments and Cottagers' Shows.

Having taken great interest in the encouragement of Cottagers in industrious habits, we have been for many years in the practice of supplying to Clergymen and others, Seeds for distribution to Cottagers at greatly reduced prices. We wish it to be understood also, that for the establishment of new Cottagers' Shows, and certain other cases in which it may be inconvenient to expend money in the purchase of Seeds, we are often willing to supply them gratis for free distribution.

We have frequently been asked to recommend a work on 'Cottage Gardening.' We know of nothing so practical as the Prize Essay, entitled 'Cottage Gardening,' by Mr. E. W. BADGER, and published by Houlston & Sons, 65 Paternoster Row. Price 3½d. post free.

*SUTTON & SONS, Seedsmen to His Highness the Pacha of Egypt.*

Extract from Suttons 1873 catalogue re Stewards, Bailiffs and Gardeners.

The centenary catalogue for 1906 was nearly 200 pages in length. The first edition was a print run of 94,000, weighing 74 tons. Special arrangements were made weeks in advance for the collection and despatch by the postal authorities at the St Martins le Grand office in Newgate Street, London.

It was decided in February 1910 that collections of flower seeds were to be sent for free to all lock-keepers on the Thames.

During WWI, bulb catalogues were produced, even though bulb production was not considered important and food production took priority. The bulb catalogue for 1914 cost £700, and for 1915 £200. Between £400 and £500 was spent in 1917. On 1st April 1918, it was decided that the seed catalogue for the next year would contain 72 pages of vegetables and 40 pages of flower seed, and 74,000 would be printed.

After WW1 in 1919, cinema advertising was discussed. Following this, two of the partners attended a private exhibition at the theatre of Barton-Hartley Ltd. They were both impressed and the board thought the cost was very reasonable; they requested that the advertising department sketch out some ideas.

In the early 1920s, coloured pictures were first used in first-class carriages on the London and South Eastern Railway. 10,000 midsummer circulars were sent out to non-customers. Tenders were put out for the production of 5,000 8-page lists for the market garden trade. Suttons already had 3,000 customers in this trade, and Mr Brown was instructed to find a further 2,000.

On 7th June 1923, the company minutes stated that the seed catalogue order for the following year would be 97,000 full catalogues and 67,500 of the abridged version.

The question of railway advertising plates arose in July 1930. The plates cost £1 each and 17/- for space; 1000 were purchased. In comparison, advertising on buses cost £1/10/- per annum.

5,000 glass ashtrays advertising seeds were purchased at a cost of approximately £300 in 1930; some were for golf clubs for advertising grass seed. Later that year, advertising was extended to LNER railway carriages as a card divided into three sections; on the left there was a coloured picture of flowers, on the right a coloured picture of vegetables and in the centre Suttons' Seeds of Reading.

This advertising was further extended to Southern Railway through Kent and the great central suburban district, to signs on bridges and on main roads, with a reflector pointing to Reading 'THE HOME OF SUTTON'S SEEDS'. In January 1931, it was agreed to spend £150 to advertise on 25 Southdown and East Surrey buses for 3 months.

Early in 1973, Suttons received several promotional orders from various companies, one of which was a magazine offer for 1.6 million packets of 'Summer Posy' – a mixture of hardy annuals, which was aimed at lady gardeners. In the same advert, readers were invited to visit their local stockists, where they could buy other colourful recent introductions, such as the Milady Blue and Milady Rose asters, and receive two free T–labels. These plastic garden labels were promoted by Mr Collins and were advertised on ITV in a 7-second advert, making Suttons the first in the seed trade to advertise in this medium. In the same week, Suttons took whole-page full-colour adverts in the *Daily Express*, *Popular Gardening* and *Garden News* and large-space adverts in the *Daily Telegraph*, *Daily Mail* and *Daily Mirror*. At the time, this was the largest range of adverts by a British seed company.

In addition, Suttons also produced a film entitled 'Suttons Seeds – the Seedsmen' as a means of promoting the company. The film, produced in the early 1970s, is a fascinating insight into the work of many people involved in the seed industry in the previous 50 years. During this time there had been many revolutionary developments in plant breeding, storage and packaging. The film was shown through the eyes of an anonymous director of Suttons Seeds, and the story was based on his observations and recollections of a lifetime in the seed business. Flowers, and particularly vegetables, had been the essence of his working life, and he talked about the job with the kind of relaxed authority that only a man with years of experience could bring. 'The Seedsmen' is a very interesting story of the work of one of the world's leading seed companies: a group of people with an enviable reputation gained by successfully giving nature a gentle nudge in the right direction. The film ended with the narrator in a state of blissful retirement, surrounded by the plants he had grown and cared for throughout the years.

### Garden Sundries and Fertilizers

As long as seeds have been sent by mail order, there has been a need for the necessary tools and other equipment. In 1873, for example, two pages of the catalogue were devoted to raffia, labels, insecticides and a range of over 50 knives and scissors. This was later extended to fertilizers, all manner of garden machinery including lawn-mowers, implements and tools, and garden furniture. In the same catalogue were galvanized verbena pegs made at the Devon and Exeter Industrial School. All these items had to be specially sourced from reliable suppliers, and often made to Suttons' own particular requirements. Some items could be despatched to the customer direct from the factory: others would be held in Suttons' own warehouses so that the whole order for seeds and sundries etc could be sent in one consignment. Sales reached their peak during the inter-war years, but delivery costs and the introduction of garden centres made the selling of larger items un-economical.

The following boxes give typical examples from the *Gardeners' Chronicle* of that peiod.

---

**Manure Peat and Charcoal, completely saturated with London Sewage, will be found a most effective manure for any crop.**

*It may be obtained from the Sewage and Manure Works, Stanley Bridge, Fulham, Middlesex @ £3.00 per ton, four shillings per hundredweight or two shillings and sixpence per half-hundredweight.*

Sewage Manure absorbed in charcoal is a first-rate fertilizer: We have tried it on French Beans. Dahlias, Roses & Cabbage plants: We put half a pint to each Rose and Dahlia, sowed it in the row with Beans and put a few pinches to each plant of Cabbage. The effect is perceptible very soon, but it will be as twice as efficacious the second year as the first.

*Gardeners' Chronicle,* 14th December 1852.

---

**The Walking Stick Blow Tube**

as now made is the simplest and most surprisingly powerful weapon adapted for killing vermin birds for preservation and etc, etc; also forms the best indoor sports, combining science with amusement.
Very readily used. Tubes 10/6d

Darts 4s per dozen, Clay Balls 1s per 100
Targets 2s each, Moulds 2/6d.

**Apply to:– E Lang
22 Cockspur Street, London.**

*Gardeners' Chronicle,* 18th April 1868.

# SUNDRY GARDEN REQUISITES.

**Appleby's Compound Tobacco Paper,** for fumigating, superior to the ordinary Tobacco Paper, 4lb. packets, 6s. each; 2lb. packets, 3s. each.

**Appleby's Common Tobacco Paper,** for the same purpose as the above. 4lb. packets, 6s. each; 2lb. packets, 3s. each.

**Tobacco Tissue.** For fumigating greenhouses, &c., manufactured from pure tobacco rolled into sheets or tissue, which allows it to consume slowly without the assistance of blowing. Pound packets, 3s. 6d. each; half-pound packets, 2s. each.

**Pooley's Tobacco Powder,** in tins, 1s. and 2s. 6d. each.

**Distributors** for the above, 2s. 6d. and 3s. 6d. each.

**Fowler's Gardener's Insecticide.** This composition easily and effectually destroys plant insects without the slightest injury to plant or tree. Price 1s. 6d., 3s., 5s. 6d., and 10s. per jar.

**Gishurst Compound,** for destroying blight, mealy bug, scale, &c., in boxes, 1s. and 3s. each.

**Wilkie's Condensed Blight Composition,** in pint bottles, 3s. 6d. each.

**Grafting Wax.** This preparation is the best which can be used in the operation of grafting Trees, Shrubs, and Plants of any description, budding Roses, &c. In tin boxes, price 1s., 2s., 4s., and 6s. each.

**Simpson's Wortley Celery Collar,** for protecting Celery before earthing up. The Collar prevents the plant from coming into contact with the earth, protects it from slugs, and secures a better blanched and more compact head. Should be used in every garden.

|            | Size No. 1. | Size No. 2. | Size No. 3. |
|------------|-------------|-------------|-------------|
| Per 100 .  | 1/9         | 2/          | 2/3         |
| Per 1000 . | 16/         | 18/         | 20/         |

**Tiffany.** A light and durable material for protecting from sun or frost. 20 yards long and 38 inches wide. Per piece, 6s.

**Improved Floral Shading,** in pieces 30 yards long, and about 4 feet wide.

**White,** stout quality, 15s. per piece.

**Ditto,** thin ditto, 10s. ditto.

**Brown,** extra strong, very durable, 15s. per piece.

**Largest Garden Mats** 20s. per dozen,

**Rofia Grass.** For price and description, see next page.

**Manilla Bast,** an excellent substitute for Cuba Bast, and quite as durable, 2s. 6d. per pound.
**Ditto,** in packets, 6d. and 1s. each.

**Cuba Bast,** for tying, 3s. 6d. per pound.
**Ditto,** in packets, 6d. and 1s. each.

**China Flax,** for tying, 2s. 6d. per pound.
**Ditto,** in packets, 6d. and 1s. each.

**Garden Gloves,** 1s. 9d. per pair.

**Ladies' Garden Gloves,** 2s. 3d. per pair.

**Wolff's Patent Pencils,** for marking wooden labels, 3d. and 6d. each.

**Wall Nails,** 1s. 6d. per 1000.

**Nail Bags,** 7s. 6d. each.

**Garden Hammers,** large size, 2s. 6d. each.
**Ditto,** small size, 2s. each.

**Shreds,** 6d. per pound.

**New Painted Shred.** This is a most useful introduction, and a sure preventative against the lodgment of insects on trees, which is so often the case where the ordinary woollen shred is used. Narrow slips (½-inch wide), 9d. per 100; broad slips (¾-inch wide), 1s. per 100.

**Painted Wood Labels,** for pots and open ground—3 inches long, 6d. per 100; 4 inches long, 8d. per 100; 5 inches long, 10d. per 100; 6 inches long, 1s. per 100.

**Yeats's Metallic Labels,** in various forms and sizes, as see next page.

**Wood Verbena Pegs.** These are remarkably cheap and answer the purpose better than pegs made of metal. We strongly recommend them. Boxes containing 250, 10d. each; 500, 1s. 6d. each; 1000, 2s. 6d. each.

**Galvanized Wire Verbena Pegs,** made by the boys at the Devon and Exeter Boys' Industrial School, 1s. per gross.

**Netting for Fruit Trees,** in different sizes.

**The Sidney Seed Sower (Patent).** All sorts and sizes of Vegetable and Flower Seeds can be sown in Drills, Pots, or Broadcast in any required quantity, by regulating the slide. By an inside fitting, Grass Seeds and Peas will pass freely, and be spread as evenly as the smallest Flower Seed. Large size, 5s. each.

*SUTTON & SONS' Amateur's Guide and Spring Catalogue for* 1873.

Page from Sutton's 1873 catalogue of Sundry Garden Requisites.

Caution.—This Catalogue is original and copyright.

# Knives, Scissors, and other Garden Tools.

| No. | | | each s. d. |
|---|---|---|---|
| 1 | Sheath Pruning Knife, large size... | | 2 0 |
| ,, 2 | Ditto | small size (superior) | 2 3 |
| ,, 3 | Pruning Knife, largest size | | 4 0 |
| ,, 3A | Ditto | large size | 3 6 |
| ,, 4 | Ditto | medium size | 3 0 |
| ,, 5 | Ditto | medium size (composition handle) | 2 3 |
| ,, 6 | Ditto | small size | 3 0 |
| ,, 6A | Ditto | medium size | 3 0 |
| ,, 7 | Ditto | small size (composition handle)... | 2 0 |
| ,, 8 | Ditto | medium size (superior) | 4 0 |
| ,, 9 | Ditto | large size | 3 6 |
| ,, 10 | Ditto | medium size | 3 0 |
| ,, 11 | Ditto | medium size | 3 6 |
| ,, 12 | Ditto | small size (composition handle)... | 2 0 |
| ,, 13 | Ditto | small size | 3 0 |
| ,, 13A | Ditto | 2 blades | 4 6 |
| ,, 14 | Pruning and Budding Knife combined | | 4 6 |
| ,, 15 | Sheath Budding Knife, large size | | 3 0 |
| ,, 16 | Budding Knife, large size... | | 3 3 |
| ,, 17 | Ditto | medium size | 3 0 |
| ,, 18 | Ditto | small size | 2 9 |
| ,, 19 | Ditto | medium size | 3 6 |
| ,, 20 | Ditto | medium size | 3 0 |
| ,, 21 | Ditto | small size... | 3 0 |
| ,, 22 | Ditto | small size | 3 0 |
| ,, 23 | Ditto | small size | 3 0 |
| ,, 24 | Ditto | small size | 2 0 |
| ,, 25 | Ditto | 2 blades | 4 6 |
| ,, 26 | Ladies' Budding Knife | | 3 6 |
| ,, 27 | Ditto | with Scissors (superior)... | 7 6 |
| ,, 28 | Pruning Knife, white handle | | 2 0 |
| ,, 29 | Asparagus Knife | | 3 6 |
| ,, 30 | Pruning Knife and Saw (superior) | | 5 6 |
| ,, 31 | Ditto | ditto | 3 0 |
| ,, 32 | Knife with two blades and botanical lens | | 5 0 |
| ,, 33 | Ditto | one blade and ditto | 4 0 |
| ,, 34 | Gentleman's Pocket Knife, three blades (superior) | | 5 6 |
| ,, 35 | Pruning Scissors, large size | | 3 3 |
| ,, 36 | Ditto | large size, japanned handles... | 3 9 |

| No. | | | each s. d. |
|---|---|---|---|
| 37 | Pruning Scissors, small size | | 2 6 |
| ,, 38 | Ditto | small size, japanned handles | 3 0 |
| ,, 39 | Scissors for cutting and holding flowers, large size | | 4 0 |
| ,, 40 | Ditto | ditto small size | 3 0 |
| ,, 41 | Vine Scissors | | 3 0 |
| ,, 42 | Propagating Scissors | | 2 3 |
| ,, 43 | Shred Scissors | | 2 3 |
| ,, 44 | Pruning Saw, 14-inch | | 3 0 |
| ,, 45 | Garden Bill | | 3 0 |
| ,, 46 | Pruning Saw and Hook | | 5 3 |
| ,, 47 | Boxwood Thermometer, 8-inch | | 1 3 |
| ,, 48 | Ditto | single degrees, minimum registering | 2 6 |
| ,, 49 | Metal Thermometer, minimum registering | | 4 0 |
| ,, 50 | Porcelain Thermometer, minimum registering, very durable | | 5 0 |
| ,, 51 | Thermometer, maximum and minimum registering, japanned case, boxwood scale (superior) | | 8 6 |
| ,, 52 | Magnet for ditto | | 0 9 |
| ,, 53 | Plunging Thermometer, oak frame, 12-inch | | 5 0 |
| ,, 54 | Pruning Shears. Extremely powerful | | 5 0 |
| ,, 55 | Sécateurs, or French Pruning Shears, 7-inch | | 3 6 |
| ,, 56 | Ditto | ditto 8-inch | 5 0 |
| ,, 57 | Grecian Pruning Saw | | 2 6 |
| ,, 58 | Garden Hammer, large size | | 2 6 |
| ,, 59 | Ditto | small size | 2 0 |
| ,, 60 | Garden Syringe, 2 roses and 1 jet | | 8 0 |
| ,, 61 | Ladies' Greenhouse Syringe, 1 rose and 1 jet | | 2 6 |

## Ivory Fruit Knives.

These are made with ivory springs, which are not liable to rust like knives fitted with steel springs.

| | | | each s. d. |
|---|---|---|---|
| A. | Ivory handle, 3-inch, single blade | | 1 0 |
| B. | Ditto | 3½ ,, blade and scoop | 2 6 |
| C. | Ditto | 4 ,, ditto | 3 0 |
| D. | Tortoiseshell handle, 3½-inch, single blade | | 2 6 |
| E. | Ditto | 4 ,, blade and scoop (superior) | 4 6 |
| F. | Ornamental inlaid handle, 3½-inch, ditto ditto | | 2 6 |

Page from Suttons 1879 catalogue listing Knives, Scissors, and other Garden Tools.

In 1873 Suttons was offering Gishurst's Compound for the destruction of blight, mealy bug, scale insects etc: it was in the catalogue up to 1955, when it was offered as 'largely for washing down glasshouses and plant frames'.

Towards the end of the 19th century, Suttons was putting its name on garden sundry items, such as the Sutton garden syringe, described as 'nickel plated, an 18-inch superior implement, fitted with an improved valve, making the working of this syringe much easier. Three roses and a jet, packed in a strong box twenty one shillings'. Another example was the Sutton Thermometer Boxwood Scale, 'registers maximum and minimum temperatures, day and night tables, showing degrees of heat suitable for various indoor plants, in japanned case with magnet 10/6d'.

In 1904 Suttons was listing two of its own named artificial manures, one for general use and one for lawns. Both of these were sold in tins from 1/6d to 4/-, or in kegs of 28 lbs for 10/6d, 56 lbs for 16/- and 112 lbs for £1 8s 6d. In the same catalogue was the Sutton Lawn Mower, offered in various sizes and prices, and also Pattison's Lawn Boots for Ponies and Horses.

# SUTTON'S LIST OF GARDEN IMPLEMENTS.

*The letters facilitate reference to the priced list below.*

A. **Spades**, best London treaded, cast-steel-faced, each, No. 1. 7½-in. × 11½-in. 4s. 6d. ; No. 2, 7¾-in. × 12-in. 5s. ; No. 3, 8½-in. × 12½-in. 5s. 6d. ; bright steel, each 6d. extra.
  **Spades**, best London treaded, solid steel, each, No. 1, 7½-in. × 11½-in. 3s. 9d. ; No. 2, 7¾-in. × 12-in. 4s. 3d. ; No. 3, 8½-in. × 12½-in. 4s. 6d. ; bright steel, each 6d. extra.
B. **Border Spade** ... ... ... ... ... ... each, 3s. 6d.
C. **Shovels**, steel, London, each, No. 1, 12-in. × 9-in. 4s. ; No. 2, 12½-in. × 9½-in. 4s. 6d.
D. **Digging Forks**, best elastic steel, bright, each, 4-prong, 5s. ; 5-prong, 5s. 6d.
  ,, ,, best closed socket ... ,, ,, 4s. 6d. ; ,, 5s.
  ,, ,, strapped steel ... ,, ,, 3s. 6d. ; ,, 4s.
E. **Potato Fork**, flat prongs, each, 4-prong, 4s. 9d. ; bright steel, 6d. extra.
F. **Border Fork** ... ... ... ... ... ... each, 3s. 6d.
G. **Scythe**, for short grass, 36-inch, riveted back ... ... each, 4s.
  ,, ,, ,, solid ... ... ... ,, 4s.
  **Scythe Stone** ... ... ... ... ... ... ,, 6d.
H. **Grass Edging Shears**, each, 8-in. 6s. ; 8¼-in. 7s. ; 9-in. 7s. 9d. ; 9½-in. 8s. 6d.
I. **Edging Irons**, each, 8-in. 2s. 6d. ; 9-in. 3s. ; 10-in. 3s. 6d. ; 11-in. 4s.

K. **Turfing Irons** ... ... each, No. 1, 7s. ; No. 2, 8s. 6d. ; No. 3, 10s.
L. **Daisy Drawer** ... ... ... ... ... ... each, 2s.
M. **Hoes**, cast steel garden ... each, 4-in. 10d. ; 5-in. 1s. ; 6-in. 1s. 2d. ; 7-in. 1s. 4d. ; 8-in. 1s. 6d. ; 9-in. 1s. 9d. ; 10-in. 2s.
N. **Dutch Hoes**, each, 4-in. 1s. ; 5-in. 1s. 6d. ; 6-in. 1s. 9d. ; 7-in. 2s. ; 8-in. 2s. 6d. ; 9-in. 3s.
O. **Triangular Hoes**, each, 4-in. 1s. ; 5-in. 1s. 9d. ; 6-in. 2s. ; 7-in. 2s. 3d. ; 8-in. 2s. 6d.
  **Spuds** ... ... P, each, 1s. 3d. ; Q, each, 1s. 3d. ; R, each, 1s. 6d.
T. **Rakes**, best garden, steel teeth, each, 4-teeth, 9d. ; 5-t. 10d. ; 6-t. 1s. ; 7-t. 1s. 2d. ; 8-t. 1s. 3d. ; 9-t. 1s. 4d. ; 10-t. 1s. 6d. ; 11-t. 1s. 8d. ; 12-t. 1s. 9d. ; 13-t. 1s. 10d. ; 14-t. 2s. ; 15-t. 2s. 3d. ; 16-t. 2s. 6d.
U. **Hatchet** ... ... ... ... ... ... ... each, 3s. 6d.
W. **Felling Axe** ... ... ... ... ... ... ... ,, 5s. 6d.
X. **Hatchet and Hammer combined** ... ... ... ,, 3s. 6d.
Y. **Fence and Rail Hammer** ... ... ... ... ,, 3s.
AA. **Mattock** ... ... ... ... ... ... ... ,, 3s. 6d.
  **Pickaxe** ... ... ... ... ... ... ... ,, 3s. 6d.
BB. **Dibber**, steel-pointed ... ... ... ... ... ,, 1s. 9d.

CC. **Special Set of Garden Tools**, comprising Hoe, Rake, Spade, and Fork. Lady's size, 13s. 6d. ; Children's size, 8s. 6d.

# THE SUTTON LAWN MOWER.

'The Lawn Mower supplied by you is giving great satisfaction. The lawn had got into a bad state owing to the previous machine breaking down, but your mower trimmed off long and short grass equally well. Of the various machines I have used I have never had one that ran so lightly or did its work so well.'—Mr. C. SIMMONDS, *Gardener to* Mrs. COURT.

'Mowing Machine, 20-inch, safe to hand, and has been used to-day. It gives every satisfaction ; quite child's play to the old one.'—Mr. G. JOSLIN, *Gardener to* Sir G. PIGOT, Bart.

THE SUTTON LAWN MOWER.

'I am very pleased with The Sutton Lawn Mower I received last spring. It has been in constant use since it arrived, and does its work very satisfactorily ; the lawn looks like velvet. The machine is the best I have ever used or seen.'—Mr. H. AVERY, *Gardener to* M. P. GRACE, Esq.

'The two machines supplied to Col. G. A. Curzon are simply perfection in all points. Lawns cannot be kept right without a good machine, which The Sutton Lawn Mower certainly is.'—Mr. F. HAND, *Gardener to* Colonel G. A. CURZON.

'The Lawn Mower is a splendid machine ; I consider it perfect.' — Mr. G. MOORE, *Gardener to* B. BARROW, Esq.

| Width of Cutter. | | £ | s. | d. |
|---|---|---|---|---|
| 8-in. | can be used by a Lady or Boy ... ... ... ... | 2 | 15 | 0 |
| 10-in. | | 3 | 17 | 6 |
| 12-in. can be used by a Lad ... ... ... ... | | 4 | 17 | 6 |
| 14-in. can be used by a Man ... ... ... | | 6 | 0 | 0 |
| 16-in. can be used by a Man on an even Lawn ... ... | | 7 | 0 | 0 |
| 18-in. can be used by a Man and a Boy ... ... | | 8 | 2 | 6 |

| Width of Cutter. | | £ | s. | d. |
|---|---|---|---|---|
| 20-in. can be used by two Men ... ... ... ... ... | | 8 | 12 | 6 |
| 22-in. can be used by two Men ... ... ... ... ... | | 9 | 5 | 0 |
| 24-in. Sutton Lawn Mower* ... ... ... ... ... | | 9 | 15 | 0 |

\* Whippletree for pony or donkey, 7s. 6d. extra.
LARGER MACHINES FOR PONY OR HORSE POWER CAN BE SUPPLIED.
Rail Carriage Paid. No Charge for Packing.

## THE PATTISSON LAWN BOOTS FOR PONIES AND HORSES (Cole's Patent).

Set of four Compactum Soles, from £1. 5s. to £2. 10s. for stock sizes. List on application.

85

Page from Suttons 1904 catalogue showing hand tools and early lawn mowers.

Quassia chips, a general insecticide, were offered in Suttons' 1906 *Centenary Catalogue*, and were still being offered in 1955. Quassia chips came from the bark of *Quassia armara*, a tree native to South America. Its benefits were discovered in 1765 by a native of Surinam, who found it contained insecticidal properties, and was also a bitter decoction for medicinal purposes.

In the late 1920s, Suttons was marketing eight of its own named horticultural fertilizers for general use and for such crops as fruit trees, tomatoes, potatoes, roses and rose tonic, sweet peas and strawberries. At the same time, the catalogues were offering a complete range of agricultural fertilizers, for autumn and early winter applications, and a complete range of own-brand fertilizers and dressings for amenity grasses, all carriage-free.

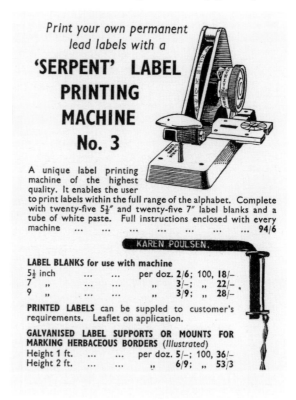

Serpent Label Machine and labels.

In 1959 Suttons introduced into its catalogue the 'Serpent' label-printing machine No.3. In the 1966 catalogue, some new items of garden sundries were listed, for example the mini-cloche.

*'The neat dome is of clear plastic and comes with a plastic pot of just the right size. Ideal for propagating house plants – ivies, geraniums, tradescantia, and similar subjects speedily rooted with the*

*help of Sutton's Mini-Cloche. Leaf cuttings from African violets can be simply propagated, the dome placed over the cuttings gives them air through the breathing holes at the top and just the right atmosphere for rapid rooting. Overall size of the cloche just over four inches tall and just under four inches wide. Set of 6 cloches and 6 plastic pots in mottled colours for 7/6d. Cloches only 9s per dozen.'*

## Agricultural and Horticultural Shows

Exhibiting at shows was a very important way of marketing Suttons' agricultural and horticultural seeds. It had its own show department until it was closed in the 1960s. The expense of maintaining a department and preparing exhibits must have been very financially demanding, and would have been a reflection of pride in the company's products and belief in the power of marketing. This self-belief was vindicated in the

Sutton's Elizabethan-style pavilion at Birmingham show 1898. Surprisingly this large building was portable!

One of Suttons' smaller portable pavilions at the Edinburgh show 1907.

many medals and trophies received over the years, both in this country and abroad.

The first tentative step towards public exhibiting came in 1837 when Suttons issued invitations to see a large display of tulips in the nursery at the rear of its premises in the Market Place, Reading: an invitation card and two tickets have survived.

The firm exhibited a selection of mangel wurzel and the swede variety Champion at the Smithfield Cattle Show, Baker Street, London in 1843, and in the Great Exhibition of 1851 was awarded a certificate and medal. In 1855, 1856 and 1857 Suttons was awarded silver cups given by the Prince Consort for the swede variety Champion. By 1857 Suttons was exhibiting at a wide variety of shows including the East Berkshire Agricultural show; the Old Berkshire Hunt show; South Berkshire show; Reading and District show and, further afield, the Birmingham Show.

In his diary of 1872, Millard wrote: 'Mr Martin John Sutton was in London today discussing the Vienna Exhibition, and told me we have been given the exclusive privilege of exhibiting.' A large exhibit of over 20 varieties of tomatoes was shown at Crystal Palace in 1887. In April 1901, Mr Grant of the show department was given permission to purchase some very good cigars for important customers! In March 1908, Suttons was given the concession to supply grass seeds to the Franco-British Exhibition at Wembley.

A large display of Suttons tomatoes on show at the Crystal Palace 1887.

As has already been stated, showing was expensive. In addition to the cost of exhibiting, Suttons donated monetary prizes for individual classes when produce was grown from their seeds. In 1912 these costs were £2,500 for agricultural shows and £1,300 for horticultural shows.

The Crystal Palace.

Suttons lawns and flower beds at the Franco British Exhibition, London 1908.

In May 1913, Suttons staged a large exhibition of flowers and vegetables for the first Chelsea Show. By 1915, the war had affected transport on the railways. The firm requested a special train to convey its exhibition to Addison Road station, which at the time was more convenient than Paddington, and after much haggling the Great Western Railway agreed to the request.

The partners noted at the Edinburgh Show in late 1914: 'It was disappointing to learn so much whisky had been drunk on 2nd December, due, as we understand to a lower type of people being present, who refused tea!' (MERL). In May 1915, a letter was received from the Royal Agricultural Show Committee, concerning 'the gratuitous giving of alcoholic liquor'. The firm replied indicating it was entirely in sympathy with these views, and was prepared to stop providing complimentary alcohol at shows.

Display of mangolds, cow cabbage and other farm crops, in preparation for an exhibition probably for the annual Smithfield Show held in London.

Swedes, mangolds, potatoes and various agricultural grasses at Edinburgh c.1911.

The Royal Agricultural Show at Bristol in 1913, showing Sutton's large portable exhibition building on the left. Attendance was 179,148 with a profit of £3,150.

Sutton's vegetable stand at the first Chelsea Flower Show in 1913.

In December 1918, Suttons was awarded the prestigious Lawrence Medal by the Royal Horticultural Society for the remarkable series of exhibits, especially the most recent one of vegetables, the seed of which had been sown in July and August. This was a great honour, as this award is seldom made and never more than once a year.

On the same day the partners sent for Mr Giles (head of vegetable and agricultural seed production) and discussed the possibility of scrapping roots altogether on the Smithfield and Edinburgh stands. Giles thought it might be advantageous to do so, and pointed out the tendency of high-class firms in other trades to turn their stands into waiting-rooms and lounges for visitors, with just one or two exhibits. The partners were favourably disposed to this plan, provided that a really good design could be found for a new Smithfield stand without exhibiting roots. If this decision was carried through, it would lead to the dropping of root classes at the Dairy Show, Birmingham, and the Edinburgh and Dublin fat-stock shows. It was agreed that Arthur Sutton would write to Webb's, Carter's, Garton's, Toogood's, Dickson & Robinson and J K King's (other seed companies) on the subject. Two weeks later, the subject was again discussed. It was agreed that Giles had the technical knowledge and, for the time being, he would still be responsible for all roots and produce for shows that year.

In January 1919, a report was issued indicating that the Chelsea show might not take place that year, as the War Office would possibly not be able to release the ground in time. It might also have proved impossible to get the authorities to forgo the entertainment tax. If either of these contingencies had occurred the show could not have been held. Fortunately, these issues were resolved and the show went ahead. There

Two horse-drawn Sutton's wagons, and three Pilgrims wagons (these were often hired by Suttons) on flat trucks, on route to a distant horticultural or agricultural show, Pre-1914.

was also a problem in March when the South Eastern Railway Company would not agree to carry the firm's horse-drawn vans on its passenger trains. However, this was resolved on the 12th March. The Chelsea Show of May 1919 was an extraordinary success in view of the fact that the armistice had taken place only the previous November. The firm was awarded a gold medal for its vegetable exhibit, and a silver-gilt Banksian medal for tulips.

In December, the *Daily Mail* asked Suttons to undertake the making and planting of the vegetable gardens for the *Daily Mail* cottages at Olympia, London, to be held in February the following year. Apparently the Board of Agriculture had approached the *Daily Mail* to have these gardens made, and the newspaper immediately contacted Suttons. It was agreed that the company should make preparations as soon as possible, and the *Daily Mail* was paying for the soil and the construction of the walls.

Early in March 1920, the question of intoxicating liquor after the Smithfield Show was again discussed, when it was learnt that Garton's did not supply any intoxicants to its customers. The board agreed it would be a good idea if the company could do likewise. In view of this, a letter was sent to Webbs of Stourbridge with a view to discontinuing this practice at the Royal and subsequent shows and to endeavour to persuade other seed houses to agree. In the meantime, Suttons would only have claret cup, hock cup, and bottled beers at shows. On 25th May it was reported by Phil Sutton that at the Oxford Show and the Bath and West Show only claret, hock and bottled beer were available. This confirmed that some companies had agreed with the firm's suggestions, at least for a year.

Suttons' exhibit at the 1922 Chelsea Show was judged as the most meritorious exhibit. The firm was awarded the Sherwood Cup for flowering plants grown from seed, and the vegetable display received a gold medal.

'The Royal Agricultural Show at Reading 6th to 10th July 1926.

'Sutton's Seeds Garden.

'This was one of the most attractive exhibits of the whole show, and one which many visitors considered alone worth the gate money. This remarkable plant breeding garden, which extends to no less than half an acre, must be the most comprehensive example of its kind that has ever been staged at any show in the world. One portion is devoted to experiments illustrating how the improvements are effected in plants both for agricultural purposes and the vegetable garden. Another section shows the work carried out for the improvement in grasses and clovers, illustrating how much better crops are secured by the employment of new indigenous types of grasses than by those generally used for this purpose. The formation of sporting turf from seed is depicted by a miniature tennis court, bowling green, croquet lawn and putting green, the latter being a model of a seaside course green, on sandy soil, showing how good turf can be obtained on poor soil. Botanists will be delighted with 'the grass garden' and horticulturalists in the methods shown for the production of vegetables and flowers for the show bench; all this embellished by beautiful beds of annuals and others which Suttons are justly famed for in all parts of the country. At one end of the garden they have created a pavilion furnished as a botanical museum.

'The Elizabethan stand, familiar to Royal Show visitors for decades past, again occupies a prominent position, this year adjacent to the Royal Stand and all agriculturalists and horticulturalists have been interested in the exhibit staged here, which comprises of typical roots of Suttons Prizewinner, Yellow Globe, Golden Tankard, Red Intermediate and Yellow Intermediate mangolds, clean handsome specimens of remarkable size, showing how greatly the farmer gains by sowing these modern varieties instead of those of low cropping and poor feeding value; forage crop plants in full growth as well as a magnificent collection of over one hundred dishes of the most tempting vegetables. One must not forget the gorgeous display of Suttons sweet peas and gloxinias, staged in the horticultural tent. (P.S. King George & Queen Mary visited the show on the 6th July. All Suttons staff were on the pavement outside their premises to see the Royal party pass on their way to Huntley & Palmers. HRH the Prince of Wales visited the show on the 8th July.)'

Reading Mercury, 16th July 1926.

In 1935, 29 of the 33 first prizes in the open classes for vegetables at the Royal Horticultural Society's Fruit and Vegetable Show were awarded to gardeners with exhibits grown from Suttons' seeds. Seven gold medals were awarded to Suttons in the same year for vegetables.

Suttons continued exhibiting at all the major shows both before and after WWII, winning many gold medals and cups for various displays. Permanent show staff were employed for the growing, transportation and erection of the stands which varied in size from the huge displays at Chelsea Flower Show to small stands at the local agricultural shows. However, by the mid-1960s the high costs of greenhouse space, heating and lighting, as well as labour charges, meant that the large stands became uneconomic and, together with other seed firms, Suttons gave up producing such elegant exhibits. The firm did still continue with smaller specialist stands and this included being regular exhibitors at the Motspur Park Show run by the National Association of Groundsmen (now the Institute of Groundmanship).

Sutton's final exhibit at the Chelsea Flower Show in 1964.

## Books and Various Publications

The first edition of *The Culture of Vegetables & Flowers from Seeds and Roots* was published by Suttons in 1884. Since then, at least 23 editions have been published, amounting to many thousands of books; although the last edition was in the 1960s, copies can still be found occasionally in second-hand shops and at book fairs. At the beginning of March 1926, it was reprinted and updated; 10,000 copies cost £1,250. An edition was also published with the same title for use in tropical, semi-tropical and temperate climates.

Suttons published many hundreds of leaflets giving cultural instructions for growing seeds for virtually every country in the world. For continents and sub-continents, such as Africa, Australia, China, India and the USA, different instructions were given for the various regions.

Suttons produced literature on a wide range of subjects, including in 1871, the first geological and railway map of England especially designed for agriculturalists. *Permanent and Temporary Pastures*, first published in 1886 by Martin John Sutton, was recognized as an authoritative work for the benefit of the farming community. By 1902 it was recorded that 16,740 copies had been sold. Several more editions were published until the early 1930s.

In the early 1900s, Suttons published editions of *My Garden Diary* with a colourful cover giving monthly reminders for gardeners and daily details of the rising and setting of the sun and moon. In addition, information on historic events and other miscellaneous facts was included. Also published were diaries for farmers and professional groundsmen.

*The Laying out and Upkeep of Golf Courses & Putting Greens* was published by Martin Hubert Fouquet Sutton in 1906, and in 1912 he published *The Book of The Links*, which was a classic of its kind. *Hardy Annuals* was published in the 1920s with a French edition; *Annuals* by Leonard Goodhart Sutton in 1931; and *The Cool Greenhouse* by Noel Sutton in 1935.

At least 9 editions of *Suttons of Reading* were published between 1902 and the 1920s, giving a brief insight into the company. In some editions, Suttons' Gold Medal Educational Cabinets are advertised. These were of polished oak, glazed, with a sunblind, and contained a collection of up to 24 species of natural grasses which were suitable for permanent and temporary pastures. The popular and botanical names, soils and localities where they are usually found, their fresh and dry weights (analyses by Dr Voelcker), and 75 glazed tin boxes of grass and agricultural seeds were included. In 1910 these would have cost 40 shillings. One of these appeared some years ago on the 'Antiques Road Show', and was valued at £200. To cover every aspect of agriculture, the company also produced similar cabinets containing specimens and seeds of uneconomic grasses all labelled and complete with sunblind, price 75/-. Other cabinets were produced for golf courses and putting greens, price 50/-, and one for cereal crops (oats, barley, rye and wheat) at 55/-. Suttons also produced cases of insects injurious and beneficial to farm and garden crops, and cases containing models of plant diseases caused by fungi, bacteria etc, which were all priced at 50/-.

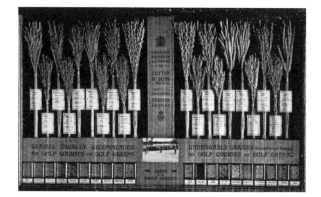

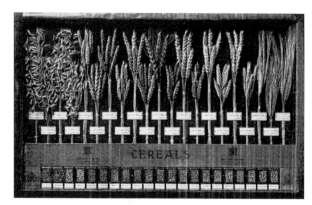

Left: Cabinet of Grasses and their seeds.
Right: Cabinet of Cereals.

Smaller cabinets ranged from 8/6d to 20/-. Suttons offered a small composite collection of useful grasses, in a japanned tin, a vasculum, with a brass handle and fittings, containing 36 varieties of grasses and giving the popular and botanical names, and soils and localities where they are found. This also contained 60 metal-capped glass bottles of grass and agricultural seeds, price 10/6d.

Suttons published many pamphlets on varying horticultural subjects. Walter F Giles, head of vegetable seed production, wrote several articles in the Royal Horticultural Society's *Journal* in the 1940s; these were reprinted, and a few have survived but are not priced, therefore they may have been given away for free. Some of the titles are: *Cauliflower and Broccoli. What are they and where do they come from?* 1941; *Interesting Types of Beans*, March 1943; *Gourds, Marrows, Pumpkins and Squashes*, May 1943; and *Our Vegetables: Whence They Came*, May 1944.

Many booklets were published on the cultivation of grass for private gardens. Over the years, these varied in price from 1s to 2/6d. From about 1952 thousands of booklets entitled *Turf Weeds, Identification and Control* were sold at 2s. These were followed in the 1960s by *The Identification of Grasses by the Foliage* at 3/-. After decimalization, these sold at 20p.

### Garden Construction Department

The first reference to Suttons' Garden Construction Department appeared in the bulb catalogue of 1922, as follows: 'For the enduring success of a garden, good planning inspired by imagination and directed by experience is the only sure foundation. In order that we may meet all the requirements of our customers in this respect we have arranged for the professional co-operation of Messrs Milner Son & White, the well known firm of garden architects, who have been responsible for the

# GRASS ADVISORY SERVICE

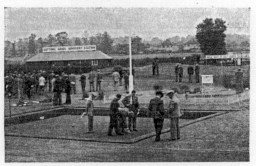

SUTTON'S GRASS ADVISORY STATION, READING

We shall be pleased to give free ADVICE BY LETTER as to the treatment of Lawns, Sports Grounds, Golf Courses, etc., on receipt of particulars.

*The facilities offered include :*

Inspection of turf and advice by specialists.

Examination of soils, top-dressings, sands, etc.

Identification of grasses.

Identification of weeds, and advice as to treatment.

Recommendations as to mixtures of grass seeds for specific purposes.

Advice on fertilising treatment and the use of turf dressings.

Suggestions on the subject of mechanical treatment of turf, including soil aeration, and information regarding various implements.

Identification of insect pests and advice on measures for their destruction.

Diagnosis of fungal attacks and suggestions for control.

If desired, a VISIT OF INSPECTION can be carried out by one of our experts, and a report subsequently forwarded on terms to be arranged.

☞ *If you have a turf problem, large or small—write, 'phone or call*

## SUTTON'S GRASS ADVISORY SERVICE, READING

Telephone : READING 54242 (Extension 41)

# GARDEN DESIGNING & CONSTRUCTION

If you are contemplating the making of a new garden or reconstructing an existing one, however large or small, our Garden Designing Consultants and a staff of experienced supervisors and foremen for carrying out any constructional work are at your disposal.

Work on industrial or housing sites will also be undertaken.

If advice and plans only are required, moderate charges will be made.

Whether planning only, or the complete laying out of a scheme by our experienced workmen is required, you will be assured of complete satisfaction.

*Herbaceous and Shrub Borders* • *Rose Gardens* • *Lily Pools*
*Terracing* • *Rock and Water Gardens* • *Paving, etc.*

*Character, simplicity, charm and restfulness are the keynotes of a garden designed by SUTTON'S of READING*

Write or 'phone:

## SUTTON'S GARDEN CONSTRUCTION DEPARTMENT

TELEPHONE **READING** 54242 (Extension 21)

Sutton's Grass Advisory Service and Garden Design & Construction adverts from 1950's catalogue.

40

Sutton's Garden Advisory Service. 1950's catalogue.

arrangement of so many of the more famous public, private parks and gardens in this country and the continent.'

This work was carried out in many parts of the country but especially in the Home Counties. Rockeries, pools, formal flower beds and lawns were all constructed under the direction of Suttons staff from Reading. However, competition and rising costs resulted in the department being closed down in 1965, when it was felt that the company would benefit by concentrating on the seed side of the business.

### Sports Ground Construction Department

The earliest reference to the Sports Ground Construction department was in Suttons' 1925 *Sports Grounds, Lawns and Golf Courses* catalogue in conjunction with Maxwell M Hart, which was well-known for the design and construction of these leisure facilities. The following year in this catalogue Suttons advertised a 'Greenkeepers' Essay Competition' in conjunction with the Greenkeepers' Association. The competition was open to all British and Continental members. Prizes to the value of 40 guineas were presented to the successful competitors, and a number of certificates of merit was also awarded.

Suttons carried out construction work for the following clubs in the 1920s and 30s:

Aldershot Grocers' Association – bowling green

HMS Fishguard, Gosport – sports ground

Landport Drapery Bazaar, Portsmouth – sports ground

St Margaret's, Folkestone – playing field

Right: Tottenham Hotspur football pitch in the course of re-construction by Suttons' Sports Ground Department, 29th April 1952.

Left: Spectators on the 14th green at Gleneagles during the *Glasgow Herald* 1,000 Tournament, in 1922, where Suttons supplied the grass seed.

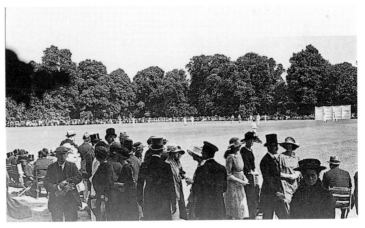

Right: Cricket match at Agar's Plough, Eton, where Suttons supplied grass seed and fertilizer. 3rd June 1922.

British Legion Poppy Factory, Richmond – bowling green

Wolverton Bowls Club – bowling green

University College Oxford – hard tennis court

Cumberland Lawn Tennis Club, Finchley Road, London – relaying grass tennis court.

The following golf clubs were constructed or renovated:

Sunningdale, Ashridge, The New Zealand club (Byfleet), Camberley Heath, Royal Porthcawl, Felixstowe, North Hants, Ballybunion, Muirfield, and in Portugal Estoril and Vidagi.

In the 1937 catalogue Suttons was promoting its Master hard tennis courts, which were constructed up to the closure of the department in the 1950s due to escalating costs.

## Shops, Stockists and Agencies

Until the mid-1930s, Suttons had sold all its seeds, plants, bulbs and sundries directly to growers, either by mail order or through its own shop in Market Place, Reading. However, many companies contacted the firm to explore the possibility of selling its seeds through shops. An office was leased at Reading cattle market from 1930 to 1964 in order to promote the sale of agricultural seed to local farmers. There was a sales office in the Central Hotel company, Dublin, in 1931.

Suttons of Cork (a company with no relationship to Sutton & Sons) asked to stock its seed as early as 1910, but the partners were insistent that they wished to supply their customers directly from Reading. The issue was well discussed by the partners, and they decided to discuss it again in the future.

For a brief period starting on 3rd December 1933, Suttons had a shop and office at Fortnum and Mason, 101 Piccadilly, London, and the following year a garden shop was opened on the first floor at 69 Piccadilly, London. In 1969 the company moved its London garden shop to 161 New Bond Street, sharing part of the premises with the Goya Perfume Company which Douglas Collins had repurchased that year. In 1974 it was relocated to 33 Catherine Street, opposite the Drury Lane Theatre.

In February 1946, it was discovered that the Christmas quarter of the electricity bill for the premises in Piccadilly had increased from an average of £1.16.6 in 1943 and £1.13.6 in the same period of 1944 to £10.17.6. The Electricity Board was contacted and investigations eventually showed that a company occupying the floor above had somehow put its cable into Suttons' meter. The result was that the other company was charged £19.17.6. It is not known if a prosecution resulted.

The first company to be given a franchise was Barrow's Stores, Corporation Street, Birmingham, on the 8th January 1934. In June 1938, Beales of Bournemouth approached the company regarding the selling of Suttons' seeds. In early August 1945, after WWII had finished in Europe, it was agreed that the number of main agents throughout the country would be increased. Representatives from the firm were sent to Newcastle-upon-Tyne, York, Southport, Manchester, Chester, Nottingham, Norwich, Cheltenham, Bristol, Cardiff and Eastbourne to find large stores which would be suitable and willing to sell Suttons' seeds. By 1958, 16 large department stores were selling Suttons' seeds, and by 1960 this had risen to 22. Later in the 1960s and 1970s, smaller retail outlets were approached with the result that, by the mid-1970s, Suttons' seeds were being sold in some 6,000 shops. Retail sales grew from around £250,000 per annum in the mid-1970s to £10 million gross over a period of 10 years, and were serviced by a sales force of 30, including area and national sales managers.

Followers of the BBC TV series 'Open All Hours' may recall the advert for Suttons' Seeds on the door of Arkwright's shop.

Although the company had moved all other facilities to the trial-ground site in 1963, the garden shop in Market Place was retained until 1973. One of the country's first garden centres was opened in 1964 adjacent to the company's new premises on London Road, Earley.

In 1985, Suttons bought its major competitor Horticultural Botanical Association comprising Carter's Tested Seeds, which had a further 5,000 retailers selling seeds, and Cuthberts, which was the major brand being sold in Woolworths and the biggest seller of packeted seeds in the UK. Dobies, a mail-order company, was also part of the acquisition. After the merger the Suttons' group had a 42% share of the packet-seed trade in the UK, which made it the largest packet-seed company in the country.

## Sales Representatives

In the early days of the company, Suttons did not employ sales representatives. Certain members of staff who had a good knowledge of horticulture and agriculture were sent to various parts of the country to call on the larger estates. Records show in November 1914 that Mr Giles, head of vegetable seed production, had the responsibility for engaging representatives. It was about this time that Suttons realized the advantages of employing such people; an example was that, for an outlay of £400, trade to the value of £4,000 had been achieved.

By October 1915, with the manpower shortage, it was suggested by Mr Giles that the firm should approach Messrs Silcocks, one of the most high-class cattle feed firms in the country, to ascertain if it would be agreeable to their travellers selling for both companies. After much consideration, the proposal was dropped.

In December 1915, three men based at Reading were sent out to obtain orders during the spring of that year.

| Rep | New trade | Total value | Expenses | Salary | MotorCycle |
|---|---|---|---|---|---|
| Taylor | £85 | £659 | £18 | £28 | (cycle) |
| Blaxill | £117 | £728 | £49 | £130 | £10 |
| Albury | £113 | £778 | £96 | £60 | £30 |

When Mr Albury went out on business, he had to wear his badge indicating that he was in a reserved occupation and could not be called up for military service.

At this time a statement was made that Messrs Dickson & Robinson had employed four men to call for business on large estates. It is recorded at the time that Suttons was not too worried by the competition, although it would 'keep an eye on the situation'. The Mr Taylor referred to above was sent for by the directors, who explained the importance of calling on customers, which he was about to undertake again. In an effort to encourage him he was given a wage increase from 35/- to 40/- per week. On the 10th May 1918, the partners agreed that, if suitable men could be found, appointments covering Dorset and Hampshire and elsewhere would be necessary to counteract Toogood, their main competitor in the area. By doing so it would be possible to ascertain during the season if prices were being cut; how far the competition could be met on the company's present terms; and whether it was really necessary to do local trade through markets, as appeared to be happening in the north.

On the 22nd May 1931 it was agreed to invite those representatives who were paid a salary, or an allowance in addition to their commission, to stay in Reading for a few days later in the summer for their first get-together. Early in July 1931, suggestions were made for dividing the country into districts, each of which would be covered by a fully-trained resident rep on the permanent staff. It was felt this was an ideal to be aimed at, but only to be achieved after some years. Leonard Sutton suggested young men from the firm should be trained for this purpose. W I Abbott who covered East Sussex was a first-class rep, and it was suggested that he should be given a wider district. Later in the month, Mr Olle was engaged to serve Kent and East Sussex, and Mr Muir for Lancashire and district. Both of these men worked those areas until they retired in the 1960s.

In 1963, the number of full- and part-time reps employed was 73; in 1967 this had dropped to 39, and by 1969 it had been reduced to 30. The main reason for this was that the farm-seed trade had been discontinued.

# 11. A Worldwide Company

Suttons was exporting seeds as early as 1841, and possibly even before this. These were sent to continental Europe, Australia, New Zealand, China, India, various parts of Africa, Canada and the Caribbean. It was truly a worldwide trade, with eventually over 100 countries supplied with various types of seeds and bulbs. The main sources of information about trading across the world are found in the directors' minutes and in some letters, leaflets and personal memories. These sources are incomplete, except for the personal reminiscences of work in India.

From catalogues of the 1870s, it is fascinating to read of the exalted list of important people to whom Suttons supplied its seeds worldwide. Among those mentioned are kings and emperors of nearly all the European countries, His Imperial Majesty the Tenno of Japan and the Pacha of Egypt. In addition to direct supply of customers from Reading, agencies were also set up and in many cases British catalogues were used, having been re-worded and priced in the local currency. Suitable collections of seeds were sent to these agents, many of whom were already selling local varieties of seeds and had an existing list of customers.

The export trade represented some 5% of the total value of the company's business, and this continued from the 1880s to the mid-1950s. Vegetable seeds have always been the more important, with flower seeds of rather less value. However, in the early days, agricultural root seed and grass seed were very significant sellers, especially to the expanding colonies, whereas the potato trade to South Africa was a huge part of the more recent business.

Suttons was famous for meticulous attention to detail when it came to packing seeds for export in order to ensure they survived the long and hazardous journeys. A commentator in 1882 wrote: 'There are two reasons why Sutton's Seeds are in especial favour in India and the Colonies. One reason is that they are genuine and unadulterated; while the other is that they undergo a process of packing originated by Suttons, and so far as we are aware not known to any other house in the trade. To give details of this mode of packing would be to divulge information which it would be wrong to give. During our visit there were huge steel tanks filled with grass and clover seeds for sowing in New Zealand and Australia; enormous zinc-lined wooden cases destined for the horticultural community of North-west India; another case addressed to the interior of Africa; while others were to find their way to the tropical climates of the West Indies and South Pacific. We also noticed a long row of packages filled with seeds for Agricultural College of Japan; and a huge pile

Farm and Garden Seeds carefully Packed for Exportation.

26    *Sutton's Farm Seed List, March 1st, 1865.*

# SUTTON'S COLLECTIONS OF GARDEN SEEDS
## FOR ONE YEAR'S SUPPLY.

1. A Complete Collection of KITCHEN GARDEN SEEDS for One whole Year's Supply (with instructions on Cultivation)    ...    ...    ...    ...    ...    ...    £3  3  0
2. A Complete Collection of KITCHEN GARDEN SEEDS, in quantities proportionately reduced    2  2  0
3. A Complete Collection of KITCHEN GARDEN SEEDS    ditto    ...    1  11  6
4. A Complete Collection of KITCHEN GARDEN SEEDS    ditto    ...    1  1  0
5. A Complete Collection of KITCHEN GARDEN SEEDS    ditto    ...    0  15  0
6. A Complete Collection of KITCHEN GARDEN SEEDS for a small Garden    ...    ...    0  10  6
7. A Complete Collection of KITCHEN GARDEN SEEDS, extra quantities, for a large Family    5  5  0

Sent Carriage Free by Rail, and 5 per cent. discount allowed for cash payment.

The sorts of Vegetables included in these Collections are those which have proved to be the most prolific, best flavoured, and most worthy of general cultivation, and of which sorts we have therefore grown large Crops of Seed. We exclude from our Collections not only inferior old sorts, but also such new ones as we have been unable to test the merits of, and which are selling at high prices. By this means, and from the great convenience experienced in supplying every purchaser with the same sorts, we are enabled to furnish a Complete Collection at much less expense than when a Gentleman or his Gardener makes his own selection; but as the latter mode of ordering is generally preferred, we have prepared an 'Order List' with columns ruled to facilitate the writing an order in detail, and which will be supplied on application.

# SEEDS OF SUITABLE KINDS FOR EXPORTATION.

SUTTON & SONS are constantly packing Farm and Garden Seeds for Australia, New Zealand, India, Africa, and other Foreign Parts, and receive the most gratifying accounts of the excellent condition in which they arrive, and of the crops produced from their Seeds.

The following *are similar to many others received* :—

*From Messrs.* CROUCH, *Portland, Victoria.* Sept. 16, 1864.

'We may remark that Messrs. Sutton's shipment of seeds have given the greatest satisfaction as far as they have been tried; the Grasses, Clovers, and Lucerne are up. We find the crop will be far too thick. If the vegetable seeds turn out as well we may say that, without exception, they are the best lot of seeds ever received in this place from Europe.'

*From* Sir R. MONTGOMERY, *Lieutenant-Governor, Punjab, India.*—May 15, 1863.

'The seeds you sent me last year answered very well, and I carried off the First Prizes both for vegetables and flowers, as you will see by an extract from the *Lahore Chronicle,* which I enclose.'

The Rev. R. G. LAMB, Green Point, Cape Town, Nov. 7, 1863.

'Your seeds have answered right well. One pinch of seed such as yours is worth a handful of the stuff sold here, which generally goes to seed before coming to perfection.'

*From* A. N. ELLA, Esq. *Queenstown, Cape of Good Hope.*—July 9, 1864.

'I may mention that the case referred to was in splendid order, looking as fresh after three months' sea, and six weeks' land carriage, as if only yesterday packed.'

*From Mr.* G. MORRISON, *Superintendent to the Government and Oude A. H. Society's Gardens, Lucknow.*—July 17, 1863.

'I received some Vegetable seeds, also some Flower seeds from your firm some 18 months ago, and they turned out first-rate.'

*From Mr.* CHAS. HASELDEN, *Boyce Farm, near Auckland, New Zealand, October 6, 1863.*

'The Grass Seeds you sent me arrived in excellent condition, and already present a luxuriant appearance, with the promise of abundant feed early in the coming season.'

*We deliver the packages free of all expense to the ship's side at London, Liverpool, Southampton, Bristol, and other English Ports;* but cannot undertake any responsibility beyond the safe delivery at the ship's side, except to effect insurance when requested to do so. Prepayment is requested for all foreign orders, and a few days' notice for packing previous to the departure of a vessel.

Foreign testimonials in the Sutton's farm seed catalogue of 1865.

# OVERSEAS

ABYSSINIA
ADEN
AFGHANISTAN
ALBANIA
ALGERIA
ARGENTINE REPUBLIC
ASCENSION
AUSTRALIA
AUSTRIA
AZORES
BAHAMAS
BALEARIC ISLANDS
BARBADOS
BELGIAN CONGO
BELGIUM
BERMUDA
BOLIVIA
BORNEO
BRAZIL
BRITISH GUIANA
BRITISH SOMALILAND
BRITISH TOGOLAND
BRITISH WEST INDIES
BULGARIA
BURMA
CAMEROONS
CANADA
CANARY ISLANDS
CELEBES
CEYLON
CHILE
CHINA
COLOMBIA
CUBA
CYPRUS
CZECHOSLOVAKIA
DANZIG
DENMARK
DOMINICAN REPUBLIC
DUTCH GUIANA
EASTER ISLAND
ECUADOR
EGYPT
EL SALVADOR
ESTONIA
FALKLAND ISLANDS
FEDERATED MALAY STATES
FIJI ISLANDS
FINLAND
FRANCE
GAMBIA
GERMANY
GIBRALTAR
GOLD COAST COLONY
GREECE
GRENADA
GUATEMALA
HAWAII
HOLLAND
HONDURAS
HONG KONG
HUNGARY
ICELAND
INDIA
IRAN
IRAQ

ITALY
JAMAICA
JAPAN
JAVA
KEDAH
KELANTAN
KENYA
LABRADOR
LATVIA
LEEWARD ISLANDS
LIBERIA
LITHUANIA
LUXEMBOURG
MADEIRA
MALTA
MANCHUKUO
MAURITIUS
MEXICO
MOROCCO
NEWFOUNDLAND
NEW ZEALAND
NIGERIA
NORTHERN RHODESIA
NORWAY
NYASALAND
PALESTINE
PARAGUAY
PERU
PHILIPPINE ISLANDS
POLAND
PORTUGAL
PORTUGUESE EAST AFRICA
PORTUGUESE WEST AFRICA
ROUMANIA
ST. HELENA
ST. VINCENT
SARAWAK
SENEGAL
SEYCHELLES
SIAM
SIERRA LEONE
SOUTH AFRICA
SOUTHERN RHODESIA
SPAIN
STRAITS SETTLEMENTS
SUDAN
SUMATRA
SWEDEN
SWITZERLAND
SYRIA
TANGANYIKA TERRITORY
TIBET
TOBAGO
TRANSJORDAN
TRINIDAD
TUNIS
TURKEY
TURKS AND CAICOS ISLANDS
UGANDA
UNITED STATES OF AMERICA
URUGUAY
U.S.S.R.
VENEZUELA
VIRGIN ISLANDS
YUGOSLAVIA
ZANZIBAR

## EXPORT ORDERS

The countries and other places overseas named on this page are among the large number to which we have exported our seeds and plants during the past season.

### THE SELECTION OF VARIETIES

This is an important factor for many countries, and where the choice is left to us customers may rely upon our sending only those sorts which, in our judgment, are likely to do well. In this connection any information as to locality and altitude that can be given will prove helpful to us.

### PACKING FOR EXPORT

Seeds intended for the tropics, or having to pass the Equator, are always dried under our perfected system and packed in hermetically-sealed tins.

### CUSTOMS AND OTHER REGULATIONS

We endeavour to keep ourselves informed of all changes in these matters and are prepared to furnish the necessary certificates, etc.

119

A Page from the 1939 catalogue, listing the countries to which Suttons exported.

The Export Office 1931. In 1937 the number of staff in this office was 24.

of hampers containing seed Potatoes for planting at the Cape of Good Hope. In addition to their new mode of packing, Sutton's have originated a special tin box, which is sealed with solder making it completely air tight, in which seeds are packed before being packed in the special wood cases lined with sheets of zinc.'

## Africa

In mid-June 1902, the packaged order for the Boer farmers was despatched. The staff in Mr Plumer's department worked from 8 a.m. to midnight on Wednesday and from 8 a.m. Thursday to 7 a.m. on Friday. The job was only just completed on time and the men were paid 8*d* instead of 6*d* per hour.

Mr Brown senior was sent to South Africa in the autumn of 1902 to meet and travel with Mr Govey, a local man who knew the territory, with the aim of establishing some agencies. Martin John Sutton stated that he would like his son Phil Sutton to accompany him, as he thought it would be a more useful education than remaining at the Royal Agricultural College, Cirencester, until Christmas as he had intended to do. Unfortunately they both caught dysentery, exacerbated by the poor weather and travelling, and returned to the UK earlier than anticipated. Fortunately, they both arrived home safely.

Suttons had been shipping potatoes to South Africa since before the Boer War in peace and wartime. In spite of this, not one tuber was lost due to enemy action, but about 200 tons were lost when the SS Clan

Consignment of seed potatoes for South Africa 1904.

Mackenzie was in collision in the Mersey and sank on the 5th November 1937. The company had signed a form of subrogation, and the insurance sum of £4,215 allowed the consignment to be replaced with Irish seed.

Early in March 1942 it was decided not to grow any potatoes for South Africa (presumably it was not known if the company would be able to export, due to the severe wartime restrictions and availability of valuable shipping space). If an order was to follow a recent enquiry, the company would take a chance and buy on the open market. This occurred on the 1st May when a company called Amm, the main agents, ordered 5000 cases of the variety 'Up to Date' and 250 cases of 'King George', which were to be bought in.

## India

'Seedsmen to the King Emperor, Reading, London and Calcutta'. So ran the proclamation on the front of Suttons' *Garden Seed Catalogue* for 1925, published for the expanding markets in India, Burma and Ceylon (Sri Lanka).

It all started somewhat earlier than this. Suttons was exporting seeds to India in the mid-1860s, when expatriates embarking for a long tour of duty on the sub-continent would take with them square, hinged tins similar to the old-fashioned biscuit tins made for Huntley & Palmers. These were manufactured by Huntley, Boorne & Stevens, another Reading company, and would be filled with packets of vegetable and flower seeds and sealed, ensuring no moisture could damage the seeds. These would have been specially selected by Suttons' experts for cultivation in the tropics. Special pre-packed formulated collections were available for this trade.

As the business expanded, the company decided to appoint agents to handle seeds imported from England. By 1912, the name of Suttons was becoming well-established, with large quantities of seeds being shipped to Calcutta; to ensure they arrived in good condition, they were packed in 200- and 400-gallon galvanized-steel sealed tanks. These were then re-used as water storage tanks, some of which adorned the rooftops of Calcutta.

Early in November 1914, Mr Stevens of the export department sailed for India to ascertain the possibilities of trade there. At the end of December, the first two letters were received, indicating that his journey was likely to prove very useful. By the 26th February 1915, he had returned and had a brief meeting with the partners. At a meeting on the 3rd March, he reported on the high position the company occupied in the public's estimation in India. A few days later, at a meeting to discuss the cost of setting up there, it was estimated that this would not be more than £2000, which would be a good investment (followed by the comment 'if the war ended favourably').

Meetings continued, and on the 17th September it was decided that the company should proceed immediately to set up a branch in Calcutta. One of the main reasons for choosing this location was the large number of European clientele living in the area. It was agreed the branch would open on the 1st May 1916 and have a catalogue ready for posting on the 31st July. This would mean Mr Stevens leaving for India at the end of October, together with a thoroughly competent book-keeper. On the 12th November 1915, all four partners met Mr Stevens and Mr Shackleford, his assistant, to say their farewells on their departure for India. They sailed the following day on the SS Arabia. By arrangement with Martin H Sutton, they were lent two special naval life-saving waistcoats which he had acquired from the Foreign Office in London. On their safe arrival in India, they were to return them to the company. He started working from the Great Eastern Hotel; soon after a move was made to Nos. 33 and 36 Park Mansions and later to 13D Russell Street, where the office remained until 2002.

On the 22nd March 1916, a letter was received from the Calcutta branch, thanking the company for its offer of seeds for General Townshend at Kut (a town on the banks of the river Tigris, about 100 miles south-east of Baghdad, where British troops had a base in WWI); regretfully these could not be accepted, as they would arrive too late.

A number of Indian catalogues were examined, and it was agreed that Suttons' would be similar of that of Pocha, an Indian company. The catalogue was prepared in Reading and taken to India for printing. Prices were converted to Indian currency. The first delivery was from packets prepared in Reading, which were sent out in specially-sealed boxes, each containing 25 packets. By the end of October, a dummy copy of the Indian catalogue had been prepared, consisting of 80 pages. This amount went beyond the estimates, and it was reduced to 64 pages. A print run of 5000 was thought to be sufficient. Trading commenced on the 1st August 1916. One of the first jobs undertaken was to communicate with the Indian jails informing them of the new branch and requesting them to send their seed orders to Calcutta, from where they would be sent to Reading for execution. Additional requirements could be supplied from the new branch. It was thought seeds should be sent in four consignments to arrive on approximately the first day of August, October, February and May. The question of packaging in Tagger Tins (a local name for a particular type of tin) or in lead or tin foil was discussed. It was agreed to commence with ordinary packets like other Indian seedsmen, but also thought desirable that some packets in tin foil and some without should be sent to Stevens for testing at the beginning of the rainy season. Other seeds to be stocked included small amounts of lawn seed, lucerne, mangel, swede and turnip. At the end of the month, a seed germinator for seed testing was sent to the branch.

Early in November 1917, correspondence from Mr Stevens in Calcutta showed that he was under extreme pressure, as deliveries of seed had gone round the Cape instead of via the Suez Canal, and had arrived very late. On 7th January 1918 Mr Shackleford said he wished to return to England at the end of his three-year contract. Mr Stevens had reported that the business was now well established, and he could employ a reliable assistant locally. The question of new premises in Calcutta was discussed.

Towards the end of March 1918, Mr Stevens raised the question of harvesting seeds in India for the purpose of acclimatization. It was apparent to the partners that this was not possible under existing conditions, but that he should be encouraged to make trials on a small scale and report the results. There was also an offer to purchase the Himalayan Seed Store business, but this was refused as it was not of much value to the company. In April, meetings were held with Mr Chambers of the Ministry of Agriculture, concerning the difficulty in obtaining export licences for Calcutta. The results were encouraging, with the promise of the appropriate documentation for India.

Early in January 1919, the question arose of Mr Stevens' return from India. Due to the war, he had stayed a year longer than originally agreed, and he must be relieved by October. There was some difficulty in choosing the right people, bearing in mind that Shackleford and Hallett would be returning. At the end of April, the partners interviewed Mr R D Pinker, who had expressed a wish to work in India. He was offered the job for about 18 months to allow for Stevens to have some extended leave and he would sail about the middle of June.

On the 25th March 1920, Mr Stevens returned to work after his leave, and the possibility of sending him to the Argentine was considered. There must have been further discussions on his future as, on the 25th May, he informed the partners he was quite willing to return to India, but pointed out that he was now aged 42 and he thought it should not be for more than 3 years. During this period, he could be training some-one to take his place. He thought the business prospects were good and, in the interest of the business, he should go back in August. A few days later his salary and commission were discussed. The partners decided to give him a present of £250 for the past year (1919–20), in addition to his commission.

Later, in view of the fact that he had been drawing a salary of £300 at the rate of 15 rupees to the pound or 4,500 rupees per annum and in addition he had been given a present of £250 which, at the rate of exchange now in force represented 2,500 rupees, making altogether 7,000 rupees per annum, it was decided to make his salary 8,000 rupees per annum and not to give him a present at the end of the year.

In 1923 Mr Stevens was appointed head of Suttons' foreign office (later known as the export office). At the end of July, a lease was signed for the Chinsurah Trial Grounds in Calcutta.

An amusing story is told. One of the clerks in Suttons' export office had a son who was applying for a job in London; he told him: 'Tell them your father works in the Foreign Office'.

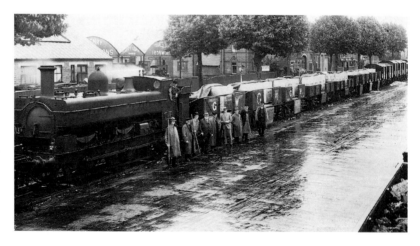

Reading's Great Western Railway goods yard in Vastern Road. An 0–6–0 pannier tank engine, with at least eight wagons loaded with seeds for export. Mr Stevens, head of the Export Department, is fourth from the right. Standing next to him, on his left is Mr Bartholomew, one of his senior clerks. Late 1920's.

Five horse-drawn wagons loaded with seeds packed in galvanized-steel tanks, ready for export. This photograph was taken opposite the old stables, 1907.

Consignment of seeds just arrived at Suttons' branch in Calcutta, 1930's.

In July 1930 Mr Pinker was appointed manager of the Indian branch and at the same time, a lease was signed for premises at 35–36 Park Mansions, Calcutta. The company was registered in India under the Indian Companies Act of 1913, and its bank was to be the Imperial Bank of India.

Until 1939 seeds continued to flow freely from Reading to India. Suttons was then involved with the bulk supply of vegetable seeds to Indian farmers. This was encouraged by the Indian Government, as it was making available good-quality seeds and improved strains, but at this stage it only involved European (temperate-type) crops. It was at this time that the British Government banned all exports of seed because of the war, and the Suttons' business was scaled down; only the manager Mr Harradence was left. The rest of the European staff was called up for military service; this included Norman Underwood, who was later re-called from active service by the Indian Government to help organize reliable seed production within the sub-continent, as serious food shortages would have occurred without the necessary seeds.

Throughout the 1940s the company was forced to change the source of seeds from imports to becoming totally self-sufficient from home-produced seed crops. Seed production was developed in areas of Bihar, Gujerat and Kashmir. Suttons was trading in European and Asian vegetables, hence the different locations.

European-type vegetable seeds were produced in the valley of Kashmir, 5,000 feet above sea level. The River Jhelum flows through its 100-mile length and 40-mile width. The climate was temperate with short sharp winters, plenty of snow covering the surrounding mountains, and hot summers. Plentiful snowfall provided a good pure water supply, making the valley extremely fertile. Rice was the staple crop, and on the terraced slopes maize was grown. European fruits such as apples, cherries, peaches, pears etc were introduced in the 19th century, as were rainbow trout which flourished in the mountain streams. Trout fishing rapidly became a favourite day out. No wonder Kashmir is called the 'Switzerland of the East'.

Gujerat and areas of the Punjab were the natural production sites for Asian varieties of tomato, cauliflower, radish, spinach etc. Flower seeds were grown at Tollygunge (Calcutta), Ranchi and later Bangalore in south India. At one time, doob grass (*Cynodon dactylon*) was an important export; huge tonnages were sold, mainly to Australia to help reclaim some of the desert regions.

Suttons' trial grounds at Tollygunge, Calcutta.

Early in December 1946, the company secretary reminded the directors that the position of Suttons in India was likely to be radically altered with the coming of self-government. Therefore it was thought they should obtain the best advice before any restrictions were imposed. By 1947, all seed imports were banned due to the lack of currency. This was also the year of Indian independence, and the partition of the sub-continent into India and Pakistan. Suttons was closely involved in the improvement of production methods, seed-cleaning and processing, with the company working alongside the Indian Government and the Directors of Agriculture in the various regions. The Indian market had opened up, with a demand for European-type vegetables. Suttons tapped into this new market, and was a pioneer in this project. Isolation sectors became established in Kashmir for the production of brassicas and all the other vegetable crops grown in these areas. To ensure its standards were maintained, the company set up a permanent office and warehouse with seed-cleaning and packaging machinery in Kashmir. Production there was now farmed out among different growers, Hindu, Muslim and Sikh, and throughout the 1960s they all worked happily together. Sadly, this beautiful valley is now at the centre of political unrest, and its once-famous and prosperous tourist industry has been badly hit.

Throughout the 1950s and 1960s, there were tight import restrictions due mainly to the lack of foreign exchange. A small amount of Snowball cauliflower seed, one of Suttons' famous varieties, was allowed to be imported. This was sold by allocation against the value of other seeds purchased, although the company realised that it was then sold on at vastly inflated black-market prices. Suttons maintained its high standards and was subject to many instances of fraudulent competition. All the wholesale production was sold in sealed tins of 500g, 250g and 100g bearing a coloured label with the Suttons' logo and copyright seal.

Look-alike products were freely sold as Suttons in the local vegetable markets. Sultans Seeds can be made to look like Suttons Seeds, and farmers who are unable to read could not tell the difference and would only know of their mistake when the crop failed.

Further information is given in Chapter 13, 'Personal Accounts of Life at Suttons', in the section by Mike Smallwood.

## New Zealand

Suttons was exporting agricultural grasses to New Zealand as early as 1841. Testimonials from customers in New Zealand were printed in Suttons' catalogues during the 1860s:

> *'In the colony, large flocks of fine sheep are being killed for future shipments, and the colonists are fattening sheep for the English*

*market and breeding the black faced and other kinds suitable for the wants of this country. Almost all of these are now fed or fattened on English grasses, and some Berkshire people may be interested to know that Mr Sutton senior shipped clover and rye grass seeds to me in 1841. Those seeds were over five months on the voyage, and were the first English grasses sown in the Auckland district of NZ. The colony since then has made rapid strides and the Reading seed firm have shipped seed for most of the rich pastures in NZ ...'*

George Graham, Hove, Brighton 12th January 1885; quoted in the *Reading Mercury, 24th January* 1885.

A page from the 1904 catalogue showing Mr T J Thomas of Markaraka, New Zealand, with a waggon loaded with produce grown from Sutton's seeds. There is also a testimonial from Mr Thomas below the picture.

Early in February 1916 the partners discussed with Mr Brown senior (head of the export department) and Mr Waight (Head of the Potato Department) the delivery problems experienced the previous year with seed potatoes for Mr Tothill's trade (Suttons' New Zealand agent). The problem was that 3,300 cases were despatched between April and July in wooden cases made on the premises, which caused considerable delay. That year's order was estimated to use 3,800 cases, therefore arrangements would have to be made for the cases to be made by a local timber merchant. Mr Waight contacted Messrs Huntley, Boorne and Stevens, a local tin-box manufacturer (which made tins for Huntley & Palmers biscuits) for a quote for supplying the tin linings for the wooden cases.

In March 1918, licences for the export trade were very difficult to obtain. One instance is recorded where the company was refused a licence to export 5 tons of turnip seed to New Zealand. Under these circumstances, the situation was explained to Mr Weaver from the Ministry of Agriculture, who expressed an opinion that something should be done. Further discussions with another Ministry man, a Mr Chambers, proved to be useful, as by the end of April licences were approved.

Walter Giles (head of the vegetable and agricultural department) sailed for New Zealand on the 19th December 1930, via the Panama Canal. He went there to see the agents, and to visit the major seed-growing areas producing vegetable and grass seed crops.

Before and after WWII the agent for all seeds was J G Ward and Co Ltd of Christchurch.

## North America and Europe

While these were both important markets for Suttons, unfortunately little useful information has survived.

# 12. Suttons and its Staff

For much of the time that Suttons has been in business, national staff welfare legislation was very patchy and working conditions varied greatly from company to company. Suttons has always had a reputation for taking care of its employees. This was partly based on an altruistic Christian outlook, but probably also based on good business pragmatism, in the belief that a happy employee was a more profitable employee. In addition there were several periods when shortages of available labour would have focussed the board's mind on providing good working conditions in relation to other competing local companies.

Each generation of the Sutton family worked in one or more of the departments to get to know the business and to gain experience, and the firm was probably small enough for the directors to know most of their workers. In the days before the National Health Service, retirement pensions and other government/national welfare organisations, Suttons' workers were fortunate to work for a company that cared, as Suttons was more involved in the welfare of its workers than most. Indeed it is probably true to say that the directors of Suttons had a paternalistic attitude to their workforce. This approach also served the company well as happy, well-cared-for workers were more likely to stay with the firm,

18 members of staff who had completed 50 years of service. May, 1944.

be loyal and give their best in return. Employees responded by showing
great loyalty in their work, and by the length of time they worked for the
company.

Duration of time employees had been employed by Suttons, 1956.

| | |
|---|---|
| *10 years and under* | *360* |
| *10 years and over* | *48* |
| *20 years and over* | *34* |
| *30 years and over* | *69* |
| *40 years and over* | *38* |
| *50 years and over* | *8* |
| *Heads of Department (years of service not given)* | *26* |
| **Total** | *583* |

Over the years, entries in the diaries, company documents and
personal reminiscences record that the company, led by the directors,
showed great care, compassion and thoughtfulness towards its workers
in the various branches and departments (MERL).

## Morning Prayers

Morning prayers were held daily from Monday to Friday at 10.30 a.m.
in the Letter Opening Room, and were conducted by local ministers and
lay preachers. In October 1915, some concern was shown about the
small numbers who attended. The partners came to the conclusion that
a special notice should be written and signed by Arthur Sutton. It was
decided that 10.30 a.m. was not the most convenient time, and that it
would be much better for prayers to be held at 9.45 or 10 a.m.

## Staff Benefits

There was a pension fund, a sick fund, a burial fund, life and endowment
insurance, a girls' saving fund and an ex-servicemen's association. The
seasonal hours were long and the wages low, but most workers stayed
on as Suttons had a reputation of being a fair employer and, although
Martin Hope Sutton was miserly with labour, he did engage extra people
at busy times (Corley, 1991–4). Treats were arranged at various times.
In 1856 when the new granary was opened, a supper, preceded by games
etc, was provided for the men, wives and children. An outing to the
Crystal Palace or another local place of interest was arranged at the end
of each season in September. There are entries in the company's minutes
recording the rewarding of workers with sums of money for inventions
or labour-saving ideas. In April 1901, an employee by the name of
Kinchin, head of the farm seed order room, was given £50 for inventing

new machinery. The sums of money are quite small by today's reckoning, but at the time these were quite substantial amounts.

In February 1902 an epidemic of smallpox had been reported. Suttons along with other firms in the town arranged for the staff to be vaccinated; this was carried out in the firm's Abbey Hall over a period of three days in March. Records show that in all cases pure sterilized lymph direct from the calf was used; many people were affected by the inoculation; and influenza was also present, resulting in many people being off work for a few days.

On the 7th August 1916, Leonard Sutton brought to the notice of the directors the distressing case of Mr Barber, who was suffering from the effects of poison gas received in one of the battles in France. Mr Barber was not making any progress, so the doctors had recommended a sea voyage, and one of the companies which Mr Sutton had written to offered to take Mr Barber to New Zealand and back for £20. It was agreed the directors would pay this, providing his family was, during his absence, supported by the Soldiers' and Sailors' Help Society. Other records of acts of benevolence include the company making an advance of £25 to Miss Biggs to help towards the expenses of her operation (13th August 1937).

Employees were encouraged to be gardeners, and were given a 50% discount on the price of seed and 20% on other items. This proved especially valuable during the 1930s' depression when Suttons' staff suffered a pay cut. In January 1917, a notice was posted stating: 'Mr L G Sutton has kindly offered land situated in Northumberland Avenue, for the purpose of allotments. It is proposed to cut some into plots of ten poles, rent to be a nominal one to defray working expenses. Anyone wishing to take up a plot (or plots) should apply on or before the 15th January, to Mr C J Durman.'

There was a Horticultural Section of the Recreation Club and, on 28th February 1918, in his diaries Mr Baskett records that the '… Club being suspended, the Partners are agreeable during the war to supply vegetable seeds to their employees for their own use as supplied to the various Allotment Associations on condition that all orders are given in for execution at one time. A seeds list will be posted at each department for which all orders must be given to the deputy head of each department and passed on to Mr Lovejoy by Friday 6th March.'

There are records of the partners ensuring that the minimum wage was paid e.g. in 1918 40/- per week. In October 1920 the Government's Unemployment Act came into force. The company obtained the appropriate forms from the local unemployment exchange and distributed them to all staff to ensure that everyone who was liable under the Act had an unemployment book. In November, the first payment of 4d was deducted from each employee for the state unemployment insurance scheme.

Dinner

OF THE FIRM OF

Sutton & Sons

TO THEIR

Heads of
Departments

WEDNESDAY,
DECEMBER
19th, 1906

At HOLME PARK.

MENU
—

Whitstable Oysters.
—
Turtle Soup.
—
Filleted Soles.    Turbot.
—
Creams of Chicken.  Mutton Filberts.
—
Roast Beef.    Boiled Turkey.
—
Sorbet of Rum.
—
King's Pheasants.    Wild Duck.
—
Salsify.
—
Christmas Pudding. Apple & Quince Tart.
Mince Pies.        Jellies.
—
Raspberry Cream & Lemon & Ginger Ices.
Dessert.

Menu for heads of department dinner at
Holme Park, Sonning, 1906, the then residence of Martin John Sutton.

Immediately after WWII, the Staff Committee asked for a 5-day week (10th May 1946). The Chairman of the Board, Phil Sutton, agreed but at a subsequent Horticultural Trades' Association meeting, the vote had gone against this. Saturday morning working finally ceased at the end of 1960; 293 were in favour, and 20 wished to continue.

A booklet of 1948 explaining the employment conditions and welfare facilities stated the following:

'Pension Fund. It was a stipulation that all permanent male staff over 20 years of age were to be members of the fund.

Life & Endowment Insurance. A special arrangement was made with two leading life insurance companies, whereby special facilities could be given to members of staff wishing to take out any policies.

Girls' Saving Fund. This was a voluntary savings fund for permanent female staff, in which they saved a percentage of their wages at very generous rates of interest which were supplemented by the company. There was also an active National Savings group for members of staff.'

From 1899 it was the custom to present hampers to all the heads of department at Christmas time. These were valued at 5 guineas for the senior heads, and 3 guineas for the others. In December 1914 the question of Christmas hampers was discussed by the board and, in view of the war, it was felt that economies could be made by reducing the value. In addition to this, an annual dinner for all heads was held each December. In 1899 it was held at Hillside, the residence of Leonard Sutton. Martin Hubert Sutton spoke after dinner of the 'depressing news from the Cape dealing with the war, the cause he thought that had led to it and the lessons to be learnt'. In 1901 the event was held at the home of Arthur Sutton at Bucklebury and in 1906 at Holme Park, Sonning, the home of Martin John Sutton.

The marriages, deaths and special wedding anniversaries of members of the family were celebrated with holidays and extra pay for the staff. The following examples are taken from Baskett's diaries (MERL).

'To celebrate the marriage of the daughter of a senior partner of the firm a whole day's holiday will be given on 29th July 1903 instead of the usual half-day.'

'The firm was closed on the 9th November 1904 when Martin John Sutton became mayor of Reading and on 2nd July 1906 Arthur Sutton invited all staff to his home at Bucklebury to celebrate his silver wedding anniversary, which had fallen earlier in the year. And in 1909 all staff were given a day's holiday to celebrate Martin John Sutton's recovery from illness.'

Directors and Heads of
Departments *c.*1955.

'*Owing to the lamented death of Mrs Martin John Sutton these
premises will be closed on Monday 6th January 1911 (for the funeral) from 12.30 to 5 p.m. Mr Sutton wishes it to be known that,
owing to the very large number of friends expected, it will to his
regret be impossible to provide seats in church for any of the staff,
except Heads of Departments and their wives.*'

*In the same year on 24th April, Phil Sutton married Miss Douglas-
Jones.*

'*Owing to the busy time it is impossible to grant a general half-day
holiday on the day of the wedding, but it will be arranged later on.*'

The following year (1912) Martin John Sutton married again. He
gave money in lieu as '... any excursion or treat would be difficult [to
arrange]. Therefore I think it best to ask individual employees to accept
the enclosed sum from me and decide for himself as to the most agreeable
way of spending it, on the half-day given in connection with my wedding
on 17th September.'

Martin John Sutton died on 14th December 1913 which led to
the following notice: 'The funeral of the late Martin John Sutton will
be tomorrow. All departments will be closed throughout the day. The

Memorial Service will take place at Greyfriars' Church at 3 o'clock which will be attended by the Corporation and other Official Bodies. As there will not be room in Greyfriars for all employees Heads of Depts will distribute tickets to certain representatives of each dept for reserved seats in the Church.

'As Beneficiaries under the will of the late Mr Martin John Sutton, we have decided to make a gift of £500 jointly for distribution amongst all those who have been in the service of the firm for a period of not less than five years immediately preceding December 31st 1913 in order that all those who knew our father best may be enabled to choose some tangible memento of one who was always their friend as well as their employer.'

## Pay

Individuals were given presents of sums of money in recognition of extra work, e.g. in September 1902, Mr Broseley was given £25 in consideration of the extra work that he had done in the absence of Mr Brown (who was in South Africa). In 1903 Walter Giles (head of vegetable seed production) wrote to the directors pointing out his difficulty in making his income meet his expenditure, owing to the extra expense entailed by travelling so much for the company in his job. It was agreed that he should have an increase of £50 p.a.

At other times, extra money was given to all the employees. On 22nd June 1897, all staff were given the day off to celebrate the Diamond Jubilee of Queen Victoria, as well as an extra week's wages. In June 1911, an extra week's wages was again given to all staff to celebrate the coronation of George V, plus two days' holiday at double pay. Heads of departments were given £5, and the monthly staff £2.

In order to keep the loyalty of key people and to help remove some of the work pressure from the partners, the heads of departments were well remunerated. Extracts from records for the 23rd July 1900 give an indication of the company's thinking at the time:

1. To give Mr Livings full responsibility as regards trusting customers and bad debts and to raise his salary by £100 to £900 per year.
2. To trust Tufnail, Giles, Lasham, Shipway, MacDonald, Grant, and Bennett more than hitherto and pay them handsomely.
3. No Partner should be requested to be in business more than five days a week.
4. Pay Heads and deputies so well that they have no inducement to leave us and thus make them our devoted servants and friends.

| Heads of Departments' annual salaries. | | |
| --- | --- | --- |
| | 1900 | 1920 |
| Bennett | £275 | £600 |
| Lasham | £250 | £500 |
| Plumer | £250 | £600 |
| Tufnail | £250 | £580 |
| MacDonald | £200 | £400 |
| Shipway | £200 | £550 |
| Giles | £180 | £850 |

In January 1912 it was deemed that no married man should be paid less than 21 shillings per week. Cost of living increases in February 1915 gave those earning less than 30 shillings per week a 10% increase, and those earning between 30 and 40 shillings a 5% increase. Suttons was obviously worried about losing staff to Huntley and Palmer, which in October 1918 paid 44 shillings for a longer working week. In response, Suttons raised wages from 35 shillings to 40 shillings per week.

| During the 1930's, the hours of work were: | |
| --- | --- |
| Monday to Friday | 9 a.m. to 5 p.m. |
| Saturday | 9 a.m. to 1 p.m. |
| Plus, for the seasonal months, January to March | |
| Evening work | 6 p.m. to 8 p.m. |
| Tea money during seasonal overtime months | |
| Men | 5d per night |
| Juniors | 3d per night |

Pay for junior office girls aged 14 years started at 11/- per week, and increased each birthday by 1/3d per week until 21 years of age. Thereafter no further rises were given, except for promotion to another job. One female junior was unfortunate enough to have her birthday on the 29th February. In a non-leap year, her increase was overlooked as there was no such day on the calendar. This oversight was noticed some weeks later and the wages sheet was altered, but she did not receive an increase for the missed weeks.

The new agricultural wages rate was increased by the Government on 4th July 1946. It was agreed that trial-grounds staff wages be increased from 73/- to 80/6d per week. Later in the month the following statement on wages was made:

'In view of the general rise in the cost of living we have decided to increase the wage scales as follows:

- The minimum wage for a clerk aged 25 will be 82/5d for a 43 hour week and 92s for a 48 hour week
- A male Seed Room Assistant at 25 will be 81/6d for a 43 hour week and 91s for a 48 hour week
- The above increases will cost the Company several thousands of pounds per annum.'

## Pensions

A staff pension fund was first mooted by the directors in March and April 1898. They decided not to adopt such a scheme, but that 3 years' wages would be paid to the executors of anyone who died after 20 years' service or more. The possibility of adopting a scheme similar to that of the Great Western Railway was considered in January 1904, but it was felt not to be suitable.

However, individuals were awarded pensions at the discretion of the partners. In April 1903, a Mr Dunn was pensioned off on account of his age, and was given a good pension plus a present of £20. At the end of January 1912, Mr Kinchin retired and was awarded a pension of £300 p.a. After he died in December 1915, the directors granted his widow a pension of £100 p.a.

A pensions meeting was held on 17th June 1921 in the Abbey Hall at midday to discuss the scheme, and a ballot for the scheme was held three days later. A pension scheme was finally set up later in 1921 as an independent company administered by Trustees, three of whom had to be elected by the staff and three appointed by the company, with an outside chairman. In the first week of June, the first contributions were deducted from all eligible male staff over the age of 21, and the directors contributed a similar amount. The Pension Fund Trust Deed was signed on the 29th January 1923.

## Profit-sharing Scheme

At the end of February 1920, Leonard G Sutton said that he thought the time had come to talk to the heads of departments about a profit-sharing scheme. A meeting was held with all staff on the 4th March. Leonard explained that the partners had made an offer of a share of the profits for the benefit of employees, and they were reminded that they had been told of such a proposal at their annual dinner. The heads were asked to express their views on this; it was added that, if this offer was accepted, it would be as an experiment for one year. The partners felt there were advantages and disadvantages, but that if they were refused, they would be pleased that the offer had been made. If the majority was to refuse, then the heads would have an opportunity to meet the partners to discuss their own thoughts on such a scheme for themselves.

A few days later, the profit-sharing offer was slightly revised, and the partners issued invitations to all employees who had been in the service of the company for at least one year to attend a meeting in the Abbey Hall. Leonard went on to say that, though they were quite prepared to reconsider the wage structure agreed in the previous April, in the coming April they wanted first to give the employees the alternative of a share of the profits. He went on to explain that it would only apply to men over 21, and would be for a trial period of one year. He was careful to point out that wage rates would remain the same, but there would be rises for merit on promotion as usual, and that he did not wish them to think that by the offer the partners were antagonistic to the unions. Staff would be given plenty of time to think it over, after which a ballot would be taken. The partners would not proceed unless there was a three-quarters majority. If they decided against it they, the partners, would be willing to reconsider the wage rates with their union representatives.

There were many discussions about the profit-sharing scheme during June. At a general meeting in the Abbey Hall, it was announced that the workforce was in favour, and that a profit-sharing committee was to be set up. The partners nominated Messrs Allum and Bartlett. F Carter and G A Rouse represented the Clerks' Union, and Barker and Goddard the General Workers' Union. At a meeting on the 19th June, it was announced that employees would receive a bonus of 8.5% and that the heads of departments would receive 2.5%. At a bonus meeting on 30th June 1921, 9% of their annual wage was given to the staff. But later that year (3rd December), wages were reduced by 5% due to the fall in the cost of living. Another 5% reduction was recorded on 2nd January 1923.

The last profit share of 8% was given in May 1946. Later that year on the 12th September, the chairman announced that the directors had decided that this scheme was to be discontinued. In its place a further 10% (a war inflation bonus), making 20% in all, was to be added to the basic wage.

## *Paid Holidays*

As well as outings, all the staff were also given annual holidays. The following notice was circulated to all staff.

**NOTICE: 15th April 1898.**

- The Summer Holiday was instituted by us many years ago with the object of giving our employees an opportunity of thorough rest and relief from the strain of work once in each year.

- The Summer was chosen as the proper season for this holiday to be taken, because it is the part of the year during which such holidays least interfere with business work, and also because Summer is the most agreeable time for holiday-making.

  *Of late these points seem to have been somewhat overlooked, and therefore we make the following announcement:–*

- All those whose wages exceed 10 shillings per week will in future be entitled to a fortnight's holiday.

- All those who receive as wages 10 shillings or under will be entitled to one week's holiday.

- No holidays in any department can be taken after the 30th November in each year.

- Those receiving a fortnight's holiday must in future take at one time not less than ten days out of the eleven working days of which that holiday consists, and can have the remaining day and also the day given in lieu of Easter Monday either as two single days or four half-days, by arrangement with their Head of Department.

- Those entitled to one week's holiday must take the whole of that week at once, having in addition the day in lieu of Easter Monday either as an extra single day or as two half-days.

Staff were expected to work hard, but were given extra time off in return. For example, in between 30th January and 20th February 1895, six half-days were allowed for ice-skating. In January 1896 it was noted that several half-days had been given for skating that month. Also on the 13th January 1908, all the staff left at 5 o'clock for skating, and in February 1908, after consultation with Mr Griffiths and Mr Plumer, it was decided the firm could not grant a half-day off for skating due to pressure of work, but agreed that all departments could leave at 5 p.m. as there was a full moon. The following notice was put up in 1912.

> *'31st January 1912. We wish as far as work permits that all should have a half-day's holiday for skating today instead of Saturday.'*

(Baskett's diaries, MERL).

An extra 2½ days' holiday were given to staff when Leonard Noel
Sutton entered the firm on 2nd June 1920.

## Unions

In August 1918 Suttons was approached by the Reading Branch of the
National Union of General Workers. A statement approved by the Board
was enclosed in all the staff's wage packets the next day.

> 'As copies of the letter addressed to the 'Workers at Messrs
> Sutton and Sons' have been handed to us, we take this oppor-
> tunity of letting it be known we wish you to feel absolutely free
> to exercise your own choice as to whether to join the National
> Union of General Workers or not. There is no doubt the position
> of workers in some trades has benefited by the co-operation and
> organisation, and the question whether our employees could be
> benefited by joining the Union is one which each worker alone
> can decide. It is as well, perhaps, for us to remind you that the
> weekly hours of work in our establishment amount to thirty
> seven and a half hours only, during a great portion of the year, as
> compared with a much greater number of hours where a regular
> Union rate of wages is paid, and that extra payment is made by
> us when working hours are longer. We have been, and always
> shall be, ready to meet those of our employees who desire to
> see us in regard to wages, and anyone wishing to approach us
> through a representative we shall be equally pleased. Whether
> our employees join the Union or not, we shall continue to watch
> very carefully the work done by each, and do our utmost to see
> that conscientious labour is recognised.'

Later in July 1919, Leonard Sutton reported that some non-union
members were under pressure from union members to join. He said
that he would interview all non-members and encourage them to join,
but would not compel them to do so. At the end of the month, he
had a further meeting with the union representative, when he said
that in the company's view it was in the best interests of all that they
should join, and they probably would, though much against their
inclinations.

At the end of May 1920, union business was again discussed when
Leonard reported that new union committees had been elected. In the
case of the Clerks' Union the result was fairly satisfactory, but in the case
of the General Workers' Union, all the old members, with the exception
of Mr Barker, had failed to be re-elected. He thought it was all the more
necessary to have three or four others nominated by themselves to make
up the General Committee to bring matters arising from the profit-sharing scheme to their notice.

## Staff outings

Between 1874 and the 1960s, Suttons arranged annual day trips for its staff and their families to various sites on the south coast. The staff were taken to Bournemouth, the Isle of Wight, Portsmouth, Margate, Wembley Exhibition [Empire Exhibition 1924]. Weymouth was considered, but wasn't thought to have enough entertainment for the staff. A special train was hired, and members of staff were given money to spend on their day off.

The annual outing in 1887 was to Portsmouth: '... as it has such exceptional attractions, not only on account of the presence of the Fleet and the opportunity of visiting the Dockyard, but also affording special facilities for Steamboat excursions to the Island and elsewhere. Every man in our employ will not only receive a return ticket for himself, also one for his wife, if married and 5/- to spend on sight seeing and refreshments. Every boy will have a return ticket for himself and 3/6 to spend. Several members [partners] of the firm hope to be able to join the excursion as usual ...' (Baskett's diaries, MERL).

For the annual excursion in 1892, a special train left the station at Reading at 7.15 a.m. arriving at Portsmouth Harbour at 9.38 a.m., returning at 8 p.m. and arriving in Reading at 10.10 p.m. On 29th July 1899, the firm went to Portsmouth and the Isle of Wight. All went well until the return journey, when the train broke down and was unable to restart on an incline. Unfortunately, there was a two-hour wait until a replacement engine arrived. A strong letter was sent to the South Eastern Railway. In June 1902 the partners commemorated the coronation of Edward VII by giving the staff double wages for that week. The announcement was made by pinning up a notice at Reading railway station on the morning of the excursion. A former employee wrote:'Every year, until the First World War, the directors hired a train and the whole firm went to the coast for the day. On the way back to Reading the director would walk up and down the platform looking into the carriages to make sure they weren't drunk. And there were these old boys, full of ale, trying to sit up and look sober.'

Other outings included a trip to the Inventions Exhibition in London on 29th September 1885 for all the staff. Each adult employee was given 3/6d and children 1/6d. On 30th April 1889, all staff were invited to a private lecture and to listen to Edison's Perfected Phonograph. This was held in the Abbey Hall, built by the company for the use of the staff in the 1870s.

On the 17th November 1899, to commemorate the marriage of Martin Hubert Sutton, the company was closed at 12.30 p.m. A special train was engaged by Mr Sutton to take all employees to London, leaving Reading at 2.05 p.m. and arriving at Paddington at 3 p.m. Arrangements

## TO OUR EMPLOYÉS.

# TRIP to the INVENTIONS EXHIBITION

TO COMMEMORATE

## Mr. LEONARD GOODHART SUTTON'S

BECOMING A

## PARTNER IN THE FIRM OF SUTTON & SONS.

This promised Excursion has been deferred until now that the evenings are sufficiently drawing in to enable the Illuminations of the Fountains and Gardens to be thoroughly enjoyed.

The Bulb Trade and preparations for the Seed Season do not admit of the Premises being entirely closed for a day, and probably all our Hands will think it an equally enjoyable plan to **make up their own Parties next week,** and go on **Thursday, Friday, or Saturday,** whichever day they can previously arrange with their respective Heads of Departments, and in this case friends will probably be able to go together.

We therefore announce that special carriages will be reserved for the use of our employés and their relatives, on Thursday, Friday, and Saturday, **October 1st, 2nd and 3rd,** by the **train** leaving **Reading Station** at **9.25 a.m.,** and in the **return train** leaving **Paddington** at **9.15** in the evening.

It will be necessary for the **Parties to be arranged at least one day in advance,** and that Mr. J. P. Jones should have a list of those who propose to go the following morning, not later than 3.0 o'clock the preceding afternoon.

A Ticket, conveying each Passenger to and fro on the Great Western line to Paddington, and on the Underground line from Praed Street to the Exhibition and back, will be supplied to each of our hands. Each married man whose wife is able to accompany him will have another free ticket for her, and will be at liberty to purchase tickets for any relatives—Adults 3/6 each, Children 1/9.

Unmarried men wishing to take one female friend can purchase a ticket for her for 3/6. In addition to the ticket (which includes admission to the Exhibition) each man in our employ will receive 3/6 to spend, and each boy 2/-. **Money and Tickets must be obtained from Mr. J. P. Jones before 3 o'clock the previous afternoon.**

*Sutton & Sons*

We take this opportunity of mentioning that the November Dinner, which was discontinued last year, will not be resumed.

S. & S.

*September 24th, 1885.*

Notice of the organisation of a trip to commemorate Leonard Goodhart Sutton becoming a partner in the firm.

were made with Mr Masekelyne of the Egyptian Hall, Piccadilly, for a special private performance. Employees were given a map, showing the most direct route from Paddington. The Hall doors were open at 6.15 p.m. Entertainment commenced at 6.45 p.m. and closed at 9.15 p.m., which allowed an hour to get back to Paddington, a distance of 2½ miles. Each employee was given a return railway ticket and a ticket for admission to the hall. Programmes were supplied free of charge by the attendants at the hall.

On the 9th November 1904, the company was closed for a holiday to celebrate Martin John Sutton becoming Mayor of Reading, and the following September a garden party was held at Cintra, when all the staff and their wives were invited to have the opportunity of meeting the Mayor and Mayoress.

In June 1906, Mr Phil gave all the employees 5/- to spend on the annual excursion to Portsmouth.

## Education

Martin Hope Sutton and his brother Alfred subsidised local schools: for example, £300 was given to Reading School when it was re-founded in 1869 (Corley, 1994–7). Alfred Sutton School on Wokingham Road, Reading, was named in honour of Alfred for his work over many years with the Schools Board in Reading.

A reading-room as well as a schoolroom was provided at one of the trial grounds for the education of the children of people employed on the company's land, as well as others in the locality. In an article in the *Gardeners' Chronicle & Agricultural Gazette* of 27th November 1852, describing a visit to Suttons' establishment, mention is made of an interesting feature of the company, in that:

> 'They have a library and reading room which adjoins the office
> on the first floor over the front shop. This is furnished with all the
> leading periodicals and standard works on gardening, together with
> Chamber's Works, the monthly volumes and other books belonging
> to the Religious Tract Society. One of the shop men acts as librarian
> and it is open to all men and boys on the establishment'.

In *Suttons' Farm Manual* of 1861, a visit to the company is described from the *Gardeners' Chronicle & Agricultural Gazette* of 9th February 1861 when the reading-room and its facilities are mentioned with the addition of history and travel books and daily newspapers.

> 'These are available at meal times and every evening after business
> hours. On application to the librarian, books can be borrowed
> to read at home. One evening recently a friendly soiree was well

THE ROYAL

## Seed Establishment.

THE FIRM have the pleasure to announce to their
Employés that they have secured the services of

# PROFESSOR DOUGLAS ARCHIBALD,

M.A,, F.R. Met. S.,

FOR A

### PRIVATE LECTURE AND EXHIBITION

OF

## Edison's Perfected Phonograph,

THE GREATEST MARVEL OF SCIENCE,

*On* TUESDAY EVENING, *APRIL 30th, 1889,*

### AT EIGHT O'CLOCK.

Illustrations by an original series of Photographic Slides with
Oxy-hydrogen Lantern and Accoustical Experiments,

TOGETHER WITH

**Loud Reproductions by the ONLY Perfected Phonograph
available for exhibition in this Country
(lent by Colonel GOURAUD),**

The LECTURE will be given in the ABBEY HALL, and
each Employé on application will be presented with a Ticket
for himself and One Friend (whose name must be given), but
all such Tickets are **non-transferable.**

N.B.—Messrs. SUTTON had this Lecture in contemplation before any
similar Entertainment in the Town had been thought of.

P.T.O.

Notice of a private lecture
and exhibition arranged
by Suttons on Edison's
Perfected Phonograph in
the Abbey Hall in 1889.

# PART I.

SOUND, in relation to the Phonograph — character of vibrations—Mode of propagation. Music—periodic ; Noise—irregular ; Speech—mixed. Königs Manometric flames. Ditto Sensitive flames. Pitch — Intensity — Quality—the complete record and reproduction, by the Phonograph. The Human Ear ; its analogy to the Phonograph.

The Phonograph of 1878. History of the Invention. Explanation of its principles.

The perfected Phonograph of 1888. History and details of machine. Improvements on old one. Manner of working it. Uses and applications. Development.

——◆——

# PART II.

Exhibition of Records from Colonel GOURAUD's Library of voices and music, including selections, among others, from the following :—

### PHONOGRAM RECORDS. (LOUD.)

1. AMERICAN BRASS VILLAGE BAND.
2. ENGLISH STREET BRASS BAND, "May Bloom," "Right Away," "Dorothy," "God Save the Queen."
3. COACH HORN CALLS } by MR. A. GOFF.
4. POST HORN  ...  ... }
5. CORNET SOLOS, "Mikado."
6. MISCELLANEOUS SPEECH, ETC. (Made on the Stage).

### LOW RECORDS.

1. TRIO (Cornet, Violin, and Piano), American.
2. PIANO SOLO, "Helvetia Waltz," and improvizations by MR. CHAS. R. C. STEYTLER.
   Piano Solo by MR. ALFRED LEE.
3. DUETS, Cornet and Piano, Banjo and Piano.
4. BANJO SOLOS.
5. COMIC SONG, in the English, French, German, Dutch, Hebrew, and Greek languages.
6. VOCAL QUARTETTE.
7. VOCAL SOLOS, "The Friars," by MR. PYAT.
   ,,     ,,    "Sewing, Sewing," by MR. BUSHELL (America).
8. MISCELLANEOUS, SPEECH, SONG, LAUGH, CRY, WHISTLING, and COUGH, etc.

### DUPLICATE.

9. { 1. Mr. EDISON's Phonogram to Colonel GOURAUD.
   { 2. Colonel GOURAUD's Phonogram to Mr. EDISON.
   { 3. Mr. GLADSTONE's Phonogram to Mr. EDISON.

Page two of the notice – the programme.

*attended by about 50 young men and clerks, shop men, warehouse-
men etc who spent a social evening with the principals of the company. Let us hope that such a consideration for the improvement of
those employed in this company may everywhere be imitated'.*

## Recreation

Recreational activities were encouraged, and facilities were provided or
funded. These included bowls, cricket, football, angling, lawn tennis,
natural science, photography and cycling.

On the 8th June 1880, the Royal Berkshire Seed Establishment
Angling Association was founded, and in 1889 the club was renamed the
Royal Seed Establishment Angling Association. This was the first section
to be formed: Martin Hope Sutton was asked to be the president and
the other partners to be vice-presidents, Mr Squire was elected secretary
and a committee was formed consisting of Messrs J Adey, J Brown, B J
Bryant, T Caudwell, G T Chandler, H D Jones and J H Millard.

| | |
|---|---|
| The vice-presidents (Alfred Sutton, Herbert Sutton, Martin John Sutton and Arthur Sutton) subscribed a guinea each | £4.4.0 |
| Martin John Sutton purchased and presented a punt costing | £9. 0.0 |
| Arthur Sutton gave prize money to the value of | £4. 1.0 |
| Members' subscriptions | £4.11.0 |
| Total | £21.16.0 |

Records of the heaviest fish caught in the first season: pike 6 lb 11
oz; perch 2 lb 7 oz; roach 1 lb 3oz; barbel 2 lb 10oz; chub 2 lb 4 oz. On
the 29th March 1881, Martin John Sutton offered to purchase another
boat to be used in the river at Caversham, and on the 24th May 1881 an
amendment was made to the Association's rules that the boats were to be
cleaned and housed immediately after the 30th November until the following June. A sum of one guinea was donated to the Reading Angling
Association. On the 29th September 1883, a fishing excursion was
organized by Arthur Sutton and Herbert Sutton to Streatley-on-Thames.
Seventy members boarded the 11.28 a.m. train from Reading to Goring
and crossed the bridge over the Thames to Streatley. In spite of continuous rain in the afternoon, a considerable number of fish were caught. At
7 p.m. the party moved to the Bull at Streatley, where a substantial tea
was provided; after this, all boarded the 8.41 p.m. train to Reading.

The 29th June 1891 is the first record of a cricket match, with an
invitation from Arthur Sutton to the cricketers and the Angling Club

for an excursion to Goring. The cricket team was to play against a local team in the recreation ground, while tennis could be played at Nunsacre, where the gardens would be open to the staff. Unfortunately some of the younger element must have drunk too much at the local pub, as correspondence survives in which the Secretary of the club wrote an apologetic letter to Mr and Mrs Sutton, and they sent back a very tactful reply.

Suttons Cricket Team pre-1914.

The Suttons opened their homes to their employees. Arthur Warwick Sutton invited staff to his home at Bucklebury. The tennis club was in existence before 20th September 1905, when it was invited to Bucklebury, and the hockey club had its first official game there on 27th September 1905.

Following a decision to form a Cricket Club, this notice was posted on 16th January 1906: 'The following have consented to act as Secretary and Committee pro tem to arrange matches and get the ground in proper condition etc. Mr Phil Sutton, Allum, Austin, Barrett, Bennett, Bowery, Hawes and Guy (Secretary). All those wishing to join the club will be invited to a general meeting towards the end of April, for the purpose of electing officers, passing rules and any other business.' (Baskett's diaries, MERL).

A notice of 12th February 1906 stated: 'As we understand there are now a good many of our employees who would like to have clubs for cricket, tennis, bowling, football and hockey, we have decided to take advantage of an offer from Mr Leonard Sutton of a lease of the Cintra Grounds for these games for the use of members in the summer evenings and on half days. We propose to call a meeting of all those who wish to join a SUTTONS RECREATION CLUB for the purpose of making rules and enrolling members.'

The Tug of War team in action at Sutton's Sports Ground at 'Cintra' c.1909.

Sutton's football team 1913/14. Mr L G Sutton seated in centre.

The partners with members of Sutton's Recreation Club c.1911.

This was followed up with the calling of a general meeting of the above Club in the Abbey Hall at 5 o'clock on Tuesday 11th April.

In the first annual report of the full Recreation Club dated 1906, the club had 345 members with an expenditure of £216.17.6d. An incident referred to in 1906 concerns the cycling section: 'A group en route to Oxford were approaching the village of Moulsford, when a slight accident occurred. One of the group received a burst tyre which caused a very loud report. The riders were bunched well together and in the commotion, two of the party were thrown to the ground and others riding close behind rode over them, and one was precipitated into some railings. Unfortunately this contretemps necessitated three of them returning to Reading by train, taking the resultant wreckage with them. Eventually the others reached Oxford and after partaking of refreshments a visit was paid to Christchurch College and other places of interest. Tea followed and in the early evening the cyclists made a start for Reading arriving home about 10 p.m.'

Also mentioned is a somewhat humorous comment concerning the collapse of the hockey section, which read: 'It has been said that all that is the matter with the poor is their poverty'(MERL).

By 1911 the membership was about the same with an expenditure of £322.12.1d. The activities and facilities then available included an air-rifle section, angling, bowls, cricket (two teams), football, hockey, horticulture, lawn tennis, photography, natural science and cycling. An extract from the 1911 annual report reads: 'The intense heat of the past summer, coupled with the absence of rain and the consequent dusty roads, made cycling out of the question as an enjoyable recreation, whilst the dried-up state of the herbage was very uninviting from a botanist's point of view.'

Suttons had an active Ex-Servicemen's Association established in 1927. They held their annual outings in April or May. In April 1949,

Sutton's ex-servicemen's outing, 1949.

three coaches took 175 members to the Charlton Athletic versus Everton match and on to the West End of London, followed by a theatre show. Members also had an annual dinner, usually in November.

The first meeting of the archery section was held at the Cintra grounds on the 6th May 1949. H C Pinker of the Wages Department was chairman, and the club was organized by Arthur Cumming, with J Hawes, an archery expert from the Harrow Bowmen, giving demonstrations of modern archery.

Suttons' Autumn Horticultural Show was held every year, and was always very well supported. Until 1954, it was held at Cintra with cricket, bowls and tennis matches also arranged for the same day, and was a most popular occasion. From 1955, it was held on the firm's premises as an indoor event.

The deeds of Suttons' recreation grounds at Cintra were presented to the Mayor of Reading, Councillor A E Smith (owner of Smith's Coaches), by Leonard Noel Sutton. The grounds had been owned by the Sutton family since about 1857. However, the late Leonard Goodhart Sutton bequeathed in his will that, in 25 years from his death, the grounds should be handed to Reading Borough Council for the benefit of the people in the area. A year or two before this, in 1955, the company had another bowling green and pavilion constructed at its main trial grounds at Earley, together with grass and hard tennis courts.

New green, constructed at the trial grounds for Sutton's bowls club, 1955.

After the move to Torquay in 1976, only the bowls club remained with many retired pensioners continuing to play at a new site in Chalfont Way in Lower Earley. This land was provided by Wokingham District Council as compensation after the A329(M) was built over the old green.

### Charity/Famine Relief

Suttons' benevolence spread far beyond its own employees. Martin
Hope Sutton was a practising Christian, worshipping at Greyfriars
Church, and in his youth he had been a Sunday-school teacher. He gave
money and support to a number of charitable works, including the
British and Foreign Bible Society, the Church Missionary Society and
the YMCA. In 1845 he gave 5% of his personal income to charitable
works; this rose to 15% in 1857 and 20% in 1868. In 1871 alone, he
gave away £2,800.

In later years, Phil Sutton was also a supporter of the British and
Foreign Bible Society, and his business secretary Mr Cairns was also
involved in the administration. At Suttons' premises in the Market
Place, a two-wheeled covered handcart with display stands was stored
in the warehouse, and every Saturday morning an employee was
detailed to wheel it in to the Market Place where Reading's weekly
market was held. Members of the Bible Society would then sell religious books and tracts from this colporteur. At the end of the day, the
cart would be returned to Suttons for storage.

Suttons was also able to help the poor and the hungry by making
charitable use of its own seed stocks. The following is an extract from
Suttons' *Farm Seed List & Agriculturalists' Manual* for 1858:

> 'Seeds Supplied For Cottagers, Reformatory and Other Public
> Benevolent Institutions
>
> 'It has been our practice for some years to send gratuitously to
> Ireland, to the Highlands of Scotland, and to certain Industrial
> Institutions in England such parcels of seeds as we happen to pos-
> sess in abundance, which has doubtless been the means of much
> good to the recipients, while it has entailed but little loss to us; for
> we always commence the following season with an entirely fresh
> stock of seeds (with the exception of a very few kinds which are
> equally good for the second year); and as it is impossible to grow or
> provide exactly the quantity of each kind of seed required for one
> year's sale, we should by carrying out our rule of selling new seeds
> only, be obliged to sacrifice numerous small quantities did we not
> make the use of them alluded to above.'
>
> 'It is gratifying to observe from time to time in the published
> reports of such institutions, that the seeds we have sent out have
> proved very useful.'

The following is from the *Annual Report*, pages 6 and 7, of Mr
Donald Ross of Oswald Street, Glasgow, who has devoted his time and
energies to the relief of the distressed crofters of the West Highlands of
Scotland:

'*In August last, having business to transact in one of the Islands, we availed ourselves of an opportunity of making extensive sojourn among the people. Having a quantity of nets, lines, ropes, salt, clothing, books, &c., for distribution, we placed the whole carefully on board a little vessel used by us in conveying meal &c., to the Islands, and then sailed for the Hebrides. The misery in which the people who have no land, and no boats or nets, exist can scarcely be credited: the children are in rags and indeed not a few were but very scantily supplied even with rags.*'

'*We visited a large number of their houses early in the mornings, and had the most ample proof of their greatest wretchedness. In dozens of houses there was not a bit of bread, and no meal. After consultation with two gentlemen in the neighbourhood, we gave nets to the most needy and deserving heads of families. In the spring of this year we sent upwards of three hundred bags of excellent seed corn to the poorest of the crofters in the Islands; and also one hundred and eighty bags of potatoes, besides a quantity (ten bags) of potatoes received from Messrs Suttons & Sons the well known seed merchants in Reading, Berkshire. Both seed corn and potatoes proved remarkably well. Messrs Sutton also forwarded a large quantity of onion, carrot, turnip and cabbage seed, for the use of the small crofters; the turnip and carrot seed yielded rich crops, and the onions, on soil well cleaned and manured, produced a fair bulk: the cabbage did not yield so well, but the soil was not in good order for its reception. It is a new era in the history of the islanders to raise carrots and onions, but we trust they will derive from this cultivation. The people are under large obligations of kindness and gratitude to Messrs Suttons for these precious gifts. We have still to lament the appearance of the potato disease in the Highlands; but in other respects there is a marked improvement. The crofters pay far more attention to farming, they cultivate their lands earlier and better; they raise cabbages, carrots, turnips & onions in their gardens, they pay more attention to education, so that, within the last six years, more have learned to read English during that period, than they did during the thirty years prior to 1850.*'

The following is from the *Report of the Industrial Schools at Bonmahon* in connection with the Irish Church Missions Society, through which Suttons had donated seeds to other schools helped by this society in previous years.

'Agricultural Teacher's Report

'*Rev, Sir – In submitting the following Report of the Agricultural School Farm, I beg to state for the information of those who take an interest in the Schools and have not yet had an opportunity of visiting Bonmahon, that the Farm is situated on the cliffs, exposed to the sea blast; and in no way best adapted for a regular course of cropping. Knowing by experience, that on the quality of the seeds in a very great degree depends the amount of produce to be realised, I feel much pleasure in bearing my testimony to the quality and purity of the seeds I had from Messrs Suttons of Reading. Their turnip seed in particular I found much superior to that I had from an Irish grower. I have tried two descriptions in the same field, and gave each the same treatment. The Irish seed gave at first a strong coarse plant, and I expected a right good crop, but I was disappointed, for it turned out poorly. The bulbs did not form well and there was too much stalk and they were of a woody and stringy nature. Messrs Suttons did not look so strong at first, but were of a healthy appearance and finally turned out remarkably well, the bulbs were of good size and did not run into stalk, and were not stringy as the other. The Mangel Wurzel and cabbage seed supplied by Suttons also held their superiority.'*

The following is the Suttons' comment on their philanthropic activities. 'The above particulars are re-published here with the hope of extending more generally the practice of providing Cottagers and others with seed and land to cultivate. The seeds we send free of charge are necessarily delayed until the selling season is somewhat advanced, that we may know what we have to spare, but should any clergymen, or the Governors of Reformatories &c., wish to purchase seeds in large quantities for similar purposes, we shall be happy to supply them at a comparatively small cost, without regard to the ordinary selling prices. '

Martin Hope also set up a committee to collect spring corn and other seeds from similar like-minded people in 1870 to help alleviate the food production problems caused by the Franco-Prussian War, 'to enable the peasant farmers of France to sow their land and save their next harvest, thus averting an otherwise inevitable famine'.

A 3-day auction of items donated by companies and landowners was held at the Reading cattle market to raise funds for the French and Belgian farmers who had been affected by the 1914–18 war. This auction was arranged by Leonard Goodhart Sutton, Mayor of Reading and a director of the company, and Martin Hubert Sutton, also a director and chairman of the executive committee organising relief for French and Belgian farmers. £3,000 was raised and passed on to these farmers.

The minutes of the directors' meetings are full of examples of Suttons making donations to outside organisations. For example on 14th April 1937, it was decided to give the sum of 1,000 guineas to the Berkshire Hospital Centenary Extension Fund, to be paid in seven equal yearly payments of £150, and to sign an agreement to contribute this annual sum for seven years in order to enable the hospital to obtain the benefit of refund of income tax.

# 13. Personal Accounts of Life at Suttons

One of the best ways of gaining an insight into the inner workings of a company is not to look at the carefully recorded company minutes, but rather to hear first-hand accounts from people who were involved in the company on a day-to-day basis.

## J H Millard: extracts from his diaries 1866–1874

J H Millard joined the company in 1860. His diaries are held in the Museum of English Rural Life, University of Reading, and cover the period from 1866 to 1874. They mostly contain mundane information on the trials of grasses, mangolds, swedes and turnips for the agricultural trade. He was very much involved in the selection for seed crops and produce for the many agricultural exhibits which Suttons staged each year, all over the country, and would often travel with one of the Suttons partners. He attended many of these shows and, with his specialist knowledge, was able to secure many orders. He was also heavily involved in the production of the farm seed catalogue. From 1870 to 1874 the diaries contain more detailed information on his daily work at the company and also snippets of his private life.

He obviously held a very responsible job at the company; this is reflected in his annual salary, which in the early 1870's was £200. This had increased to:–

| 1879/80 | 1880/81 | 1881/82 | 1882/3 | 1883/4 | 1884/5 |
|---------|---------|---------|--------|--------|--------|
| £950 | £1,000 | £1,000 | £1,000 | £1,100 | £1,100 |

Sometime in 1886 he made a request to the partners, that in view of his importance in the company structure he might be considered to be made a partner. Unfortunately this was refused and he left, and with a friend set up a rival business marketing agricultural seed. Sadly after three years they were faced with bankruptcy. Abstracts from his diaries are given in different chapters throughout this book.

## H R Baskett: extracts from his diaries 1895–1928

H R Baskett joined Sutton and Sons in 1895. He was a statistician and worked directly with the partners of the company on sales. His diaries are held in the Museum of English Rural Life, University of Reading. He recorded the day-to-day details of the company, the partners and their families, the staff and national and international events that affected the life of the company and its employees. Abstracts from his diaries are given in different chapters throughout this book, and are recounted in his own words and the words of Suttons' official notices.

### When We Were Boys Together (Reminiscences of Nearly Sixty Years Ago by a Reading Man in Australia)

*G.C.J., Summer Hill, New South Wales. August 9th 1908*

The paragraph in the *Standard* of June 27th, referring to Mr William Deane's retirement from a long and honourable service with Sutton & Sons, brings vividly to my mind a number of persons and happenings of long ago, when Mr Deane and the writer were boys together at the old-established seed shop in Reading's Market Place. In those days the title of the shop was John Sutton and Sons, old Mr Sutton, the founder of the firm, being then in the land of the living, though, practically, Messrs. Martin Hope Sutton and Alfred Sutton ran the business.

It would be an easy matter for me to name everyone of the employees at that period, but I will name a few only, as required in this narration, and that is chiefly about the boys employed, of whom I can remember Rose, Ballard, Pearce, Deadman and another to be named presently. Rose was an old boy, and left soon after my entry into the service, then came Ballard and Pearce, both Crown Street schoolboys, as I was also, and both my seniors in point of age. Then came another boy, and coming as he did from the Blue Coat School as an apprentice to the firm there was quite a flutter amongst us, because in those days a Blue Coat boy was not only envied, but a very much admired person by less fortunate lads. How well I remember their smart and natty appearance as they marched two by two, every Sunday morning to old St Lawrence's Church; and even at this distant period they remain photographed, as it were, in my mind's eye. All looking strong and healthy, clean, warm and comfortable, which many a poor boy in those days was not. True, many of St Lawrence's boys were clad in semi-charitable uniform suits provided by the school authorities, partly from penny contributions by the scholars and partly from donations by superintendents, teachers and other good friends. The garments were warm and comfortable, and a Godsend to many a poor boy, yet despised by the parents of others as being 'charity clothes'. Yet these hyper-sensitive people were only too glad to see their boys clothed in the quaint garments of the Blue Coat School, for which they paid nothing at all. All the same every boy worth his salt thought it the finest thing out to be a Blue Coat boy, and parents with any sense eagerly sought to have their boys entered as scholars in the famous school, then at the corner of London Road and Silver Street. There was no degradation in a long blue, frock like garment, corduroy breeches, yellow stockings and low shoes; to wear linen bands hanging from their necks as the parsons wore theirs; and flat caps that would not stay on their heads, even if they attempted to wear them; which they rarely did.

This new boy's name was William Deane, and I never knew a boy I had quite the same regard for as I had for the ex-Blue Coat boy, who hailed from Sonning, and despite the passing of 58 years, I see him now just as he appeared when he came among us in a short blue waist jacket, grey trousers, and a peculiar kind of cloth cap, much in vogue with boys in the early fifties [1850s].

He was my senior by a year or two, but he never put on airs or domineered, as old boys are apt to do; on the contrary, he was always kind, amiable, helpful; thoughtful too, when others were frivolous and flippant. Being an apprentice, the new boy was a cut above the rest of us; which however made no difference; he was always a good fellow – sort of Social Democrat, or, at any rate a good Radical, as I think most of us boys were in those days. And what games we had! Quiet games of course, but none the less hearty and amusing, and sometimes, I fear, we sorely tried the patience of Mr. Martin (Sutton) and Mr Alfred (Sutton) not to mention the lesser lights as Messrs Stewart and Messenger, the shopmen. It was during the winter evenings that we used to play up. The busy season being on, we were kept on later than usual sending out catalogues, etc; we were all in a bunch, one folding, another addressing, another sticking on stamps, and so on. Ballard was a dry, comical fellow, and would say something funny to set us laughing, and that was my weakness. Anyhow it caused trouble, and I was considered the chief offender. On the whole we were good boys, and in the daytime gave little trouble; we were each one separately employed, in the shop, warehouse, or nursery – and woe to the boy who attempted to play pranks within sight or hearing of either Mr Leaver (the late Henry Leaver) or Mr Rivers, foreman of the Forbury Nursery.

Now, after a lifetime of loyal and honourable service to a world-famed firm, the friend of my boyhood retires upon his laurels and a well-earned pension [he retired on half-pay]; and none is better pleased than myself to learn that his worth was so highly esteemed by his employers. Seas and oceans divide us, and 13,000 miles of ocean voyaging is no joke when one is in his seventies, yet I trust my old friend, in his leisured dignity, will sometimes think of the other old boy down under who, while his friend has been assisting to build up a great firm, has been doing a little bit towards building up a 'newer Britain in another world', as a famous Australian once said.

Be that as it may, it is my hope that the Blue Coat boy of over half a century ago, now a handsome, elderly gentleman, I'm sure, will live for many a long day in ease and comfort, and keep a correspondence commenced a few years ago. In these days of fast mail boats and penny postage (from one end at least), two old friends may talk to each other by proxy (the useful 'drop of ink'), even though we may never meet in person.

Old Reading is still very dear to me, though 50 years an Australian; and the Standard's fine illustrations give me a world of pleasure, while my Australian friends take an interest in such an ancient town, and express surprise at the excellence of its newspapers. That being so, I hope to keep in touch with the old town for the remaining years of my life: and to hear from time to time from those I esteem, not the least of whom is William Deane (see box on indentures in Chapter 3 'The Reading Years').

## Harry Jermey

To look after the Market Place premises in 1920 during both night and day, there were three uniformed fireman, Messrs Ryan, Palmer and Chandler, who all lived in houses owned by the firm in Abbey Square. The first two were soon to retire, to leave Harry Chandler to hold the fort with various non-uniformed staff who already worked in the seed rooms. During the summer all the hose was collected from various departments, to be taken out to the yard and tested under pressure, and nobody was more careful than Harry. Each piece of hose was marked with an indelible pencil to indicate which department it was to be returned to, and all that for the Potato Department was boldly marked with a T. When questioned if we had the right hose, Harry indignantly replied 'Certainly it is: this is the Tater Department!'

1942 saw me making my first journey to Scotland for planting, rogueing and lifting potato crops, and each year after that I made three journeys north. The October/November journey also covered the lifting and boxing for export to South Africa of anything up to 800 tons of the variety Up To Date. Our agents in South Africa were Messrs E J Amm & Sons of Johannesburg. I had the pleasure of meeting members of the family on several occasions when they visited Reading. They were most excellent business associates and people of great integrity.

The small stream which passed through the centre of the trial grounds in a westerly to easterly direction is the overflow from Whiteknights Lake. For many years it was an open ditch some 5 feet wide and about the same in depth, with grass banks which needed to be cut. On one particular occasion a marvellous character known as Tom was assigned to this work. Unfortunately he had a slight stutter, and was not to know the new man sent by the foreman to help him had an identical impediment.

In a very short time, Tom thinks he is being mimicked, and the new man has a punch on the jaw and is in the bottom of the ditch! It was however quickly sorted out, and they worked together for many years.

The Potato Department must have been the last office to have a female typist, purely by reason that the general atmosphere of the department was always thought to be not quite right for ladies: this would be about 1938. Miss Riddles arrived from the Correspondence Office and in due course she was asking me why some of the staff had nicknamed her Jimmy. After a long time and much pressure from her, I gave the reason and lo and behold I was in the dog-house.

As the war progressed and labour was difficult to secure, we had to turn to prisoners of war. The Italians arrived first and did not last very long, then the German POWs arrived and no fault could be found in their ability to work. However it was discovered they were making men's and women's slippers at the camp in the evenings and bringing them in to sell to staff. We then found our sack– and bag-tying string and cord was being cleverly woven to make uppers and soles, and afterwards being dyed to various colours. This had to stop. Miss Riddles became friendly with one of the Germans, and at the end of the war they were married.

An event which only lasted for a short time after I joined the firm in 1920 was the annual dinner of the Recreation Club held in the Abbey Hall at the end of November or early December, when various sporting and horticultural cups were presented. This affair was about the only one, apart from the heads of department function, when intoxicating liquor was available. On the stage to entertain were members of staff: Charlie Owen (piano), Freddy Boucher (violin), Denny Tompkins (violin), and his brother on the cello, and at the first function I attended was a magician and his lady assistant specially brought from London. The next year we had to be content with sketches by Charlie Cheer (ledger office) and Charlie Owen (cashiers), and comic songs rendered by Percy Spong (electrician). For many years, Percy entertained at functions all over the town and the immediate area. He was on one occasion engaged for the annual dinner of the Reading Bowling Club, and during the rendering of the famous song 'My Word You Do Look Queer', the president of the club died as he sat listening to it. Reg Bryant was the Secretary of the Recreation Club, and the most difficult part of the job was collecting the annual subscription of 5/- for adults and 2/6 for juniors.

The Recreation Club also put on a great sports afternoon in the summer in conjunction with the Horticultural Show. The sporting arena at Cintra was all correctly marked out under the supervision of Taffy Lovegrove (Grass Dept), who was an official at the Reading Athletic Club. The events included all the usual races of 100, 200, 440 yards, half-mile and mile, plus tilting the bucket, inter-departmental tug of war and all children's races.

### Jane Sutton: Memories

**My father's stories**

When my father was small, he was often taken into the Forbury gardens where he gazed up at the lion on its plinth, high above his head. He was therefore very disappointed when he went to the zoo and saw such a small lion in a cage! [The Maiwand Lion is a huge statue commemorating the Afghan war of 1879/80, and the men of the Royal Berkshire regiment who died in the campaign].

During the Second World War, it was not unusual for my father to go for lunch at the Great Western Hotel, the white building near the station which still stands today. One day, he had artificial flowers in a vase on his table. He called the waiter and asked him 'When Mr Palmer comes here for lunch, do you give him imitation biscuits to eat?' 'No, Sir' was the quick reply – and the vase was whipped away!

**The trial grounds**

It was always a pleasure to visit the trial grounds when I was a child, with its rows of brightly-coloured flowers, the wonderful conservatory with gloxinias and other pot plants, a blaze of colour. A visit to Slough trial grounds also meant meeting Mr Balfour and to see his plant-breeding work, especially of *Digitalis* with flowerets all around the stem.

When I was four or five years old, it was a treat to see the huge carthorses at both trial grounds. Joe stands out in my memory as the horse who kept the others awake at night! In Reading, I was allowed to ride on the back of a horse as it trod carefully between rows of plants as the weeds were hoed out. Along the adjacent railway line, the great green Great Western Railway engines and their cream and brown livery coaches rushed by.

**The Market Place office**

My father's office was the centre of our visits to Reading, whether on a shopping spree or *en route* to boarding school. During the Second World War and late into the 40s, travel was mostly by train and hence the necessity to start from Reading station. A visit to the sundries department to collect things for the new term was a treat. This contained a treasure trove of pencils, rubbers, paper clips etc! Going through the wooden passages, passing iron-wheeled barrows being pushed with sacks of seed on them with their characteristic noise and smell, is so memorable. And then after an evening out in London, there was the eerie atmosphere of the garage as we came to collect our parked car late at night.

When I was in my teens, I spent several days in different departments, for example the seed-testing lab and notably with Mr Naylor in the soil-testing lab. These were valuable insights that helped me later at university.

### Out and about

It was a privilege to travel with my father to visit golf courses. A visit to Gleneagles was amazing for a teenager, as was Rapallo (Northern Italy) just after the end of the war. On this second visit we had Mr Lovegrove with us, who was a specialist on grasses and turf maintenance.

In the autumn, we often went up to the east coast of Scotland to check the quality of the seed potato crop.

Then there was the Royal Show which in those days moved around the country. It was a great experience seeing the cattle, horses and other events.

The spring, of course, meant a visit to the Chelsea Flower Show, and the pride with which I looked at the inevitable gold medals placed in front of Suttons' displays! When I was at college in London and had digs near the Royal Hospital, I would bicycle to the show-ground on the Saturday morning as the stand was being dismantled, and be given a huge bunch of flowers to take back to my room.

### Trying it out!

Sometimes my father would bring home a vegetable or some fruit from the trial grounds. Potatoes were his speciality, and I especially remember my first taste of the small purple, salad potato Pink Fir Apple. And then if seeds were needed, we were quite happy to eat the melon around them!

### Underwood Mission Hall

In the early 1930s, Whitley estate was being developed. My mother and father saw an area set aside for a bowling green behind the Community Hall. They asked if it could be given to them to build a church, which they considered was more important. It was opened in 1937, and has since been enlarged twice and is still a thriving church. My father was the chairman of the Trustees for the rest of his life, right up to his final illness in 1963.

### Prayers

Board meetings always started with prayer as Suttons sought to be a Christian company. Each day there was a time for voluntary morning prayers, for which the electric bell rang out through the old building. A different minister came in from the churches in town each day. My father led Monday mornings, and I can remember attending occasionally. When my father died, Daphne Sutton received a kind letter from the man who was responsible for organising the prayers, then of course at the new trial ground site.

## John Cox

John Cox worked at Suttons from 1931 to 1976. He started as an office boy, and finished as company secretary. The following pieces are his memories of the company, and how it worked.

### Reading Market Place: Sutton's Seed Shop

The Victorian Gothic stone-faced premises with prominent words ROYAL SEED ESTABLISHMENT – SUTTONS SEEDS, letters carved and heightened in gold, was impressive, and was intended so. It had two shop windows but no goods were displayed, merely an interior screened with meshed curtains. The double entrance doors, made of seven feet high or so plate glass with elaborate large brass handles, were guarded by a member of the 'Corps of Commissionaires', one Sgt. Kelly, ex-Irish Guardsman, tall, slim and dressed in a tailor-made navy-blue uniform and a pill-box hat with the initials S & S in gold braid on the peak and on the jacket lapels.

His duties were clearly defined: to disperse any boys who might loiter in front of our premises, to salute with a great flourish each of the Suttons' partners upon their arrival for business each morning, and at the same instant to grasp with his left hand the handle of the entrance door and open it. In the case of the senior partner, this duty also extended to relieving him of his leather briefcase and with ceremony escorting him to his office door. Certain senior staff were permitted to enter and leave by using the main Market Place entrance (all other staff had to use the warehouse entrances). If one was well regarded by the supreme guardian, the commissionaire, one might receive a salute, a certain confirmation that one's status within the company was assured. This privilege was jealously guarded and enforced. In addition, the use of the special toilet was available to those senior staff who were issued with a personal numbered key.

On Saturday mornings, market day in Reading, he oversaw the correct position for the British and Foreign Bible Society's colporteur stand in the Market Place, the stand on wheels having been stored in Suttons' warehouse during the previous week. Should customers wish to buy seeds or obtain horticultural advice, he would be expected to open the door into the shop area: the customer would firstly have to skirt around the huge coke-fired heater, then looking up, a little awe-inspired, see the dark mahogany counters with perhaps a bowl of sweet peas or a container of blue trumpet gloxinias from the glasshouses. Behind the counters were rows of small drawers, each with a ring handle, and labelled with a different variety of vegetable or flower seed, and smartly-dressed, black-suited assistants, often with a flower in the buttonhole in their lapel. In a small annexe at the rear of the shop was a boy dressed in a blue uniform, whose duties each morning included cleaning the brass door handles and the company's registered name plate, stoking the fire heater with buckets of coke obtained from the stack in the yard, and most importantly running to the seed warehouse for the seed of species or cultivars that were not available in the shop drawers, so that customers were not delayed. All would be carried out with quietness and decorum, as would be expected in the 'Are you being served' atmosphere of the Royal Seed Establishment.

As may be appreciated, with so much of the old building being fitted out in wood, the fire risk was such that the 'No Smoking' rule had to be strictly enforced. Similarly, as the Sutton family supported the Bible Society and overseas missionary work, and was upright in its civic responsibilities, no intoxicating drinks were allowed on the premises. That is with one exception, though how that situation had arisen is unknown.

It had become the custom for many farmers to take twelve months to pay their seed account. When ordering their current seed requirements of say grass seed, mangolds etc., certain local farmers would bring their cheques for the amount owing to the Market Place and, with a wink and a nod to Sgt. Kelly, they would be escorted to a small side waiting-room, curtains drawn, away from prying eyes and given a little salute. 'The Chief Cashier will be with you in a minute, Sir'. The company walk-in safe, a brick-built vault like in a bank, with a heavy metal door for safekeeping of ancient records, wages, cash etc was located adjacent to the cashier's office. It was known to few that on a shelf at the rear were bottles of whisky. The glasses and a bottle, hidden under a white serviette, were taken to the waiting-room. With due ceremony, the farmer and the cashier drank a toast to the new year's harvest, the cheque was handed over to cover last year's account, and was duly receipted. The farmer departed to spit hands at the cattle market, and the cashier returned to count his money. Sgt Kelly then rinsed the glasses and put the bottle back in position on the shelf in the safe. It was strange how these bottles emptied so quickly. His step was slightly wayward as he returned to his post, guarding the premises and dreaming of more wealthy farmers coming to pay their debts.

### Male Clerks

Men all wore dark suits, collar and tie. Each had a wooden cupboard near their desks and upon arrival their jackets were taken off, neatly folded inside out and their well-worn office jacket, ink-stained, linings frayed, with elbow patches, put on. If their shirt sleeves were worn or cut down, they put on a pair of false starched wrist cuffs.

### Conversations overheard

To new office boy:

*'Find Mr Hancock, he is the foreman in the vegetable seed room, and bring back a large packet of rail seed.'*

Director to secretary:

*'Don't bother to knock at my door when you want to see me: I leave all my indiscretions at home.'*

### No Smoking on the premises – just take snuff

A certain director enjoyed his cigarette. Mid-morning he would call out to his secretary 'Just going round to see the solicitors' or '...local magistrates court.' Out of his office he would go, bowler hat on, down the main corridor. The commissionaire would salute and open the door. A short walk to the local public gardens, light up the cigarette. Heavenly bliss! By mutual understanding, the director and any member of staff whose duty took him into the town and crossed his path would recognise each other, but stare straight ahead and walk past; such a common-sense business relationship.

The snuff-takers could be recognised by those with a trained eye: they would walk calmly to the selected colleague who was busy shuffling papers at his desk. All of a sudden, both would drop from sight, the snuff-box came out from the waistcoat pocket, the lid was adroitly flicked open, fore-finger and thumb, snuff to the left nostril, snuff to the right, a cough, eyes slightly watery, both would in unison stand up. The visitor would nonchalantly walk back to his own desk, and await a return visit. But the tell-tale sign of a snuff-taker is the surplus snuff spattered on their jackets! And don't forget to tell the office boy: 'Slip out of the back entrance to the King's Road tobacconist for next week's supply of ¼ oz SP snuff (cost 9*d*).'

### Office Juniors: Girls

The first girls employed in the offices were either shorthand typists or office juniors. To preserve their modesty and to deflect the improper glances of the male office staff, it was decreed that they should be issued with overalls. 'Green in colour, long-sleeved, calf-length with cream-coloured cuffs and collars; front buttons held in place by metal slit pins. Two outfits per employee to be changed bi-weekly; laundered by the local laundry company. The girls to visit Messrs Jackson, Kings Road for personal fittings.' In fact at this time, the issue of overalls was probably a Godsend to many who may well have owned but one skirt and a jumper.

### Wages

Only a few senior higher-paid staff had a bank or building society (savings bank) account. The great majority were paid weekly on Fridays in cash.

At this time there was some concern for security, as there had been local robberies in town. The (National) Westminster Bank was but two doors away from the main entrance, but it had an open yard at the rear abutting onto a Suttons building. A pulley with sufficient rope to reach to ground level had been attached to the outside and top of the Suttons building. Every Friday morning, at a pre-arranged time, the chief cashier would lower the pulley. Bank staff would emerge from their rear door, money notes and coin in strong bags would be hooked to the pulley, which was duly hauled in by the cashier. Complete security had been achieved unseen by the outside world.

### Shows

During the summer and autumn, large agricultural shows were held all around the country: Bath and West, the Royal, Royal Counties etc. Suttons had a wooden portable pavilion in which they met farmer customers who were then discreetly entertained in a curtained-off section to light refreshments, Stilton cheese, beer and whisky, all ordered by the show departmental staff from local Reading suppliers. Surplus refreshments were returned to Reading for the next show. Of course it was very difficult to estimate the exact quantity for each show, so that it was prudent to over-order rather than to run out of stock.

However, it seemed to be the duty of certain members of staff to test the quality of the returned cheese and drinks; at a time when the head of department was away, the office would suddenly be empty. Yes, our farmer customers must have the best-quality refreshments as we have the best-quality seeds!

### *Ron Butler*

My earliest memory of working at Suttons is the very cold winter of 1947, my first year, when every day, after cycling five miles through ice and snow I arrived at the office and attempted to thaw out by the tiny gas fire, the only source of heat. In the large office with a lofty ceiling this took some time, but eventually I was able to begin work, sitting at a large high desk, almost Dickensian!!

One of my first jobs was to list and store all the vegetable seed samples as they were taken by the warehouse staff. Then at the appropriate sowing time, I had to assemble each subject and put them in order of variety maturity and, after checking the samples, they were then entered into the trial book, numbered and sent to the trial grounds for sowing. The numbers per subject varied from a dozen or so up to 350–400 for peas each year. Suttons grew their trials of swede and turnip on a farm in the Scottish borders. Once the various samples had been entered into the trial book, they had to be carefully packed into a hamper, together with large wooden labels and various other items. Then two men set off by train for Berwick station to sow the field-scale trials, returning again in the autumn to lift the roots for inspection and to select the finest specimens for seed production work.

An early lesson I was taught was that accuracy in all aspects of the business was more important than speed. Whenever a bag of seed was opened, it must firstly be checked with the label to ensure that the subject, variety and grower's code were as required, and again at the end of every operation to re-check the label details. However, I recall just one occasion when this obviously had not been done carefully enough, because savoy seed had been used instead of Brussels sprout. A storeman had misread Savoy Rearguard for Brussels sprout variety Market Rearguard and, both being brassica, it did not show up from a visual inspection of the seed. Some thousands of packets were filled and sent out to customers, and it was not until the young plants were checked in the trial field that the mistake was noticed. Immediately an emergency plan was put into operation. All members of staff had to abandon their own work for one or two days, so that every one of many tens of thousands of orders could be scrutinised. Every customer who had been sent the incorrect seed was then sent a fresh packet of the true seed, with a covering letter of apology. In addition to this, a half-acre of land at the trial grounds was immediately sown with seed so that plants could also be despatched in time for transplanting. Although it was a costly mistake, the company obtained a great deal of praise and goodwill for the prompt action taken. The storeman who had many years of careful service with the company received a reprimand, and I am sure he was even more careful after that.

In the peak season, January to March, I spent part of each day in the Putting Up Room from where the orders for the market-garden customers were executed. This involved weighing up individual items of vegetable seed for each order, in sizes from ¼ oz to 4 lb in paper packages, gradually working through the whole order which was then carefully checked before despatch. Later, with the advent of foil packaging, most lots were pre-packed at the start of the season.

From the spring through to autumn, I spent a lot of time at the trial grounds recording maturity times and other data in all the trials, and learning to identify the many different varieties. I worked with a number of colourful characters at the trial grounds, men who had spent their lifetime growing trials, going away as members of rogueing gangs, especially for peas in the summer, or selecting fine typical plants for shows. They could always be relied on to make the best of any plant or root, turning it 'best side up' ready for when the directors came to inspect them. I also recorded in the trial books the deliberations of my bosses, and noted any action to be taken in regard to specific lots of seed. Armed with this information, I was then taken out to seed crops and given instruction as to the necessary rogueing, gradually taking over as crop inspector which included visits to the main seed-growing areas of Europe. In England, the chief areas were east Kent and Essex around the Colchester area, where I would spend many weeks a year inspecting the various crops. In fact I got to know the road between Reading and Colchester so well, no motorways in those days, that I used to say I could drive it blindfold, something that almost came to pass on one occasion when the fog was so thick that it took me 6 hours to get home, and no car heaters or windscreen washers, either.

Although we were working for competing companies, we often met up with rogueing gangs from other seed companies and there was a healthy respect between us. Even abroad, we often encountered other members of the English seed trade, and it was reassuring to know that in all the main seed-growing areas there were friends or contacts nearby, as the main agents there often acted for several foreign seed companies. As with all travelling, not all things went smoothly, with the occasional delayed or cancelled plane or train. We once had a hard job persuading the taxi driver to take us to our hotel in Ancona in Italy, only to find when we did arrive that it had been requisitioned as a shelter for local people put out by an earthquake. However, we managed to find lodgings elsewhere and were able to reach our crops, which thankfully were unaffected. My worst occasion was on my very first journey beyond Europe, when I was booked to visit four or five areas of India for our seed company there on a fact-finding mission in 1971. About half-way to Calcutta, we were informed by the captain that war had broken out between India and Pakistan and that our flight would be diverted, with all passengers for India being disembarked at Beirut. After several attempts the next day, I eventually got a flight as far as Bombay but, on arrival there, found utter chaos and no possibility of travelling further. On the best advice, I abandoned my journey and managed to get a plane home. A long weekend away, but not what was planned. I did in fact manage two trips to the sub-continent later, which were very informative and worthwhile.

We were very fortunate in having a thriving recreation club during my early years, with football and cricket teams, as well as tennis and bowls and indoor facilities. Later the company built some superb tennis courts and a bowling green, which was often used for county matches, at the trial grounds at Earley, all of which were a joy to play on. I was also involved with the annual horticultural and craft show, and the competition was quite keen. Mrs Collins became very supportive of this event during her time with the company.

As time passed, I took over the vegetable-seed purchasing department, which involved either growing the required amount of seed or buying from specialist suppliers, also finding the best new varieties for the catalogues each year. Once the company had arrived in Torquay, we had to set up and run a new trial ground. Not only did we check out all seed lots here, but also had a show garden especially for the new varieties. It was at the annual press days that I got to know all the principal garden writers and broadcasters quite well. There are two who will always be remembered with affection for their sincerity and hard work. Firstly Arthur Billett, who built up Clacks Farm single-handedly from an arable field to the mainstay of 'Gardener's World' from the mid-1960s to the early 1980s, and who never varied when asked for the best tomato for the gardener, namely Alicante. Secondly, Geoff Hamilton, who produced so many and varied gardens. We had many long telephone conversations, and I could often see the results of our discussions in the next few programmes of 'Gardener's World'.

Finally I had the privilege of organising and setting up the new trial ground facility at Ipplepen, where all the various trials can easily be seen, and it is a popular spot for holiday visitors in the summer, as well as keen gardeners.

## Gerry Westall

A few recollections passed on to me from some old friends and colleagues at Suttons Seeds.

With such a large staff, there were at least three or four qualified first aid people. One man in particular was 'Dick' Emery who, if you had got something in your eye, would ask you to sit on the chair. He would then open his drawer, take out a match and sharpen it to a fine point. Holding your eyelids apart, with finger and thumb, on seeing the problem, he would gently use the pointed match to remove whatever it was and show it to you and say 'There it is'. Over the years, he must have done this scores of times with no ill-effects.

Arthur Austin was a WWI soldier who lost a leg. He told me after the amputation he was travelling across France on a train full of wounded soldiers and was asleep on a lower bunk. Suddenly he awoke and felt something dripping on to his blanket. Knowing it had been raining he thought there must be a leak in the carriage roof. However after a while he realized it was blood from a wounded soldier on the upper bunk. He immediately called a medical orderly, but often wondered if the man survived.

Another well-known character, I will call him Tom, unfortunately had a rather pronounced stutter. One day I went up to him and said 'Is Bill in today?' to which Tom stuttered 'h-h- hee's g-gorne to the O-O-Orspital.'

'Oh', I said, 'Nothing serious, I hope.'

Tom: 'H-h-hee's g-g-gorne to h-h-have an h-h-hexray.'

To which I replied, 'Has he broken a bone?'

Tom: 'N-n-no, h-h-hee's g-g-gorne to s-s-see if there's a-a-any effing w-w-work l-l-left in him!!!!!'

On reading through the company records, I came across the following two entries:

On the 6th March 1903, a problem arose concerning two employees who had been doing work outside of the firm. One was a ledger clerk, and the other a potato picker. They had been employed in music and chimney-sweeping respectively in their spare time. They were told they must give up either this or our work. The ledger clerk agreed immediately not to do outside work again for money. Whereas the other man said he preferred chimney-sweeping, and left with a week's wages.

It is recorded that on 1st January 1910 one employee who was in Market Place which was overlooked by one of the partners' offices was seen handing what appeared to be a betting slip to a bookie's runner. When questioned, he replied 'It was not a betting slip; I only purchased a raffle ticket.' The partner believed him, but the considerations of the board on the following Monday are not recorded.

## Michael Smallwood: Suttons in India

I started my career in the seed trade with Suttons in April 1956, straight from school. I spent my first two years on the London Road trial grounds, an area of some 75 acres, bounded by the old Great Western Railway and the Southern Railway lines. In the summer, railway passengers would admire the very colourful display of flowers and vegetables.

My first year was spent in the greenhouse complex, in the centre of which was a large central cast-iron pavilion which was used solely for decorative floral displays. This was connected by walkways to a further range of greenhouses. All of this was heated by two monster Robin Hood boilers which had to be stoked with coke 24 hours a day by hand! This required duty men to work shifts until midnight, and then come on again at 6 a.m. The trial grounds manager at this time was Harold Kemp. The glasshouses were under the control of Fred Ilott, a man of short stature with a clipped moustache and wearing a flat cap, with the air of a sergeant-major. He was strict but quite fair in dealing with the staff.

My second year was with the outside staff and the foreman Harold Fowles, who had been with the company since 1924. The glasshouse staff did not have much to do with the outside gang, as they thought themselves somewhat superior! At that time Suttons still used horses on the grounds; I can picture horse-drawn wagons, used mainly for clearing the fields and transporting manure. The real name of the man who led the horses was Bill Murrell, but he was known as 'Baldy', for obvious reasons.

After National Service I returned to Reading in 1959 as a junior boy in the agricultural grass seed department, managed by Gilbert Pitts. The office manager was Tom Joy, who was an amazing character; he sat in the corner of the office, and spent all day on the phone talking to customers, formulating grass mixtures for different prescriptions for various soil conditions, locations and prices, which he did without the aid of a slide-rule or calculator. Occasionally, we were given special mixtures to price, and it took us ages.

One day when I was particularly bored, Mr Noel Sutton sent a message saying he wanted to see me in his office after lunch. I had no idea what it was about, and I had a couple of hours to speculate. I thought perhaps he had noticed our bored expressions as he walked along the corridor. To my surprise and amazement, he asked me what I thought about going to work in India for the company, and he gave me a few days to decide. It did not take long to accept: it released me from the boredom, and at the time a salary of £1,000 a year sounded quite tempting to a 21-year-old in 1960. I was probably getting at the time £300 to £400 p.a. A contract of employment was drawn up in which I was referred to as the 'mercantile assistant'. There cannot have been many such one-sided contracts around at that time: it probably had not been re-written since about 1910, and was a real relic of the colonial days, full of what I should and should not do. I was to work for 4 years without a break or home leave; I was not to marry for the term of the contract; if I left the company, I was not allowed to work in the seed industry for 5 years etc. The only thing that was in favour of the 'mercantile assistant' was the £1,000 per annum.

Nevertheless I signed the contract and took off for Delhi in April 1961 on a BOAC Comet, which promptly broke down at the first stop at Cairo. We had to wait a couple of days while a spare part was flown out from London, and we were put up in the newly-constructed Hilton Hotel. For someone who had been living in lodgings in Reading the

week before, this was really something. We had trips to the Sphinx and
the Pyramids on camels, all at the expense of the airline. Eventually we
arrived at Palam Airport, New Delhi: the heat was unbelievable, as were
the smells and sights; wild dogs, cows free to roam anywhere, beggars
and bicycles.

I should explain there were three other ex-Reading employees work-
ing for Suttons in India: Larry Holmes was based in Calcutta, Maurice
Eymore in Bangalore and John Hodges in Kashmir. Larry was shortly to
return to Reading, John was to take over as manager in Calcutta, and
I was to run the Kashmir operation as Superintendent, Suttons Seeds,
Kashmir.

In the 1960s Kashmir's population was 90% Muslim and 10%
Hindu. The Hindu were mainly the most educated and owned land,
whereas the Muslims were the craftsmen and labourers. This always created a certain amount of conflict and hence today Kashmir state is still a
disputed area, and a source of much unrest between India and Pakistan.
However, we spent many happy evenings in the house of our Hindu land-
lord drinking Kashmiri 'kava' (a green spicy tea), talking with a group of
friends who included Hindus, Muslims, Pathans and Sikhs.

When I arrived in April 1961, I was to work with John Hodges for a
few months learning the trade. Kashmir with its temperate climate was
an ideal place to produce biennial seed crops such as cabbage, carrot,
turnip, kohl rabi etc.

My job was to control the production of quality seeds by the traditional method of rogueing and selection. Every crop in every field had to
be inspected on a number of occasions. Some locals could be quite devi-
ous, so it was quite a challenge. They knew that, if they supplied inferior-
quality seeds, I would not pay for them. All deliveries were sampled and
trialled.

Fresh seed would start to arrive in our warehouse in July. It all had
to be dried, cleaned and packaged immediately. We used Metal Box
tins, which came flat. We had our own reforming machinery and tin-
sealer. Sowing time in the plains began with the monsoon in late July-
August, which meant we had to work 24-hour shifts seven days a week
to get the seeds to the markets throughout the Indian sub-continent.
This frantic rush went on for about eight weeks. Consignments of tins
were packed 50 at a time into wooden boxes, all of which had to be
sealed and banded to avoid contamination. They left the warehouse
on a horse-drawn trailer and were taken to the State Transport Office
to start a 200-mile lorry journey to the nearest railhead, from where
they would go by rail to their final destinations. The first deliveries
were sent off to Calcutta for the retail market: wholesalers and farmers bought the rest of the crop. The whole process from production

through packaging, sales and distribution occupied most of the year. Hard work, but happy memories.

Nearly halfway through my first contract, I was able to obtain permission from Noel Sutton to marry, and in December 1962 Margaret came out and we were married in All Saints Church, Srinigar. Sadly the church was burnt down in anti-British riots in 1967. However, it was made clear that the salary I was being paid was not envisaged as that of a married man, but the company was not prepared to pay me any more.

It is hard to believe that none of the Sutton family had ever visited their Indian operations in over 50 years. In 1966, we were all delighted to receive Mr Douglas Collins, who had purchased a controlling interest in Suttons. Our Kashmiri growers were very impressed with him. Douglas had a great interest in farming, so he easily understood the methods of growing, and was instantly able to relate to our growers. After his visit, we were dealt with far more understandingly from Reading.

Life was never dull: we relied on a daily flight into the valley for mail. In the early 1960s, Dakotas with pre-war technology were the only planes on the Kashmir route. If the weather was bad, there were no flights, sometimes for up to three weeks in the winter. There was no radar, and the planes literally flew between the mountains. One did crash, and was not recovered until the spring when the snow had melted. We also had fairly regular earthquakes, as Kashmir is just off the Hindu Kush fault line. Luckily our house was of mud construction, so happily it just swayed with the earthquake movement; even so it was quite frightening.

We lived on the banks of the Jhelum River protected by a 15-foot-high mud bank. On a number of occasions the water got dangerously near the top: the sound of the swollen river rushing through the trees was quite off-putting. Pakistan was continually sending out infiltrators from across the border, and sometimes gunfire broke out. One fairly serious incident happened very near the house, but we slept through it. We also went through the 1965 Indo-Pakistan war when we were literally trapped in the valley for a few weeks when Margaret was 6 months pregnant!

In the 1960s there were still a few retired Indian Civil Service personnel living in the valley, mainly widows who could not face coming back to England after spending most of their lives in India. There was an English padre, bank manager and a few missionaries working in the hospital and school, and that was it.

It was a time we remember very happily, and I have never regretted accepting Noel Sutton's invitation to work in India. I was fortunate to have worked there for eight years (1961–1969).

# 14. The Suttons

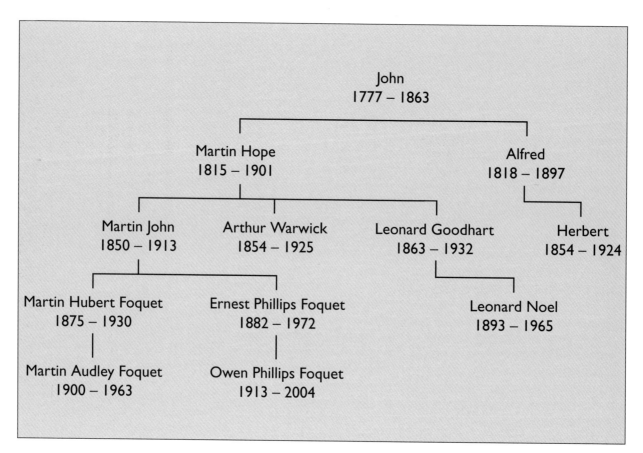

'Family Tree' of the Suttons Partners and Directors.

The Sutton family is perhaps one of the greatest horticultural dynasties of all time. The most remarkable and possibly unique thing about Suttons is the fact that, for well over 150 years, the company and its myriad of departments were run by five generations of the one family. When Owen Sutton retired in 1979, the link between Suttons and the Sutton family was broken.

In order to give the reader an insight into the individual contribution of notable members of the Sutton family to the company and to society, we have included this series of mini-biographies. For completeness, a brief biography of Douglas Collins, who was instrumental in the survival of the company in the 1960s, is included.

MARTIN JOHN SUTTON
(eldest son of Martin Hope Sutton),
Born October 25th, 1850.

MARTIN H. FOQUET
SUTTON (eldest son
of M. J. Sutton),
Born Nov. 28th,
1875.

MARTIN HOPE
SUTTON, Born
March 14th, 1815,
Died October 4th,
1901.

MARTIN A. FOQUET SUTTON,
Born September 1st, 1900.
(Son of M. H. F. Sutton, and great grandson of M. H. Sutton).

### FOUR GENERATIONS.

———

The last portrait taken of the late

# Mr. MARTIN HOPE SUTTON.

Photograph taken in 1901 of the four generations of the Sutton Family.

### John Sutton (1777–1863)

John Sutton was born in London, one of three sons and three daughters of James Sutton (1744–1789). His grandfather, Charles, had been a miller in Newbury. The children were orphaned at a young age, and were brought up by their father's partner in the company of Sutton and Winckworth, flour factors and mealmen. John and his older brother James were apprenticed to the company. At the turn of the eighteenth to the nineteenth century, they left London for Reading to take over their inheritance of a mill on the Kennet. John set up as a corn factor at King Street in 1806. He married Sarah Norris of Shinfield, and they had three sons and three daughters.

The company nearly foundered in 1815 when the Dean, Marsh & Co. Bank went bankrupt (Corley 1991–3). John had a £950 overdraft from the bank, and at the same time a buyer in London defaulted. It was during this catastrophic year that his second son, Martin Hope, was born.

Both John and Sarah suffered from ill-health. As a young man, John had been advised by his doctor in London to take three glasses a day of a fortifying wine. His health deteriorated and, by 1827, he was unable to manage the firm, and Martin Hope was brought in to help in the warehouse and then in the office. Later on, Martin Hope helped his father overcome his addiction by occupying his time in the business.

John Sutton was a proud man and he 'could not believe the humiliating doctrines contained in the Christian religion' of the day. He worshipped at the Unitarian Church until it closed for lack of funds in 1820. Then he attended St Laurence's, where he 'entirely omitted those parts [of the liturgy] where he considered it wrong, though [he was] very particular in repeating audibly as well as fervently praying in those parts which met his views'. He was a free thinker, and did not follow any particular political -isms of the day; 'he was a moderate and quiet whig...' (Corley, 1991–3).

He became a widower in 1834, and did not invite people socially to his home. None of his daughters married. He died at his home, Southampton Villa, on the 31st May 1863, and is buried in Reading Cemetery.

> 'He was a strict man whom I feared rather than loved, but as a child considered him to be 'the wisest and best man in the town'. John Sutton was 'always respected in rather an uncommon degree by the inhabitants of [Reading] where he had lived nearly thirty years a respectable tradesman. His word was really as good as his oath'.
>
> Martin Hope's comments on his father (Corley, 1991–3).

### Martin Hope Sutton JP (1815–1901)

Martin Hope Sutton was the second son of John and Sarah Sutton. He was born in a difficult period for his father and was given the name of Hope '… as an expression of faith that a bright future was in store for him' (Cheales).

He survived measles and whooping cough as a child through the devoted nursing of his mother. His father was worried about his son's health and, thinking that a career in surveying would be less damaging to his health, he sent him to train with F Hawkes of Friar Street. However, Hawkes only used him as a clerk and so Martin Hope returned to the family firm at the end of December 1833, after only 3 months. As an adult he survived pleurisy, a condition not helped by hard work in the garden and by leaving the shop door open so that passers-by could see the peas and beans for sale. He complained about a bad back when attending church services in 1842, and indeed for a while conducted much of the important company business from a sloping sofa! In a post-script to a letter sent to Martin John Sutton in 1894, he complains that his eczema has become very bad, day and night. He was very impressed by the speeches of Joseph Livesey (who visited Reading in 1837–8), who founded the Teetotal Temperance Movement, and as a young man his health improved when he gave up alcohol.

He was taken out of school at the age of 13 to help his ailing father run the company. He worked in the warehouse initially, which was very hard for a shy young boy working with the men. Two years later, he moved into the counting-house.

'Cintra' Lodge a residence of Martin Hope Sutton and later Martin John Sutton.

He was a hard-working, industrious young man with a great love of botany. His father actively dissuaded him and tried to prevent him studying the subject. He refused to let him deal in seeds during working hours; consequently he continued his study of botany and the buying and selling of seeds in his spare time. In 1828 he started to sell seeds in the name of John Sutton. In 1832 and 1833, he sold the seeds in bags with the labels written by his sisters. He was made a full partner in 1837. Martin Hope was very industrious all his life; he rose early and went to bed late; and he took very little money out of the firm.

In comparison with his father, he was very sociable, dressed fashionably, attended functions and dinners, and played cards. But he stopped playing cards when he met Charlotte Trendell, the daughter of a local watch-maker, in 1840. Charlotte was a member of an evangelical church, and her religion had a very profound effect on Martin. They married 4 years later in St. Mary's church, Reading, and moved into a house on Southampton Street. Their two children died in infancy, and Charlotte died of consumption in 1846.

'Work proved his main solace, and it was the distress in Ireland [1846–7] which at that time required continuous exertion' (Corley, 1994–7). His energies were put into breeding disease-resistant potato cultivars for Ireland, as well as supplying seed of fast-growing vegetable species.

Two years later, in September 1848, he married Sophia Woodhead (d. 1896), daughter of William Warwick of Whitley, and they had five sons and four daughters: Martin John, Ernest William, Arthur Warwick, Claude Hope, Leonard Goodhart, Laura Sophia, Eveline Mary, Jessie Constance and Florence Rosa. They lived at Portland Place, next to one of their nurseries. All the children suffered from ill-health, particularly Martin John, his eldest son, probably due to the poor sanitation. Martin Hope finally admitted that 'our present home evidently disagrees with our children's health', and they moved to the healthier area of Cintra Lodge in 1857 (Corley 1994–7). This house remained in the Sutton family until it was given to Reading Corporation in 1955. He gave many garden parties, as well as allowing the grounds to be used by his employees for sport.

Fortunately for the company, he had been recommended as a seedsman to the Queen and Prince Albert, and he advised on grasses and forage crops for the Windsor farms as well as on the planting for Osborne House, where he was a frequent visitor. Queen Victoria almost certainly offered him a knighthood, for when an honours tout approached him in the 1880s, he made it clear that he could have received one much earlier had he wished it. The Queen remained on friendly terms with him however, and indeed he received presents from her at Christmas time, including on one occasion a pair of goats!

He refused to be involved in most of the civic duties of the town, but he was a Justice of the Peace. He took a keen interest in local and national affairs and, in comparison with his father, was an ultra-radical, but his sympathies were with his religion. He was a very strong evangelical Christian. He belonged to and gave his time and money to the Evangelical Society, British and Foreign Bible Society, Church Missionary Society, Church Pastoral Aid Society, Religious Tract Society, London City Mission, Young Men's Christian Association (he opened a branch in Reading, and had the first meeting at his home), and he furnished the City Mission Home in Ventnor at his own expense. He taught at a Sunday school in Reading; many of the young people who attended and were taught by him went on to become employees. He started a Ragged School in one of the most disreputable areas of Reading, and later built a room for the pupils. He started a Penny Bank to encourage thriftiness, which was managed by a clerk from the Reading Savings Bank, and it was in use until the Post Office Bank started. He instituted morning prayers at the firm. Employees could also attend concerts and addresses by the London Evangelization Society. He set up Mildmay Hall, which is today used by the Progress Theatre, and had a rhododendron cultivar named after him. As detailed in chapter 12, he gave a considerable proportion of his income to charity.

He retired in 1888 at the same time as his brother Alfred, but his sons despaired about his interference in the firm even when they were nominally in charge. He refused to argue with his sons, but left letters on the table for them to read. He died on 4th October 1901.

'The success achieved by Martin Hope Sutton affords another illustration of the proverb, 'Seest thou a man diligent in his business? He shall stand before Kings." (Cheales)

### Alfred Sutton (1818–1897)

Alfred Sutton was the third son of John Sutton. He joined the firm at the age of 14, and became a full partner in 1843 when the firm became John Sutton and Sons. He managed the seed and bulb trade in 1832, when Martin Hope worked for F Hawkes for a few months.

In the same year that he became a full partner, Martin Hope had such a severe back problem that Alfred had greater responsibility for running the firm. Martin Hope was so depressed that he discussed with Alfred the possibility of one of them becoming a missionary. But when Martin Hope returned to full health, this possibility was discussed no more.

Although they were partners, Martin Hope was the driving force. Alfred was a nervous, sickly man, a condition which was exacerbated by the pressure his brother put him under. When Martin Hope was on his honeymoon on the Isle of Wight, Alfred received daily letters from him directing the firm. Alfred wrote back:

> '*I am become so nervous through your absence and something else [his letters?] that I often cannot hold my pen steady. I have often been unable to refrain from tears and am continually sighing.*'

In 1851, he was living with his wife, Ellen, and three children at seven Market Place (1851 census), and ten years later he was living at Portland Place (next to their trial ground) with 10 children (1861 census), but nothing is recorded of any of the health problems from which Martin Hope and family suffered while living there. In between these two moves, he lived at 1 South Place, South Street. Latterly he lived at Greenlands, in Redlands Road, where he died.

In conjunction with Martin Hope, he financed the building of schools, mission rooms, cafés and workmen's restaurants in different parts of Reading, including a coffee house known as the British Workman (Boase, 1901), long before School Boards and temperance hotels came into existence (Cheales). When the first election for the new School Board took place in 1871, after the 1870 Education Act, Alfred topped the poll. He remained on the School Board until 1886.

The two brothers worked together harmoniously and successfully until 1888, when they both retired on the same day, leaving the huge business they had built up in the hands of the younger generation. Alfred died in August 1897.

Alfred and Ellen produced 11 children. One of their daughters Edith, became notable in her own right; but like the other female members of the Suttons she was not involved in the running of the family business.

## Edith Sutton JP (1862–1957)

Edith became a school manager in the 1890s, and was elected to the School Board in 1901 (Alfred Sutton and George Palmer had previously been members after it was set up under the Education Act of 1870), and was co-opted to the Education Committee when it was set up in 1903 (Alexander, 1985). In 1904 she sought to persuade the council to consider the issue of votes for women and free meals for needy children. Following the 1907 Qualification of Women (County & Borough Councils) Act, she was elected unopposed for Battle Ward to the Borough Council and held the seat until 1931. Ann Cook (Cook, 1970) suggests that she may have been the first woman in the country so elected (*Reading Mercury*, 1907). She joined the Labour Party in the early 1920s, having been active in the Christian Social Union (Yeo, 1976;

*Reading Mercury*, 1906, and *Reading Standard*, 1909). Alexander gives the view that her gender and, from 1920, her adherence to the Labour Party are the reasons why the seniority principle failed to secure her election to the Aldermanic Bench until 1931, and her belated election as Mayor for 1933–34; she retired from the council in 1945. She had also been a JP since 1920. In 1954 she was the third Sutton to be made a Freeman of the Borough (Kemp, 1996). The house at 12, Northcourt Avenue was built for the Sutton family, and Edith lived there until they moved to no. 24 where she lived until her death in 1957 at the age of 95.

### Martin John Sutton JP (1850–1913)

Martin John Sutton was born on 25 October 1850, the eldest of five sons and four daughters of Martin Hope and Sophia Sutton. He was educated at Blackheath Proprietary School, and joined the firm aged 16. He became a partner in 1871, and was made head of the firm in 1887, holding this position for 26 of his 47 years of service.

Martin John Sutton in his office c. 1911.

He was married twice, first in 1875 to Emily Owen, daughter of the late Colonel Henry Fouquet RMLI who died in 1911, and secondly in September 1912 to a young lady in her early 20s, Grace, the eldest daughter of Mr C T Studd. His first marriage produced two sons, and a daughter who, in 1903, became the wife of the Reverend B Staunton Batty, the vicar of Wargrave.

For most of his life he suffered from indifferent health and was advised by his doctors to live outside Reading. He moved house regularly, and resided at Kidmore End before moving to Henley Park, then Holme Park, Sonning (where he took an active interest in local affairs), and finally to Wargrave Manor.

These illnesses and his unsettled life probably sprang from difficult relations with his father and his brothers over, for example, extravagance in all branches of the firm, and the brothers' habit of spending to the limit of their incomes (Corley, 2004).

He was a very religious man and, as well as doing much to further the causes of temperance, Sunday observance, missionary work and the YMCA, he also used his influence to try and bridge the divide between the Church of England and Nonconformists.

He was a great believer in research and investigation, and he carried out research on his firm's trial grounds and on his own farms. From his work on the quality of pastures, he wrote the book *Permanent and Temporary Pastures*, which was first produced in 1886. It became a classic, and was reprinted many times. He also published papers on wheat-growing, rural education and the agricultural depression.

> 'Mr Sutton has, in conjunction with Dr J A Voelcker, conducted here [Dyson's Wood] a series of manure experiments on several of his grass fields'.
> *Agricultural Gazette*, 16th January 1888.

These experiments were laid out in a similar manner to those at Rothamsted Experimental Station. He also took a great interest in the breeding of roots and grasses, as well as breeding Red Poll and Dexter cattle, Southdown and Welsh Mountain sheep and Suffolk Punches.

At the French Exhibition in 1878, Martin John was decorated by the President of the French Republic with the Cross of the Legion of Honour in consideration of the distinguished services he had given to agriculture, while in 1901 the French Government further recognised his efforts in the improvements of grass and arable husbandry in France and in England, and especially in the advancement of agricultural education in both countries, by presenting him with the insignia of the Ordre du Mérite Agricole. In addition, he was made a Knight of the Order of the Hospital of St John of Jerusalem in England.

He extended the company's trading to New Zealand, Australia and the East and later to the USA. He travelled extensively on the Continent, where he saw M Vilmorin, with whom he carried out seed selection for cultivars adapted to different soils and climates. [Vilmorin founded a seed and nursery company which became one of the largest in France. It is now in the same group as Suttons]. In 1900, he was asked to serve on the seeds committee appointed by the Ministry of Agriculture to examine the sale and regulation of seeds.

He wrote many letters to *The Times* on education, particularly rural education, government of the Church of England and the effects of the movement away from laissez-faire to protectionism. He argued that the loss in wheat acreage and decrease in wheat prices due to the importation of wheat from the colonies was leaving the country vulnerable. He argued for support for wheat-growers from a tax on either imported food or manufactured goods.

> *'The fact is, this country is in such a dangerous condition in consequence of its artificial and inadequate food supply that we dare not run the risk of riots and internal commotions which any rise in prices would entail. It is blind folly to allow this country to be without 6 weeks' supply of food and yet be scandalised because we find our arsenals depleted of other munitions not more really necessary in times of war'.*
>
> The Times, 31st December 1903

For some years, he was a member of the Free Library and Museum Committee. He was a Justice of the Peace: at one period he served on Oxfordshire County Council and, at the time of his death, represented Sonning and district on Berkshire County Council. He was also a member of Berkshire Education Committee, a life Governor and a member of the Council of University College, Reading, a Fellow of the Linnaean Society, a member of the National Agricultural Examination Board, Smithfield Club, London Farmers' Club and Southern Counties Shows, governor and for 23 years a member of the Council of the Royal Agricultural Society of England, and member of the Council of the Bath and West Agricultural Society.

In December 1903, together with his life-long friend G W Palmer (of Huntley and Palmer biscuit fame), Martin John Sutton was presented with the freedom of the Borough of Reading, in recognition of his '... having distinguished himself in promoting the interests of agriculture in the country, of his lifelong work in furtherance of the commercial prosperity of the borough and in the support of various benevolent institutions, especially those having for their object the welfare of young men and of his generous gift to the Corporation of a statue of His Majesty King Edward VII, as a permanent memorial of the Coronation of His Majesty'(*Reading Chronicle*, 19th December 1913).

The inscription on the statue read: 'This statue was presented to the town by Martin John Sutton, eldest son of the late Martin Hope Sutton, who for 86 years was resident in this borough.'

In accepting the freedom of the borough, Martin John Sutton expressed his sense of the great honour which had been conferred on him as a private individual. He added:

> 'I feel sure it is not so much my career, as that of my father thus to recognise. It is to that father that I owe all that I am and any good things that I possess. You refer to my work in agriculture; if I have been able to show how two blades of grass can grow when only one grew before, it is only by continuing and perfecting the researches which he instituted. Your resolution speaks of efforts of a philanthropic character, and special works amongst young men. How can I help following in the steps of a father whose whole life was devoted to such work? He founded the first Church of England YMCA ever founded in England. You refer to the statue of King Edward, which His Royal Highness Prince Christian has come so graciously to unveil. My only excuse for presuming to present it to Reading, is that I am the oldest son of one whose passionate loyalty to the Throne was known to all, and during his long life received many tokens of condescension and regard both from our late beloved sovereign Queen Victoria and our present King'.

Martin John was chosen as mayor of Reading in 1904, although he was not a councillor. He died on the 14th December 1913 of a heart attack, following the use of anaesthetic for dental treatment. His body was conveyed to his Wargrave Manor home before being buried in St Andrew's churchyard, Sonning. He must have been held in high esteem by his colleagues as, in the following February, a notice was posted within the company stating: 'It is thought that many of our employees might like to have a portrait of the late Mr Martin John, and a number have been prepared for this purpose. All those who wish for one, can be supplied on applying to their Head of Dept.'

### Herbert Sutton (1854–1924)

Herbert was the third and youngest son of Alfred and Ellen Sutton. He married Emma, daughter of Dr William Watkinson Mackey of Reading. He entered the firm in 1875, was made a partner in 1881 and retired in 1898 due to ill-health. He attended St John's church where he was a member of the Church Board. By nature he was conservative and had been chairman of the Reading Conservative Association. He purchased St Laurence's vicarage in Valpy Street and gave it to the Dairy Institute, part of University College, Reading, plus £1,000. He retired to Bournemouth and died in Swanage on the 17th October 1924.

### *Arthur Warwick Sutton JP, FLS, VMH (1854–1925)*

Arthur Warwick was a son of Martin Hope. He was educated at Malvern College and the Royal Agricultural College, Cirencester. He became a partner in the firm in 1876 and a senior partner in 1913, and retired in August 1921 owing to illness.

'Sutherlands' – residence of Arthur Warwick Sutton from 1884 to 1888; and later it was the home of Leonard Noel Sutton.

He married Arabella Constance in 1881, and they moved to Bucklebury Place, Bucklebury, in 1893. In 1894, he founded the Bucklebury Fireside Club. This was probably the most influential local social organisation during the pre-1914 years. It attracted many male members from Bucklebury, Midgham and Woolhampton, and offered a wide range of educational, sporting and other leisure activities.

'The Fireside Club was founded by Mr Arthur Warwick Sutton of Bucklebury Place, a senior partner in the firm of the Reading seedsmen. He expressed the purpose of the club as a means whereby "they might be able to know each other better, and by meeting together he might be able to exercise some influence and try to point them to if they needed above all others, the knowledge of our Lord and saviour Jesus Christ". The club was situated in the grounds of the house. The main entrance to the house was via the lodge in Carbins Woods Lane, clearly marked AD 1893. The other entrance was some 100 yards further along the lane towards Bucklebury, marked today by the West Lodge and the red-bricked Fireside Cottage. The clubhouse was on the left-hand side some 30 yards along the lane leading to Woottons that separates the cottage from the new Home Farm (then the Laundry Cottage). This was the venue for concerts, lectures and general meetings, with a smaller room for a Friday evening Bible Study and other group meetings* *or classes. The grounds were an excellent setting for football and cricket matches and, in 1905, held a private golf course. In the next year a rifle range was added and, in 1912, a recently-built gymnasium attracted some 60 men to be drilled by Ed Stagg (army reservist). The club benefited from Mr Sutton's experiences when he had established a similar club for young men in 1880 in Silver Street, Reading.*

*By 1896 the club had 112 fully paid-up members. The Fireside rifle range was officially opened in May 1906 by General Sir John Watson VC. There were 121 members in 1905; this had gone up to 171 in 1906, when the Suttons celebrated their silver wedding.*

Garden Party at Bucklebury Place 2nd July 1906 to commemorate the Silver Wedding Anniversary of Mr & Mrs Arthur W Sutton. On the bridge left to right Martin John Sutton, Mr & Mrs A W Sutton, on the extreme right Leonard Goodhart Sutton.

*'Mr and Mrs Sutton left the house at the beginning of 1915 for London and, at a farewell gathering, William Matthews reminded the assembled members that they had met for the past 19 years and had enjoyed good companionship amongst all classes thanks to the efforts and generosity of Mr Sutton. In the course of his response, Mr Sutton reported that he had received letters from parents to say that, thanks to the club, their sons serving at the front were the best shots in the unit.*

*'The home was placed up for auction and purchased by Dr Carl Langer who maintained the tradition of the Fireside Club, which continued to flourish with the particular support of Mr J Henshall, club secretary and the head gardener at "The Place".'*

*(Trigg J, personal communication)*

He published several papers on horticultural research, and he was the first member of the family to be elected to the Council of the Linnaean Society. In 1918 he was appointed to the National Board of Agricultural Education. He was awarded the Victoria Medal of Honour by the RHS for his services to horticulture. Prior to and during WWI, there was much concern with some of the corrupt practices being carried out in the trade. Arthur Sutton attended meetings in London with regard to illegal payments made to head gardeners, who at that time had great control over the placing of large seed orders. His recreations were Eastern travel, golf, shooting and fishing, and his special hobby was lecturing on Eastern travel; one of his publications was *My camel ride from Suez to Mount Sinai.*

He moved to Bournemouth because of failing health, and died on 15th April 1925 at Clifton Road, Southbourne. He left an estate of £112,793, but left no legacy to any religious sect or charity (except to the YMCA) as 'I believe it is a man's duty to give in charity during his life time such proportion of his income as in the sight of God he may deem right'. However, he did give the freehold of the premises of the YMCA, Garrard House, Friar Street, Reading, and the Fireside Mission and Workman's Club, Silver Street, Reading, to the National Council of the YMCA ('these together cost me less than £10,000') for perpetual use of the same by young men, lads and working men of Reading, and stock yielding £100 per annum for permanent endowment of Garrard House.

## Leonard Goodhart Sutton CBE, JP (1863–1932)

Leonard G Sutton was the youngest son of Martin Hope Sutton. He was educated at Wellington College and the Royal Agricultural College, Cirencester, where he obtained his diploma in agriculture in 1883. He toured the seed-growing districts in the UK and on the Continent before spending time in the various departments of the firm. In 1885 he became a partner. The flower department was under his personal supervision, and he was considered one of the greatest experts on flower culture. He was Chairman at the time of his death, and had given 46 years' service to the firm.

'Hillside' one time residence of Leonard Goodhart Sutton and later Noel Sutton.

He married Mary Annie, daughter of Colonel W J Seaton, and they had five sons and one daughter. His daughter, May, married Major J Chater Jack, and they had three daughters. Leonard was already a widower when WWI broke out in 1914 (his wife died in August 1900). His five sons served in the Army, but within the space of about 18 months, four were killed. Lt. Eric Sutton of the Royal Sussex Regiment was killed in 1916, Lt. Wilfred Sutton of the Royal Berkshire Yeomanry was killed in 1917, and Lt. Eustace Sutton of the Royal Engineers and Lt. Alec Sutton of the Rifle Brigade were killed in 1918. His remaining son Captain Noel Sutton served with the Royal Berkshire Yeomanry during the war.

Leonard Sutton always wore a black suit and bowler hat. It was his custom to walk round every department once a week, and he would stop and talk to anyone and ask questions. His bowler must not have been very comfortable, for he often took it off and laid it on the nearest desk, before continuing walking round the department. Three departments later, the office boy was told 'Go and find Mr Leonard's bowler'.

He was made a JP in 1906 and, from 1909 to 1929, represented Victoria ward on Reading Borough Council. He was elected mayor in 1914, just after the start of WWI, and remained mayor for two years. During this time he raised three Reading companies of Royal Engineers, all of which saw active duty at the Front. In 1925–26 he was mayor for the third time. During this period he had the honour of welcoming King George V and Queen Mary when they visited the Royal Agricultural Show, and the Prince of Wales (later Duke of Windsor) on the opening of the new Caversham Bridge. He was awarded his CBE in 1920 for 'valuable public service in Reading during the war'. He declined a knighthood offered to him after the war. He became an honorary Freeman of the Borough in 1931. At the presentation the then mayor, Councillor F G Sainsbury, described him as: 'An outstanding personality, a true English gentleman, beloved by his fellow citizens, a God-fearing man, ever willing to lend a helping hand to the poor and needy, ever ready to undertake responsibilities and duties for the furtherance of the Christian and social life of the town, and one who will ever be remembered as a gentleman, who lived a life for the good of others'.

His interest in education led him to be chairman of the Reading Education Committee for 17 years; a member of the governing body of Reading School, and later chairman; trustee of St John's school; an almoner at Christ's Hospital; representative governor of Royal Holloway College; member of the Council of Reading University College, and upon the College receiving its charter as a university, he was elected vice-president of the Council of Reading University, while in 1930 he succeeded Dr. Alfred Palmer as president of the Council of the University; president of the Reading Schools Football Association; and vice-president of the Berkshire Schools Athletic Association.

He took a great interest in the Berkshire Territorial Association, and seldom missed a meeting or a visit to the summer camp. When the Association was founded in 1908, he was one of the original co-opted members, and in 1911 was elected chairman.

He maintained a great interest in agriculture, and was a governor and vice-president of the Royal Agricultural Society of England, president of the Royal Counties Agricultural Society, vice-president of the Royal Horticultural Society, fellow of the Royal Geographical Society and of the Linnaean Society, and served on the Government Seeds Advisory Committee. Closer to home, he was vice-president of the Reading Allotments Society and the Reading and Pangbourne Gardeners' Associations. He became a member of the Council of the Reading Chamber of Commerce when it started in 1903, and was elected president from 1915 to 1921.

He was a deeply religious man, and devoted a great deal of time and money to St John's Church, Reading. He continued his father's and elder brother's interests in missionary work, and was a subscriber to the Church Missionary Society and the British and Foreign Bible Society; he also sat on the National Assembly of the Church of England as a representative of the Oxford Diocese, having been elected by the Reading Ruri-decanal Conference. He was also vice-president of the NSPCC and, for 21 years, secretary of the local branch and later chairman of the executive committee, vice-president of the Reading YMCA, chairman of the Berkshire Branch of the British Red Cross Society, chairman of the Queen Victoria Institute for Nursing in Reading, and vice-president of the Royal Berkshire Hospital in 1921.

He lent his support to many sporting bodies: among the offices which he held were president of the Reading Wednesday Football League, president of the Reading Working Men's Regatta, and vice-president of the Berkshire Lawn Tennis Association. He was also a member of the Berkshire Playing Fields Association, and sat on the provisional committee when that association was formed, in response to an appeal by the Duke of York. Mr Sutton succeeded the late James Simonds as president of the Reading Amateur Football Club, and was vice-president of the Reading Cricket League for over 20 years.

There are many other bodies with which Leonard Sutton was associated. He was an ex-officio member of the Reading Public Libraries Committee, a member of the Reading Council of Social Welfare, president of the Reading Dispensary Trust, a trustee of the Reading Municipal Charities, president of the Reading & District branch of the British Sailors' Society, president of the Reading Branch of the British Empire Shakespeare Society, chairman of the Reading Girls' Club, and for 30 years the treasurer of the Reading Philanthropic Institution.

He died on the 8th June 1932 at his home, 'Hillside', in Allcroft Road. On hearing of his death, the King and Queen sent a sympathetic telegram to his son, Noel Sutton, which read: 'The King and Queen have learnt with regret of the sudden death of Mr Leonard Sutton and assure you and your sister of their true sympathy with you in your loss. Their Majesties know how greatly Mr Leonard will be missed both in the horticultural world and in the municipal and social life of Reading'.

## Martin Hubert Fouquet Sutton JP, FRSA, FLS, FRGS (1875–1930)

Martin Hubert Fouquet was a son of Martin John and Emily Owen. He was educated at Harrow and Christchurch, Oxford.

He was a partner in the firm, a Justice of the Peace, fellow of the Royal Geographical Society, fellow of the Linnaean Society and a Fellow of the Royal Society of Arts. He wrote *The effect of radioactive fertilizers on plant life*, *The Book of the Links*, *Electrification of seeds by the Wolfryn Process*, and a 9th edition of *Permanent and Temporary Pastures*.

He married Eleanora, daughter of Colonel Mouton, in October 1899 (308 employees attended the ceremony); they had two sons and three daughters. They lived at Erlegh Park within Whiteknights Park, where he died on 27th March 1930.

The name Fouquet, which he and other members of the family bore, stemmed from the Suttons' descent through Emily Owen from the English branch of the old French family of Fouquet, the chief of whom was Nicolas Fouquet, Lord High Treasurer of France under Louis XlV, and thought by many to be the 'Man in the Iron Mask.'

N.B. Some members of the Sutton family were given the name Fouquet. Documents give a number of different spellings of this name even for the same person at different times! For clarity, we have used only one spelling.

## Ernest Phillips Fouquet Sutton MBE, FLS, VMH (1882-1972)

Ernest Phillips Fouquet Sutton, known as Mr Phil within the company, was the great-grandson of the founder of the firm, John Sutton, and the son of Martin John Sutton. Mr Phil was educated at Trinity College, Cambridge, and the Royal Agricultural College, Cirencester. He joined the firm on 1st May 1906, 100 years after it was founded. When he started as a junior partner, he used to rise at 5 a.m. to help open the post in Reading at 7 a.m. At the time, he was living with his father near Henley, and he travelled in by bicycle during the winter and on horse-back in the summer.

During WWI he served in France as an officer in the Royal Artillery. Later he was seconded to the Army Service Corps, and put in charge of growing vegetables on 4000 acres of land in France to feed the troops.

Mr Phil was a leading authority on vegetable cultivars and seed production, and was a member of the Council of the Royal Horticultural Society from 1948 until 1965. In 1952 the RHS awarded him the Victoria Medal of Honour, the highest award the Society can bestow.

A past-president of the Smithfield Club, a governor of the Royal Agricultural Society since 1926, and a vice-president and steward of the horticultural section of the Bath and West Show for many years, he was a familiar figure at the principal agricultural shows, including the Smithfield Show in London.

He continued his father's interest in English Kerry and Dexter cattle, and was president of the associated society in 1915 and 1922. He formed the 1st Henley Scout Group in 1908, and later was a District Commissioner for the South Chiltern Division for 34 years.

He married Hilda Douglas-Jones in April 1911. They were married for 61 years, and had a son and two daughters.

He retired in January 1966, having been a director for 60 years and chairman for the previous 33 years. He spent his final years at Pinemead, Upper Warren Avenue, Caversham, and died on 12th August 1972. Following a funeral service at Greyfriars Church, Reading, he was interred at St. Andrews, Sonning (*Reading Mercury*, 17th August 1972).

### Leonard Noel Sutton MA, JP (1893 –1965)

Leonard Noel was the eldest son of Leonard Goodhart Sutton, and the only son to survive WWI. He was a captain in the Berkshire Yeomanry, and was allowed home after the death of his four brothers. Even so, his ship was torpedoed *en route* through the Mediterranean. He later commanded the 395th (Berkshire Yeomanry) Field Battery, Royal Artillery, retiring in 1937 with the rank of major. He married Dorothy Jeans in the late 1950s.

He joined the firm on 2nd June 1920, and to celebrate this event the employees were granted an extra 2½ days holiday. He became a director in the firm in charge of flower-seed production, and travelled widely visiting Australia, New Zealand and many other countries. He was author of *The Cool Greenhouse*, and was never happier than when engaged in the breeding, selection and cultivation of flowers.

Like his father, he carried out many civic duties. He was High Sheriff of Berkshire 1933–4 and was made deputy Lieutenant of the County in 1936. The following year, he was appointed a Justice of the Peace for Reading. For nearly half a century, he was a member of the Senate and Council of Reading University, and was a governor of the Royal Berkshire Hospital and a member of the Board of Management. He was also a member of the Territorial Association of Berkshire and held the Territorial Decoration.

For many years, Leonard Noel was deputy president of the Berkshire Red Cross Society. He had wide interests in many of the social and philanthropic activities of Reading, and had been president of the Reading and District Boy Scouts' Association and of the Reading Athletic Club, and a treasurer of the Reading Philanthropic Association. He was a trustee of the Thames Valley Savings Bank, serving on the committee of management. The Reading Dispensary Trust was another of his interests, and he was president of the Reading and District Gardeners' Mutual Improvement Association.

He died at his home 'Sutherlands' in Christchurch Road, Reading. The funeral service was held at St John's, Reading, the church where he worshipped and served as a trustee, churchwarden and sidesman.

The name of Sutton lives on in Sutton Court, a sheltered housing complex in Culver Lane, Earley, built on the site of Iles nursery. It was opened by Mrs Noel Sutton in 1962 (*Reading Chronicle*, 15th October 1965).

### *Martin Audley Fouquet Sutton (1900–1963)*

Martin A F Sutton was the fifth generation of Suttons. He was born in September 1900 and was educated at Harrow, Pembroke College, Cambridge, and Harper Adams Agricultural College; he was a fellow of the Linnaean Society of London. He joined the company on 2nd October 1923, and was made a partner on 1st December 1926. He carried on the work of his father (Martin Hubert), grandfather (Martin John) and great-grandfather (Martin Hope) in prescribing mixtures of grasses and clovers for meadows and pastures, the breeding and selection of special strains of grasses for amenity and agricultural purposes, and studying the effects of cutting, diseases, insects, irrigation, fertilizers, root growth etc on turf growth. He was a practical man and was involved in experimentation at the trial grounds, as well as analysing the results thoroughly. He helped to establish the culture of fine turf as a scientific study needing the care and attention of a qualified groundsman, and inaugurated week-long courses of instruction at Reading for those wishing to improve their theoretical and practical knowledge of turf matters.

In 1912 his father had published *The Book of the Links*, which was a classic of its kind. Martin Audley published a successor *Golf Course:*

Mr Audley Sutton.

*Design, Construction and Upkeep.* In 1950, he published a further edition of *Lawns and Sports Grounds*, which had its origins in a pamphlet written by his grandfather 80 years previously, and was first published in 1933. He was the editor of *Turf for Sport*, a magazine produced by the company, and was the joint author of a number of technical bulletins, one of which was on grass growth through bitumen for use as runways for aeroplanes. In 1930 he read a paper before the Royal Horticultural society entitled 'Lawns: their formation and upkeep', which was later published in booklet form.

He took an interest in the company's general advisory service which dealt with the horticultural problems; took a close interest in the firm's soil-testing laboratory and seed-testing stations; supervised the seed potato department; and was a founder-member of the National Association of Seed Potato Merchants, and served as the first President for 3½ years.

He lived at Park House, Upper Redlands Road, Reading, from 1934 to 1941. Around the end of World War II, he moved to Green Trees, Greenham Common, Newbury, which had a large collection of rare trees and shrubs. The arboretum had been started by Bruce Johnson, and Martin Audley added many more from around the world, including the rhododendron 'Martin Hope Sutton'. He married twice, and had one daughter from his first marriage.

He was, for many years, an Inspector in the Special Constabulary, and he collected models of vintage railway engines. He continued the family tradition of being an evangelical churchman, and was for many years the treasurer of the Reading Auxiliary of the British and Foreign Bible Society, and co-founder of a Mission Hall in south Reading (Underwood Mission Hall). He also devoted a great deal of time to the YMCA, and was chairman of the Youth Work Committee of the Reading branch for nearly 30 years.

He was a kind and well-loved man, and one of his contemporaries wrote of him that 'the grass is better and greener where he has trod'.

### Owen Phillips Fouquet Sutton (1913–2004)

Owen Sutton was the fifth generation of Suttons to work for the company, and was the only son of Phil Sutton. He attended Harrow School, and spent some years studying estate management before entering the firm; he became a director in 1937. Initially he worked in the vegetable seed production department, which involved a considerable amount of travel to British and European contract growers. On the death of his cousin Martin Audley in 1963, he took over the grass advisory service and grass seed department. He was a keen games player, and had first-class expe-

Mr Owen Sutton.

rience of most ball games played on grass; cricket, soccer, hockey, golf
and tennis, which gave him a practical understanding of the problems of
groundsmen, greenkeepers and parks superintendents (Moore, 1964).

He was the last family member to be on the board when he stepped
down in 1977, although he continued to act as a consultant for a time
after the move to Torquay and he retired at the end of November 1979.
Owen was married twice and had three daughters, but no male heirs to
continue the family line.

### Douglas Collins (1912–1972)

Douglas Collins was born at Waltham St Lawrence, Berkshire, on
the 31st January 1912. His family often holidayed in France and
Switzerland, which gave Douglas the opportunity to speak fluent French.
This led him to begin his working career as an office boy in a Monte
Carlo hotel. His next job was in the office of a paint and varnish manu-
facturer in Birmingham, where he graduated to become a sales represent-

ative. About this time, he became interested in the making of cosmetics, and was running a small company.

He had been keen on sailing and, by the time WWII started, he was already on the Navy's Supplementary Reserve, from where he was automatically drafted into the Royal Navy until he was demobbed in 1945. During the war, his company had been kept going by a small and loyal band of employees. For a while, he worked for a firm of stockbrokers in the City, as well as keeping an eye on his cosmetic and new perfumery business.

He became involved with the British Lion Film Company in 1954, and 3 years later, was asked if he would be prepared to take up the post of chairman, which he accepted. During this period, he continued to consolidate and increase the perfumery business into what became the world-famous Goya company. He sold the company in 1960, and as a result became a millionaire (Collins, 1963).

In 1964 he became associated with and worked for Sutton Seeds, and eventually purchased the company. With his varied and skilful knowledge, he was able to return the company to a profitable concern. He was appointed chairman of the National Seed Development Organisation in the late 1960s, a company owned by the Ministry of Agriculture to exploit and sell all new varieties resulting from public research. This included vegetable, potato and cereal crops bred by British research stations. His other interests were building, farming and writing. Tragically, he died of a heart attack in 1972.

Douglas Collins.

# 15. Appendices

## Conversion tables

### *Money*

Money referring to prices before the decimalisation of sterling in 1971 is expressed in pounds (£), shillings (*s*) and pence (*d*) and after that date in pounds and pence (p).

| | | |
|---|---|---|
| 12d | one shilling (1/-) | 5p |
| 20s | one pound | 100p |
| £1 1s | one guinea | £1.05 |

### *Weights*

| | | |
|---|---|---|
| one ounce (1oz) | | 28.35g |
| 16oz | one pound (lb) | 0.454kg |
| 14lb | one stone | 6.35kg |
| 112lb | one hundredweight (cwt) | 50.80kg |
| 20cwt | one ton (t) | 1.02 tonne (one tonne = a metric tonne) |

### *Length*

| | | |
|---|---|---|
| one inch (in) | | 2.54cm |
| 12 in | one foot (ft) | 0.31m |
| 3ft | one yard (yd) | 0.914m |
| 220yd | one furlong | 0.201km |
| 1760yd | one mile | 1.609km |

### *Area*

| | | |
|---|---|---|
| square inch | | 6.45cm$^2$ |
| one foot square (ft$^2$) | | 0.093m$^2$ |
| 9ft$^2$ | one square yard (yd$^2$) | 0.836m$^2$ |
| 4840yd$^2$ | one acre (ac) | 0.41 hectare(ha) |
| 2.47ac | | one hectare |
| 640ac | one square mile | 259ha |

### *Volume*

| | | |
|---|---|---|
| 8 pints | one gallon | 4.55 l |
| 8 gallons | one Winchester bushel | 36.37 l |
| 8 bushels | one quarter | 290.96 l |

## Notable dates in the history of Suttons Seeds

1806    The start of the business of John Sutton, Seedsman. King Street, Reading

1833    Broadsheet catalogues produced.

1836    Martin Hope Sutton becomes a partner. The sale of vegetable and flower seeds becomes important.

1837    Move from King Street to Market Place, Reading.

1840    Start of mail order business with the penny post and new railway network.

1846    Irish famine relief. Suttons provide quantities of quick maturing vegetable seeds to help provide food after the potato famine.

1856    The first bound catalogues for gardeners are produced.

1858    The oldest surviving Farmers' Year Book.

1869    Seed Adulteration Act. Suttons install their own seed testing laboratory.

1871    Royal Warrant granted by the Prince of Wales.

1873    Expansion and new building on existing site at Market Place, Reading.

1874    First mention of the firm's annual days out by train, (to Hastings).

1883    First foreign visit to see Continental seed growing.

1884    Royal Warrant granted by Queen Victoria.

1903    New glasshouse range built at trial grounds.

1913    Purchase of seed business of J Veitch and trial grounds at Langley.

1916    The opening of the Indian Branch.

1923    First Market Garden catalogue.

1962    The move from Market Place to London Road, Earley.

1964    The end of the Sutton family control of the business.

1965    Introduction of 'Harvest Fresh' sealed packets.

1976    Move from Reading to Torquay.

1985    Acquired Carters, Cuthberts and Dobie brands.

1990    Opening of new trial grounds at Ipplepen.

1998    Move from Torquay to Paignton.

2006    Suttons celebrates its Bicentenary.

# 16. References

The major source of information has been the Sutton archives in the Museum of English Rural Life (MERL), University of Reading. These archives contain a wealth of information on the company from the directors' minutes to diaries of employees, pamphlets, letters, catalogues, etc, which extend from the early nineteenth century to 1976, when the company left Reading for Devon.

Gerry Westall has a large collection of Suttons' ephemera, some of which have been used to illustrate many points in the book.

Reading Local Studies Library (RLSL) in Reading Central Library has provided information from census data, trade directories, voters' lists, *Reading Mercury, Reading Chronicle, Berkshire Chronicle, Reading Observer,* and *The Times.*

## *Suttons' publications*

A list of these can be found in the section 'Books and various publications' in chapter 10 'The Art of Selling'.

## *Primary sources*

*British Trade Journal*, 1st February 1877

*Builder Magazine*, 1873

**Cheales, A B,** *Martin Hope Sutton of Reading.* A few noteworthy incidents connected with the life of Martin Hope Sutton of Reading gleaned from authentic public and private documents, private publication, 1898 (RLSL)

**Cook, A F,** *Reading 1835–1930 A community power study* (PhD thesis), University of Reading, 1970

**Corley, T A B,** 'The earliest Reading Bank: Marsh, Deane & Co., 1788–1815', *Berkshire Archaeological Journal*, vol 66 pp 121-8, 1971-2

**Corley, T A B,** 'The making of a Berkshire entrepreneur. Martin Hope Sutton of Reading: 1815–40', *Berkshire Archaeological Journal* vol 74 pp 135-143, 1991-3

**Corley, T A B,** 'A Berkshire entrepreneur makes good: Martin Hope Sutton of Reading 1840–1871', *Berkshire Archaeological Journal* vol 75 pp 103-110, 1994-7

Corley, T A B, 'A Berkshire entrepreneur's final years: Martin Hope Sutton of Reading 1871–1901', *Berkshire Archaeological Journal* vol 76 pp 94–101, 1998–2003

Corley, T A B, 'John Sutton', *Oxford Dictionary of National Biography* vol 53 pp 391–2, Oxford University Press, 2004

Corley, T A B, 'Martin Hope Sutton', *Oxford Dictionary of National Biography* vol 53 pp 398–399, Oxford University Press, 2004

Corley, T A B, 'Martin John Sutton', *Oxford Dictionary of National Biography* vol 53 pp 399–400, Oxford University Press, 2004

Elliott, B, 'In the beginning …', *The Garden*, vol 129 (2) pp 92–95, 2004

*Gardeners' Chronicle,* 27th November 1852

*Gardeners' Chronicle,* 9th February 1867

*Gardeners' Chronicle,* 11th January 1873

*Gardeners' Chronicle and Agricultural Gazette,* 27th November 1852

*Gardeners' Chronicle and Agricultural Gazette,* 9th February 1861

*Gardeners' Chronicle and Agricultural Gazette,* 18th April 1868

*Gardeners' Chronicle and Agricultural Gazette,* 16th January 1888

Hodder, T K, 'Sutton's at Reading', *The Journal of the Royal Horticultural Society* vol 81 (5), 1956

*Journal of the Royal Agricultural Society of England* (second series), vol xxv Part II

'Mr Martin Hope Sutton of Reading', *Proceedings of The Fireside Club*, date unknown, pp 364–368 (RLSL)

Huxley, A, Harvest Fresh Packets, *Amateur Gardening*, 1967

Moore, W, Turf for Sport, vol IV, 1964

'Souvenir of a visit to Messrs Sutton's seed establishment', *The Farmer and the Chamber of Agriculture Journal*, 22nd May 1882

Sanchez-Giraldez, H, 'Peas from the Pharaoh', *Seed News*, vol 45 p 7, 2005

Trigg, J, Before the fountain, private publication, 1995 (RLSL)

Trigg, J, As we were, private publication, 1997 (RLSL)

Yorke, E, *Reading Directory,* 1839

## Books

Alexander, A A, *Borough Government and Politics, Reading 1835–1985,* George Allen & Unwin, London, 1985.

Boase, F, 'Alfred Sutton', *Modern English Biography*, vol III R-Z, Netherton & Worth, Truro, 1901

Collins, D, *A nose for money*, Michael Joseph, London, 1963

'Douglas Collins', *Who was Who*, vol 7, A & C Black, London

Gorer, R, *'The Gardenesque Garden 1830–1890'* in Harris, J, Editor, *The Garden. A celebration of one thousand years of British Gardening* (The guide to the exhibition presented by the Victoria and Albert Museum, May 23 to Aug 26 1979), pp 47–55, New Perspectives Publishing Ltd, London, 1979

Kay, F G, *Pioneers of British Industry*, p 338, Rockcliff, London, 1952

Kemp, P, *Northcourt Avenue. Its History and People*, Northcourt Avenue Residents' Association, Reading, 1996

'Arthur Warwick Sutton', *Who was Who*, vol 2, A & C Black, London

'Leonard Goodhart Sutton' and 'Martin H F Sutton', *Who was Who*, vol 3, A & C Black, London

'Martin John Sutton', *Who was Who*, vol 1, A & C Black, London

Yeo, S, *Religion and Voluntary Organisations in Crisis*, Croom Helm, London, 1976

## Web sites

Suttons Seeds http://www.suttons.co.uk
Suttons of India http://www.suttonseedsindia.com
Postal Orders http://www.postalhistory.org.uk/research

# 17. Index